Policing the Victorian Town

The Development of the Police in Middlesbrough *c.* 1840–1914

David Taylor
Professor of History
University of Huddersfield
UK

First published 2002 by
PALGRAVE MACMILLAN
Houndmills, Basingstoke, Hampshire RG21 6XS and
175 Fifth Avenue, New York, N.Y. 10010
Companies and representatives throughout the world

PALGRAVE MACMILLAN is the global academic imprint of the Palgrave Macmillan division of St. Martin's Press LLC and of Palgrave Macmillan Ltd. Macmillan® is a registered trademark in the United States, United Kingdom and other countries. Palgrave is a registered trademark in the European Union and other countries.

ISBN 0-333-652398 hardcover

This book is printed on paper suitable for recycling and made from fully managed and sustained forest sources.

A catalogue record for this book is available from the British Library.

Library of Congress Cataloging-in-Publication Data

Taylor, David, 1946 May 10–
    Policing the Victorian town: the development of the police in
    Middlesbrough c. 1840–1914 / David Taylor.
        p. cm.
    Includes bibliographical references and index.
    ISBN 0-333-65239-8 (cloth)
        1. Police–England–Middlesbrough–History–19th century.
    2. Police–England–Middlesbrough–History–20th century.
    3. Middlesbrough (Eng.)–History. I. Title.
HV8196.A6 M537 2002
363.2'09428'5309034–dc21   2001058326

10 9 8 7 6 5 4 3 2 1
11 10 09 08 07 06 05 04 03 02

Printed and bound in Great Britain by
Antony Rowe Ltd, Chippenham

Policing the Victorian Town

Also by David Taylor:

THE NEW POLICE IN NINETEENTH-CENTURY ENGLAND
CRIME, POLICING AND PUNISHMENT IN ENGLAND, 1750–1914

To Becky, Ruth, John, Barry and Jamie

Contents

List of Tables	viii
Acknowledgements	x
Maps	xi
1 Introduction: Urban Growth, Social Order and Policing	1
2 The Birth of the 'Infant Hercules': Urban and Industrial Growth in Middlesbrough, *c.* 1840 to the 1870s	14
3 The New Police in Middlesbrough: From the 1841 Improvement Act to the Early Years of the 1856 County and Borough Police Act	25
4 The British Ballarat? Crime in Middlesbrough, *c.* 1840–70	52
5 The Police and the Public *c.* 1840–70: The Limits of Policing by Consent	78
6 The Years of Maturation: Urban and Industrial Growth, *c.* 1870–1914	100
7 Expansion and Professionalisation: The Middlesbrough Police, *c.* 1870–1914	112
8 The Police and Crime in Middlesbrough after 1870	142
9 The Police and the Public from the 1870s to 1914	171
Notes	185
Bibliography	211
Index	221

List of Tables

2.1   Middlesbrough: selected demographic characteristics, 1841–71   21

3.1   Police/population ratios in selected boroughs in the mid 1850s   38

3.2   The Middlesbrough police force, 1857–70   40

3.3   Middlesbrough police weekly wages rates, 1857–71   40

3.4   Comparative police wage rates, 1857–70   41

3.5   Length of service of Middlesbrough police officers, 1854 to 1869   42

4.1   Prisoners tried at Northallerton Quarter Sessions, 1835–69   54

4.2   Distribution of indictable crimes in the North Riding of Yorkshire and Middlesbrough, 1835–55 and 1856–70 and the Black Country, 1835–60   56

4.3   Serious crime in Middlesbrough, 1858–69   57

4.4   Percentage distribution of petty crime in Middlesbrough, 1855   66

4.5   Petty crime in Middlesbrough, 1858–69   67

5.1   Assaults on the Middlesbrough police in the 1860s   87

6.1   Principal occupations in Middlesbrough, 1871–1911   101

6.2   Middlesbrough's industrial structure, 1871–1911   101

7.1   Length of service of Middlesbrough police   114

7.2   Range of experience of Middlesbrough police officers, 1870–1914   115

7.3   Rank and age structure of the Middlesbrough police force, 1882 and 1889   116

7.4   Career outcomes of Middlesbrough police recruits, 1856–69 to 1900–14   118

7.5   Career outcomes of long-term policemen   121

7.6   Wage rates in the Middlesbrough police force, 1871–1912   126

7.7   Growth rates in real earnings for three career categories in the Middlesbrough police force   129

7.8   Growth rates in real earnings in three Middlesbrough industries   130

A7.1 The growth of Yorkshire borough police forces,
      1871–1911   135
A7.2 Police/population ratios in selected Yorkshire boroughs,
      1871–1911   136
8.1   Reported indictable crimes in Middlesbrough, 1870s
      and 1880s   144
8.2   Indictable crimes in Middlesbrough known to the
      police, 1903–13   144
8.3   Offences against the person known to the police,
      1903–13   145
8.4   Cases tried at Northallerton Quarter Sessions in the
      1870s and 1880s   150
8.5   Middlesborough prisoners tried at Northallerton in the
      1870s and 1880s   151
8.6   Offences dealt with summarily in Middlesbrough in
      the 1870s and 1880s   153
8.7   Cases tried summarily in Middlesbrough, 1903–13   154
8.8   Principal street offences in Middlesbrough, 1903–13   157
8.9   Offences tried at Middlesbrough juvenile court, 1910–13 168
8.10 Middlesbrough probation orders, 1908–13   169
A8.1 Other police activities in Middlesbrough, 1903–13   170

Acknowledgements

In writing this book I have become indebted to many people. I would particularly like to thank the staff of the Cleveland Country Record Office, Middlesbrough, Middlesbrough Public Library, the North Yorkshire County Record Office, Northallerton, and of the libraries at the Universities of Teesside, Durham and Huddersfield. In addition, my thanks go to colleagues at Teesside and Huddersfield, particularly Dr Bertrand Taithe (now of Manchester University) and Dr Philip Woodfine, who were kind enough to read through and comment in detail on earlier drafts of this book, and also to the anonymous reader whose supportive but perceptive observations were of great help in the final stages of writing. I am grateful to the University of Teesside and Middlesbrough Council for permission to use material that first appeared as 'The Infant Hercules and the Augean Stables: a century of economic and social development in Middlesbrough, c. 1840–1939', in A. J. Pollard, ed., *Middlesbrough: town and community, 1830–1950*, Stroud, 1996; the editors of Journal *of Regional and Local Studies* for material which first appeared as 'Crime and policing in early-Victorian Middlesbrough, 1835–55'; and the Cleveland and Teesside Local History Society for permission to reproduce material from their *Middlesbrough's History in Maps*, 1980. As ever my greatest debt is to my wife, Thelma, who not only read and commented on the book at all stages of its writing but whose encouragement kept me going when I was close to abandoning the whole project. However, the book is dedicated to our children, who were wonderfully supportive but ensured that I maintained a proper sense of proportion through their constant amazement that anyone could spend so much time exploring the lives of long-dead policemen in a somewhat less than idyllic part of northeast England.

Maps

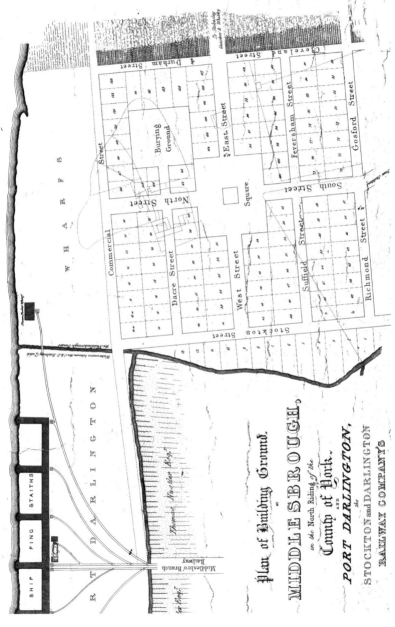

Map 1: Middlesbrough in 1830

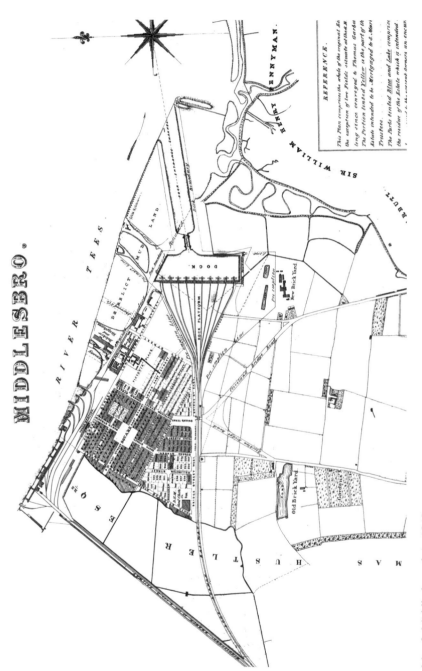

Map 2: Middlesbrough in 1845

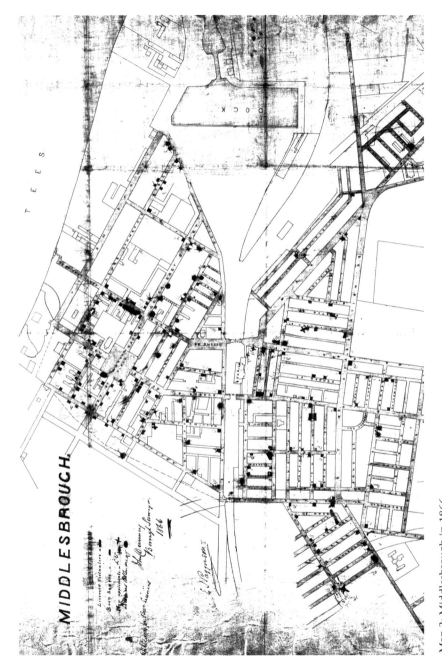

Map 3: Middlesbrough in 1866

Map 4: Middlesbrough in 1874

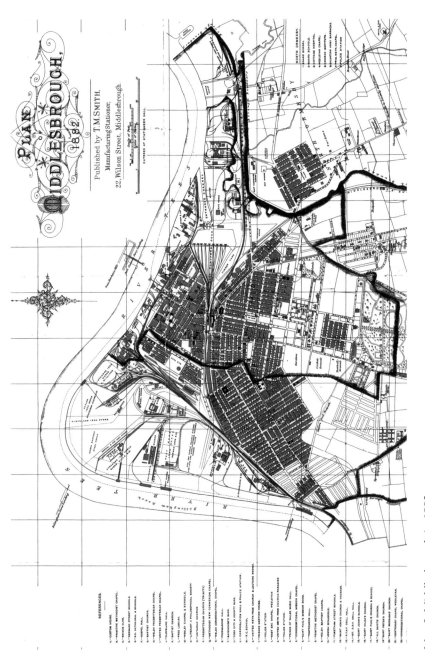

Map 5: Middlesbrough in 1882

1
Introduction: Urban Growth, Social Order and Policing

This is the story of an initially small but rapidly expanding community in the north-eastern corner of the north riding of Yorkshire, and the way in which its founding fathers and their successors set about creating and maintaining an acceptable degree of order and decorum in a town which, especially in its earlier days, had many of the qualities of a frontier settlement. More specifically, it is the story of a police force, from its creation and early vicissitudes to later, more stable times, and the work of its members. In part, this is an unashamedly local study that seeks to recount in detail the experience of a small group of men in one particular part of England over a period of some seven decades. However, despite its local focus, this book also throws light on the wider process of the creation of a policed society in the Victorian and Edwardian periods.

Over the last twenty years or so there has been an upsurge of interest in crime and policing in modern England and Wales. Emsley and Steedman have established the broad picture of police development while others such as Swift have provided valuable insight into local variations.[1] Similarly, the broad pattern of recorded crime has been delineated, notably in two important articles by Gatrell, while the creation of a policed society has been placed in a broader context of the rise of respectability.[2] Notwithstanding the recent spate of publications, our understanding of the evolution of policing and its impact upon crime is still dominated by two outstanding books that first appeared twenty years ago or more. David Philips' *Crime and Authority in Victorian England*, if not the first, was and is an outstanding study, firmly rooted in a detailed analysis of the Black Country, that provides an authoritative refutation of the highly-charged interpretations of crime in nineteenth-century England that relied too heavily and uncritically on literary sources such as Dickens.[3] This ground-breaking study was complemented by David Jones's insightful *Crime, Protest, Community and Police in Nineteenth-Century Britain*, which contained a series of studies that considered crime and police in rural and urban contexts and also in parts of Wales as well as England.[4] Although he and Philips share a common concern for the complex inter-relationship between criminals, the police and their wider community, not least in his work on Merthyr Tydfil, Jones modified Philips' emphasis on the relatively low levels of violence in mid-nineteenth-century Britain.

It is into this broad context that the study of Middlesbrough should be placed. It will be argued that, although in the long term a stable police force was created that contributed to the 'civilising' of a town that can rightly be considered to be a frontier settlement in its earliest days, the process was slow and that significant parts of the local community remained turbulent and threatening well into the last quarter of the nineteenth century. Middlesbrough was unusual in being a new town. Its growth from a negligible 'out-of-the-way place' in the 1820s to a town of some 120,000 inhabitants on the eve of the First World War unsurprisingly caught the popular imagination. The frontier town of the early-Victorian years – the 'British Ballarat' as Briggs described it – never entirely cast off its rough-and-ready image.[5] The town was clearly atypical and the experience of its police force necessarily unusual. However, the town's dramatic growth brought out in stark relief the problems faced, albeit in less extreme form, in many other parts of the country. Discussion of nineteenth-century urbanisation is enriched by a consideration of the distinctiveness of Middlesbrough, but the history of the town and of its police can only be fully appreciated when set in the wider context of Victorian urban and industrial development.[6]

During the nineteenth century the long-term processes of urbanisation and industrialisation accelerated at a rate that brought about a fundamental transformation of the country. Not only did the overall population grow but also the balance between town and country shifted significantly and irreversibly. People moved away from the hamlets and villages of England to the towns, especially the new industrial towns, as the centre of gravity of the country's economy shifted from agriculture to industry. Bolton and Burnley, or Halifax and Huddersfield, such were the exemplars of the new urban-industrial centre spawned by the classic 'industrial revolution'. At the micro level certain communities were transformed, though there is a danger of overstating the rate and extent of change in macro terms. Agriculture was still the largest single employer of male labour in the mid-nineteenth century, while in the late-nineteenth century the services sector was as important as the industrial to the well-being of the nation. But there can be little doubt that by the early twentieth century a series of profound and inter-related changes had taken place that had changed the face of the country, the nature of society and, perforce, the ways in which it was governed.[7]

The growth of towns and cities evoked mixed emotions. There was a very positive side: urban life was associated with wealth and culture. The town embodied the human triumph over nature. Here could be seen the visible signs of progress, order and civilisation that under-pinned a tradition of civic pride. But there was an equally negative side: towns were associated with major threats to order. To many respectable men and women, not just of the middle classes, they were 'physical and moral sewers' from which emanated threats to the well-being of the nation – disease, crime and disorder – that aroused considerable and continuing concern. There was something of a paradox in the fact that the town (or city) was living testament to progress, order and civilisation but created its own problems that threatened the existence of these virtues. The paradox could only be resolved by developing new ways of organising and governing society. The policeman with his bull-dog lamp, casting light into darkness, became a very apt symbol of the new urban order and the wishes of its ruling elites. Indeed, he was intended to be more: he was to be the embodiment of that wish to civilise urban society.

The association of towns and cities with crime and disorder has a long tradition but there was a qualitative change in the nineteenth century produced by the interaction of a number of different factors. The first has to do with the scale and pace of urban growth. Awareness and discussions of urban problems, even in the mid-eighteenth century, were dominated by the situation (real or imaginary) in London. The 'Great Wen' was of a size that set it apart from all other towns and cities. London never lost its absolute dominance in terms of brute size, but its relative importance in public perception declined as provincial centres burgeoned. Although their continuing dependence upon London meant that no genuine provincial 'capital' developed, the spectacular, distinctive and well-documented growth of Manchester and Liverpool, the emergence of medium-sized industrial towns in the west riding of Yorkshire, south Lancashire and the midlands, the expansion of old and new ports, and the appearance of sizable spa towns, transformed the face of England. The town, with its potential and problems, was an inescapable living presence across most of the country by the mid-nineteenth century.

The growth of towns and cities, lightly regulated in many ways, brought a variety of problems, of which the maintenance of social order is the most relevant to this study. The expanding towns, especially in the first half of the nineteenth century, grew because they attracted large numbers of people, often young and unmarried, lacking roots in the locality and less subject to normal social discipline. It is important not to exaggerate the disruption that took place: most migration was short-distance, many incomers had family or friends. However, it is equally important not to overstate the smoothness with which the transition from rural to urban took place, nor to underestimate the fears that were engendered by these unprecedented developments. A sudden influx of 'strangers' not only put pressure on physical resources but also put pressure on the social fabric of a town. There could be resentment between 'natives' and 'comers-in' as well as tensions between different migrant groups. Overcrowding in clearly defined parts of town could exacerbate these frictions. Small communities, characterised by face-to-face contact and codes of behaviour, often informally enforced, were gradually replaced by larger communities which were more impersonal and in which the informal 'ties that bind' were less secure, or at least, so many contemporaries believed.[8]

This situation was further compounded by the transition from a society characterised predominantly by vertical links to one characterised by horizontal links. Although less fashionable than some years ago, the question of class in modern English society remains a complex and contentious issue.[9] Historians will continue to differ in their assessment of the emergence, extent and nature of class in the eighteenth and nineteenth centuries and of the relative importance of class compared with gender or ethnic divisions. Few would contest, though, that there had been a shift from a world in which orders and interests were seen as the central notions around which the social order was structured to one in which class (however imprecisely defined) played a major role. For many influential (that is propertied and educated) Victorians there was little doubt that the lower orders or working classes were not just a group apart but represented a serious threat to the civilisation which they, the elites, embodied. The toiling classes were an essential element in the generation of wealth but they were also (potentially at least) a major threat to civilisation. There was a perceived need to control and discipline the public activities of the working classes in particular that dated back to the late eighteenth century but which was felt more keenly in the 1830s and 1840s. The 'new police' were undoubtedly seen as a defence for the law-abiding against the anti-social and criminal, and had an important and growing part to play in this process of social disciplining.

The emergence of larger, more impersonal, less cohesive urban communities was problematic enough in itself but the situation was further complicated by the emergence of new values and new expectations. At least four elements are worthy of note. First, attitudes towards personal security and public order changed. Behaviour, individual or collective, which once had been acceptable (or at least tolerated), was no longer so. There was less tolerance of interpersonal violence and growing criticism of boisterous and disruptive group behaviour. This impacted on society, and particularly working-class society, in a number of ways. Traditional forms of protest, for example food riots or mass demonstrations, were reconceptualised with greater, almost exclusive, emphasis on threats to order rather than expressions of the rights of free-born Englishmen.[10] Traditional recreational activities, bull-running in Stamford, Shrovetide football and so forth, were similarly stigmatized. Even long-established work practices, notably for street-traders and itinerant salesmen, came under threat as order in public places became increasingly prized, at least among certain of the opinion-formers and law-makers of Regency and Victorian England.[11] Second, ongoing changes in the construction of masculinity were intimately related to the increasing intolerance of violence. A reaction against the libertine discourse of the Regency aristocracy led to greater emphasis being placed on male gallantry and protectiveness towards weaker members of society. The dismantling of the 'Bloody Code' in the 1820s and 1830s was accompanied by a growing critique of 'barbaric' violence by parliamentary reformers and judges. Self-control was increasingly seen as a distinguishing feature of English men. Violence between men and, even more so, violence perpetrated by men on women, children and the elderly, was correspondingly condemned.[12] Third, and also closely linked to the new attitudes towards order, there was a growing desire to improve standards of public behaviour, thereby bringing respectability and decorum to the streets. Again, once-acceptable behaviour came under attack from those who wished to suppress vice and reform morals.[13] Finally, there was also an economic dimension to the new desire for order and decorum. Ill-disciplined, immoral men and women with their irregular lifestyles were unsuited to the increasingly structured and disciplined work practices of the factory and workshop. It is no coincidence that a reforming employer such as Wedgewood saw the reform of his workers' morals outside work to be related to and as important as the creation of a work discipline for them when employed at work.

The desire to re-moralise society was part of a wider religious revival dating from the late eighteenth century. This crusade was given added urgency by the growing awareness that religion – at least organised religion, especially in the form of the Church of England – played but little part in the lives of large numbers of ordinary men and women. Indeed, here was to be found, or so it was argued, the source of the problem. Lacking the saving influence of religion, growing up little better than the heathens of Africa or Asia (as they were seen), the working classes of urban England could hardly help but be immoral, ill-disciplined and given over to a life of crime![14]

Crime, like the poor, was an ever-present phenomenon, but perceptions of crime were not unchanging. During the last decade of the eighteenth century and the early years of the nineteenth, perceptions of and attitudes towards crime appear to have shifted significantly. Put simply, an older view, that crime was an inevitable but relatively marginal and unthreatening part of the natural order, was replaced by a newer view in which crime was a central (if soluble) problem of society.[15] The concept of crime was re-created and in the process of reconstruction took on a far greater significance. The multifaceted anxieties of a society undergoing fundamental change were displaced onto 'the criminal' who became folk devil and scapegoat.

The coming together of these different elements – more and larger towns, less cohesive communities, demand for new standards of security, order and discipline, the diminishing impact of Christianity and the new threat of crime – led to a reconsideration of the means of preserving order and their underlying principles. Unsurprisingly, this debate was initially focused on and largely restricted to London. Arguments about police reform in the capital rumbled on from the second quarter of the eighteenth century, if not before, and culminated in the debates and decisions of the 1820s from whence emerged Peel's Metropolitan Police in 1829.[16] However, it was obvious that the debate was not simply about London. It is a measure of the scale of the problem in the eyes of the political leaders of the time that the Whig government in 1832 considered a bill that would have introduced a national and centralised system of policing. The bill was never introduced to parliament and police reform took a different form but unmistakably this was a major political issue of the day. The extent of the provincial debate on policing has often been overlooked but, as Philips and Storch have recently demonstrated, this was a major issue in local politics across the country.[17] The precise significance of the 1839 Rural Constabulary Act will remain a matter of debate, but it cannot be denied that this piece of legislation was an important step in the evolution of modern policing during the second quarter of the nineteenth century, culminating in the 1856 County and Borough Police Act, which provided a framework of policing across the country.

The rapid growth of existing towns created a worrying range of difficulties, but the dramatic growth of a new town (Middlesbrough) posed problems of a different magnitude.[18] Here, old structures (of whatever nature, physical, social or political) were not swamped by growth, as happened in other fast-growing towns, they simply did not exist but had to be planned and created *ab initio*. The Owners of the Middlesbrough Estate, the town's founding fathers, undoubtedly had a plan for the physical layout of the new community and a vision of how that community was to be regulated. The physical environment was to be laid out symmetrically and growth was to take place in an orderly and regulated fashion. In addition, conditions were to be laid down governing the conduct of public life. Middlesbrough was to be an ordered and orderly place. The reality was starkly different. The original settlement (see Map 1) was soon swamped by the flood of workers who poured into the town. People lived in temporary accommodation – in mud huts and tents, on keelboats and steamboats – as infilling of the original site took place. The original gridiron pattern was subverted as streets were extended eastward and, more importantly, as the town sprawled southwards and westwards. Within a generation a new town was growing up south of the railway line (see Maps 2 and 3). Urban growth was not ordered and the new community was not orderly. Disorder and disease – made manifest in the dock riot of 1840 and the cholera and smallpox outbreaks of 1852 – presented very real threats. The original committee set up to govern the new town soon proved inadequate to the task. An Improvement Act was petitioned for and was passed by parliament in the summer of 1841.[19] This act was a statement of intent made in the face of great adversity. It would provide a framework within which the town was to be run (a framework that was further developed on acquiring borough status) but in itself did not guarantee success. The creation of a safe and healthy, well-run community depended upon the ability and determination of the founding fathers and the growing number of people employed by them. This study examines the way in which one part of the wider problem, the threat of crime and disorder, was tackled.

The book is divided chronologically into two sections, reflecting two distinct long phases in the development of the town. The first concentrates on the years from *circa* 1840 to 1870. These were years of long-term expansion in demographic and economic terms. They were also the years in which the founding fathers had to tackle a range of major problems which, while not unique in themselves, had occurred on an unprecedented scale. More specifically, these were the early years of policing in the town. The town's police force was founded in the early-1840s and effectively refounded in the mid-1850s. Unsurprisingly, these were years that witnessed considerable difficulties in the creation of a stable and effective police force and that also witnessed consider-able anxiety for the moral well-being and future of the town. There was a brittle confidence about the town and its future. The second period from the 1870s to the Great War saw continued economic and demographic growth but at a slower rate. The town's heavy industries faced greater competition, which tempered the boom of the mid-nineteenth century, but at the same time the local economy also diver-sified and matured. The original political elite, dominated by the iron and steel trade, was augmented by new men, many from retailing. Maturation also characterised the general governance of the town and the development of the police. The second and third generation of policemen who tramped the streets of Middlesbrough in the late nine-teenth and early twentieth centuries were a less volatile, more disci-plined group as policing became a recognised long-term career for a small number of men. The brash and often brutal 'British Ballarat' gradually succumbed to the forces of order. The anxieties and fears, clearly visible in the 1830s and 1840s, and so close to the surface in the 1850s and 1860s, were gradually, though partially, dispelled. The town never entirely threw off its reputation for violence but, even though it had spilled over its original borders, it gradually lost its frontier charac-teristics. Fears and anxieties were less apparent or more deeply buried by the last quarter of the century.

The Middlesbrough police are the main focus of this study. Consequently, certain aspects of the town's life are relegated to the periphery. The wider socio-political development is treated only as contextual material. This is not the place to write at length on the tem-perance and anti-gambling movements in the town, nor of the broader political evolution of Middlesbrough, except in so far as it impacts directly on the central issue of policing. Similarly, while the threat of criminality is of central importance, there is not here a systematic analysis of the ways in which Middlesbrough's criminals were pun-ished. Once again, this is an issue that is touched upon only when it impacts directly on policing.

The account that follows is in many important respects an 'official' history, looking from the top down, because it depends heavily upon such sources as the minutes of the committees of the Improvement Commission and later of the borough of Middlesbrough as well as the various reports and statistical returns produced by the chief constable. The archival evidence reflects varying needs and perceptions. At any one time the central government sought annual information on particular issues (habitual criminality or habitual drunkenness, for example) that reflected its particular concerns; the watch committee had its own agenda, as did the chief constable. Indeed, the response of the latter had a significant impact on the surviving historical record. The earnestness with which Edward Saggerson produced his reports contrasts with the more minimalist approach of his successor William Ashe.

The statistical evidence of crime in the town is particularly problematic. Recorded crime is not a record of actual crime and changes in the level of recorded crime cannot be assumed to reflect changes in the true incidence of crime. The recorded crime rate was affected by changes in the definition of crime as well as by changes in policing and prosecution behaviour. In a legal system that still depended upon the action of the victim in prosecuting an offence, there was considerable scope for the exercise of discretion and, as a consequence, there was considerable and fluctuating variation between the incidence of crime and its prosecution through the courts. This was particularly true of petty crime where the actions of a crusading individual, a determined watch committee or a zealous chief constable could have a significant short-term impact on the official figures. Finally, the situation is further complicated by changes in the administration of justice. Summary justice was extended significantly over the course of the nineteenth century, notably through the 1847 and 1850 Juvenile Offenders Acts, the 1855 Criminal Justice Act and the 1879 Prevention of Crime Act. There were also important changes in the collection of official crime statistics, in 1833 and 1856, and later in 1893, that make long-term analyses highly problematic.[20]

Although varying in the level of confidence they place in the statistics, historians as diverse as Gatrell and Hadden, Jones, Rudé, Philips and Williams have all argued that useful conclusions can be drawn not simply about the working of the criminal justice system but also about the state of crime.[21] The validity of crime statistics (and thus their value to the historian) has most recently and most provocatively been challenged by Howard Taylor, who has argued that they 'largely reflected supply-side politics'.[22] The muted enthusiasm of ratepayers for financing prosecutions, the parsimony of the Treasury and an underfunded police that had 'a great disincentive to prosecute and a strong motivation to keep the crime figures down' resulted, to all intents and purposes, in a conspiracy that created a fraudulent 'English miracle' of declining Victorian crime rates. On closer examination the argument is less compelling than first appears to be the case. There is little or no evidence either of direct Treasury interference or of the actual (as opposed to alleged) impact on prosecution. Indeed, Howard Taylor concedes that 'further detailed research is necessary, both at the local and national level, to determine the full effect of Treasury and local parsimony on prosecutions level'. Similarly, the bold assertion that 'chief constables were forced to cover up and do nothing about the true extent of crime in their localities' and that 'they had to produce figures of recorded crime that confirmed the number of prosecutions brought' is unsubstantiated. There is also, in general terms, an inherent implausibility in the argument. It is difficult to believe that, at a time when concern for the protection of person and property was increasing rather than decreasing and when the local press provided detailed coverage of events, that police chiefs would have been able to maintain a 'public illusion' if in fact there were 'vastly more offences [being committed] but most criminals got away without prosecution'. More specifically, there is no evidence to suggest that prosecutions in Middlesbrough were seriously constrained by financial considerations, nor that successive police chiefs during and after the 1850s were powerless to act and merely compiled figures that perpetuated comforting myths. This is not to say that all crimes were prosecuted. Clearly they were not and there were people in the town who wished to see more done, especially against drunks. Nor is it to say that all the crime statistics are beyond question. Clearly certain series had major flaws, but the preoccupation with indictable offences is misleading, as by far the greater part of police intervention was for non-indictable offences.[23] Rather it is to argue that, while the criminal statistics were the product of a complex interaction between criminals and prosecutors (and as such reflect the determination and ability to prosecute as well as the level of offending behaviour), they provide valuable, if approximate, information on the state of crime. In other words, it will be argued that the decline in crime rates in nineteenth-century Middlesbrough reflects a real change and was not a confidence trick played on a gullible public by the local police and other local and national actors in the criminal justice system.

There are other problems with the official record, not least its incompleteness. The minutes of the Improvement Commission are tantalisingly sparse. At times they hint at heated debate about the state of the police but merely record the bare bones of a decision. At a more mundane level they do not provide a complete record of the men who served as police in the town. Indeed, this problem remains serious until the 1860s. The documentary coverage is more complete for the later years, though there remain some surprising omissions – most notably the absence of annual reports for certain years – and the approved destruction of old police records by chief constable Riches, acting as a new broom in the 1890s, is a sorry loss.[24] None the less, there is a greater volume of material for the latter part of the nineteenth century but it retains its official, and therefore inherently limited, quality.

As a consequence, the voice of the ordinary policeman is rarely heard, or at least rarely heard directly. The policeman appears in the record more often as a problem, a man to be disciplined or dismissed for some breach of regulations. Less commonly he appears as a success, a man to be praised for bravery or devotion to duty. But what the ordinary policeman thought of his job or his position in society is beyond the surviving record. Indirectly he expressed his dissatisfaction by demanding more pay or resigning for better-paid or less-arduous employment; indirectly he expressed his commitment by making a career of policing or by acting in ways that put him in danger. Very rarely did he express himself directly, or, if and when he did, it went unrecorded. Similarly, the voice of the policed occurs infrequently in the official record. To some extent this can be offset by consulting the local press. Editors and correspondents undoubtedly commented on the way in which the town was policed, but the opinions thus expressed were drawn from a narrow section of society. Those who felt most directly the force of policing – the working classes in general, the unskilled and the Irish in particular – rarely, if ever, wrote to the local press. Consequently, they also appear most commonly as problems: threatening figures accused of serious crime and sent to assize or quarter sessions, or faintly comic figures whose pathetic criminality provided humorous copy for the journalist dispatched to the town's petty sessions. Once again, their experience and opinions can only be reconstructed indirectly.

The story that unfolds in the following pages does not follow a simple 'whiggish' pattern of progress. The model of an efficient new police introduced to combat rising lawlessness and quickly and warmly accepted by the public has but a partial application to Middlesbrough.[25]

That there were major threats to law and order in the town during the 1830s and 1840s is beyond dispute but the response, in terms of policing at least, was half-hearted and parsimonious. New policing in Middlesbrough effectively dates from the mid-1850s but the creation of an effective body of men took several years. Progress was made, especially after the 1860s, but improvements in policing did not go unchecked. Indeed, the early twentieth century was to witness a minor crisis in the town force as suitable recruits became more difficult to find. Turnover rates, which had been falling steadily for 30 years, began to rise again in Edwardian Middlesbrough. At the same time, though not simply as a consequence of the difficulties of recruitment, there was an upturn in the incidence of crime in the first years of the twentieth century, which contrasted with the falling rates of the Victorian years. Furthermore, there was from the outset considerable opposition that manifested itself in collective and individual hostility to the police, which declined over time but never disappeared.

The history of policing in Middlesbrough, however, does not conform precisely to 'revisionist' interpretations of police history, much in favour in the 1970s and 1980s, with their emphasis upon social control and class conflict. There was more to policing than social control. The rhetoric of 'the fight against crime' had some substance and was not simply a cover for more partisan, class-based actions. There was also a welfare dimension, formal and informal, to police work in the town. However, there is little doubt that the police were seen by many local politicians and local citizens to be key agents in the disciplining of the working classes and especially the 'poor Irish' of Middlesbrough. For all that, intention did not guarantee outcome, and it is clear that the wishes of the watch committee, for example, were mediated by the more pragmatic considerations of chief constables and, perhaps more so, of ordinary constables. Furthermore, attitudes did not always divide along class lines. Indeed, in the middle decades of the nineteenth century there were persistent complaints about the conduct of the police expressed by middle-class critics on behalf of working-class victims of police insensitivities and brutality. Similarly, it is clear that the working-class response to the police, even in the earlier years, was not uniformly hostile. That said, nineteenth-century Middlesbrough was a town with deep divisions – class, ethnic and gender – and the police, charged with enforcing order and thus effectively preserving the *status quo,* were (and were seen to be) agents of an elite which sought to discipline and even improve the behaviour of the population at large. The tensions thus engendered were not fully resolved but, partly as a result of the development of policing within the town and partly as a result of broader changes in society, conflict lessened and Middlesbrough, not unlike many early twentieth-century towns and cities, became accustomed to being a policed community. This creation of a policed community, this creation of a *modus vivendi* between police and policed, over a relatively short period of time and in such distinctive and difficult circumstances, was a considerable achievement. The credit for it rests largely but not exclusively with those charged with the responsibility of policing the town; and within that group due credit must be given to those who implemented policies on the streets of Middlesbrough and not simply to the senior officers who supervised them. Victorian policemen can easily be caricatured and their importance overlooked. They were more than loyal servants of the local watch committee, more than insensitive 'domestic missionaries' or arbitrary enforcers of class-based legislation, and more than avuncular and jovial (and rather jokey) bobbies. They were also men, often with limited training and skills, performing, albeit imperfectly at times, a difficult job in difficult, even dangerous, circumstances. Certain individuals were 'heroes', others 'villains' but as a body of men they emerge from the historical record as a less than perfect group but one increasingly characterised by a willingness and ability to contribute to the development of the town as a community. These were the men who were to play a major role in the transformation of the 'British Ballarat'.

2
The Birth of the 'Infant Hercules': Urban and Industrial Growth in Middlesbrough, *c.* 1840 to the 1870s

The history of policing in Middlesbrough cannot be properly under-stood without an awareness of the highly distinctive economic and social development of the town.[1] Middlesbrough experienced a rate of population and industrial growth unparalleled by any other town in England. There was something almost superhuman about the town's early industrialisation that was captured in Gladstone's oft-quoted reference, made on his visit in October 1862, to the 'infant Hercules'. The distinctive and dramatic growth was to pose particular problems for the police charged with the responsibility for upholding the law and maintaining order and decorum in what was, at times, effectively a frontier town that would not have been out of place in America or Australia. That said, Middlesbrough shared certain characteristics with other towns and cities in England and Wales. The rapid growth of the iron industry in south Wales, for example, gave rise to tumultuous, male-dominated communities in places such as Merthyr Tydfil. Similarly, the problems associated with a relatively large immigrant, especially Irish, population were to be found both in large cities, notably London, Liverpool and Manchester, but also in smaller towns such as Wolverhampton.

Economic developments

The agrarian-based settlement of 1801 with its 4 houses and 25 people was to become a major industrial centre from the 1830s onwards, but the census enumerators who tallied the 154 inhabitants in 1831 could scarcely have envisaged the transformation that was about to take place. The combination of growing demand for coal, the development of the Stockton and Darlington Railway and the navigational limitations of the river Tees created a window of opportunity that was exploited to great effect by Joseph Pease and his Quaker colleagues, who in 1829 became the Owners of the Middlesbrough Estate and the founders of the modern town. The extension of the railway to Middlesbrough was completed in December 1830 and the first coal was loaded at the new staithes a month later. Joseph Pease's initial estimate of annual exports, made in 1826, forecast a total of 10,000 tons. In 1831 some 150,000 tons of coal were shipped out. Two years later coal exports had more than doubled to 336,000 tons. The scale of activity had exceeded Pease's wildest hopes and acted as a powerful engine of change for the local economy.

Additional staithes were built on either side of the originals to cope with the dramatic growth of coal exports, but it soon became apparent that this was not the most effective way of shipping coal on a tidal river. The desirability of a constant water level necessitated the building of a new dock and, after a visit by Thomas Cubitt in 1836 to draw up plans, the decision to build was taken in 1838 by the Middlesbrough Owners, who in return gained the monopoly of all coal carried past Stockton. Four years later the work was complete. Ten coal staithes, capable of loading at 16 tons per hour, had been erected, and there was space for some 3,000 coal wagons and 150 ships in a dock complex that covered a total of 15 acres, 6 of water and 9 on land.[2] Impressive though this investment was, it could not safeguard the town's economic future. Success was threatened when competition from nearby Hartlepool grew considerably, and as the extension of the railway to that town and the completion of the Victoria Dock in 1840 resulted in Middlesbrough losing its shipping advantage. By the early 1840s the Hartlepool and Dock Railway Company was carrying a third more coal than its rival Stockton and Darlington Railway Company. The dangerous nature of the river Tees from Middlesbrough to its mouth, coupled with the problem of silting up, made Middlesbrough less and less attractive to coal exporters in the 1840s. By the end of the decade it was becoming obvious that coal exports were falling and the future was looking bleak. Yet salvation was closer to hand than anyone realised.

In response to the considerable demand created by the expansion of the railways in the region, Henry Bolckow and John Vaughan, with the support of Joseph Pease, established their ironworks in 1839 to the north of the original town and adjacent to the river Tees in what was to become Vulcan Street (see Map 3). Two years later the rolling mill, also in Vulcan, Street started production of rails for the

Stockton and Darlington railway. By 1846 production had reached 20,000 tons, mainly in the form of rails and bars, but the company also had machine-tool facilities that enabled the production of small and medium-sized steam engines to take place. The support of Pease was essential. Among other things he ensured that orders from the Stockton and Darlington railway came their way. Indeed without this support Bolckow & Vaughan might well not have survived the slump of 1847. Iron manufacturing was not the preserve of one firm. Among other early companies were Gilkes & Wilson, responsible for the Tees Engine Works, also in Vulcan Street, and later in 1852 the Tees Ironworks, which was built on marshy ground near the eastern end of the Middlesbrough Estate. Once again, the Peases were involved in financing the enterprise. It is no coincidence that these industrial leaders also played a prominent role in the political life of the town.

All iron producers faced problems of fluctuating demand and uncertainties about the supply of iron ore. The former problem was a recurring feature of the iron and steel trade, but the latter was solved in dramatic fashion with the discovery of iron ore in the nearby Eston Hills in 1850. The first quarry, the aptly named 'Bold Venture', produced over 1,000 tons of ironstone a day. In little more than 5 years ironstone production in Cleveland had risen to over a million tons a year. The local iron industry was revitalised and experienced a period of unprecedented expansion. Bolckow & Vaughan established blast-furnaces and ironworks on newly reclaimed land in Middlesbrough and Eston in 1852. In 1853 Bell Brothers set up an ironworks across the Tees at Port Clarence and the Teesside Ironworks of Messrs. Snowden & Hopkins was also started that year. The industry expanded in the districts immediately surrounding Middlesbrough. In 1854 Sir Bernard Samuelson established a blast-furnace at South Bank and the Cochranes did likewise at Ormesby. The outbreak of the Crimean war provided a further, albeit short-term, boost. By the middle of the decade there were some 14 blast-furnaces in Middlesbrough and a further 14 to the east of the town, producing some quarter of a million tons of iron. The balance of economic power in the town was clearly shifting. What is more, the new entrepreneurs were determined to maximise their position through cooordinated action. In 1855 the first meeting of the Cleveland Ironmasters' Association took place in the *Talbot Inn*, Middlesbrough. A new presence had been established which was to have a profound effect on the subsequent development of the town.

The growth of the iron trade was stunningly spectacular. New firms, such as Fox, Head & Co. and Gilkes, Wilson, Pease & Co. entered alongside established producers, but no one rivalled the enterprise of Bolckow & Vaughan. When, in 1865, they became a limited liability company with a capital of £2,500,000, they employed some 8,000 men. Long-term growth was punctuated by slumps in the late 1850s and mid-1860s, and booms, most notably in the early-1870s, when the Franco-Prussian War disrupted European production and greatly increased the demand for British iron. By the early 1870s the Cleveland District, with some 90 blast-furnaces, was producing over 2 million tons annually, or one-third of the national output of pig-iron. Production was heavily concentrated in the Ironmasters' District of Middlesbrough, located to the north-west of the town in the loop of the Tees (see Map 4) and further east along the Middlesbrough to Redcar railway, but its social impact was felt much more widely.[3]

The expansion of pig-iron manufacturing was paralleled by the growth in production of malleable iron via the puddling process. No evidence survives from the earliest days but it is known that in the early 1850s there were two major puddling plants: the Middlesbrough Ironworks of Bolckow & Vaughan and the Teesside Ironworks of Snowden & Hopkins and, in all probability, a total of 30 puddling furnaces. By 1863 there was a total of 191 puddling furnaces in Middlesbrough including 68 owned by Bolckow & Vaughan and 55 by Hopkins & Co. A fall in demand and a disruptive strike, following a decision to cut wages by 10 per cent, checked expansion but rapid growth resumed in the late 1860s and early 1870s and peaked in 1873 when the number of puddling furnaces in the town topped 400. The newly-formed Britannia Iron Co., whose driving force was Sir Bernard Samuelson MP of the Newport Ironworks, accounted for 120 of them compared with the 100 of Hopkins, Gilkes & Co. who had succeeded Bolckow & Vaughan as the second largest producers. The expansion of the railways and the growth of iron shipbuilding created buoyant demand conditions that underpinned this expansion. However, the dominance of iron production was ended by the long-term development of steel production, and was precipitated by the dramatic depression of the mid-1870s.

With the rapid expansion of iron-making came growth in the engineering and shipbuilding trades. In 1842 the York & Darlington Railway Co. opened an engineering shop. The leading light was Edgar Gilkes who, with Isaac Wilson, took over the works in 1844 before amalgamating with the Teesside Ironworks to create Hopkins, Gilkes &

Co. Teesside Iron and Engine Works. In 1843 Bolckow & Vaughan, concerned with securing an outlet for their iron production, also established an engineering works while the Teesside Bridge & Engineering Works was formed in 1850. The earliest shipbuilding yards in Middlesbrough had produced wooden ships. As early as 1840, William Cudworth, a Middlesbrough man, launched the first steam ship, *The Fortitude*, on the Tees. In 1858 Rake Kimber & Co. made the first iron ship at Middlesbrough, the *De Brus*. The Backhouse and Dixon shipbuilding yards opened in 1866, while in 1873 Raylton Dixon & Co. shipbuilders were founded. In addition, there were a number of smaller manufacturing industries including chemical, wire, tank and boiler works.

Heavy industry was of fundamental importance to the development of the town, but there were other industries that played their part. The rapid growth of the town and the accompanying demand for housing meant that the building and ancillary trades were an important source of employment. Such was the demand for bricks and tiles that the Owners had to open a second brick yard to supplement the original that had been in existence since before the founding of the town. In addition, skilled tradesmen such as cabinetmakers and watchmakers were a small but significant element in the local economy. So too was the Middlesbrough Pottery, which had been founded in 1835 by Richard Otley as a deliberate attempt to diversify the town's economy. Similarly, retailing and even leisure provisions developed from the earliest days as it became apparent that there was a rapidly growing and concentrated mass market in and around the town. Postgate, reflecting on the town's earliest years, was struck by the 'considerable number of tradesmen with their families' attracted to the town by the opening of the port in 1830.[4] The leisure trades were also present from the outset. Visiting shows provided occasional highlights, but the commonest form of entertainment and escape, for men at least, was to be found in the many inns and public houses that sprang up. White's Directory for 1842 listed some 28 inns and taverns, and 9 beer houses as well as 5 brewers in the town.

The development of the Ironmasters' District and the growth of the dock area were of considerable economic importance to the town, but they also had a wider social significance. The dock area quickly acquired a reputation for drunkenness, violence and prostitution that posed particular problems for the town's new police. The grim expanses of the industrial centre posed different problems. Policemen, including those paid by private companies, had to guard against industrial thefts, but long, inclement winter nights tempted several men to shirk their duty and seek comfort in one of the works' cabins.

Demographic and social developments

At the start of the nineteenth century there was an insignificant settlement of 4 houses and 25 inhabitants on what was to become the town's site. Thirty years later there was little sign of the changes to come, but the opening of the rail link and the dramatic expansion of coal exports transformed the little village. By 1841 the population had risen to 5,463. Population growth in the following decade was less rapid, though renewed economic activity in the 1850s and 1860s saw the town's population soar to almost 40,000 by the census of 1871. Joseph Pease's dream of a planned community of some 5,000 inhabitants was swept away by economic and demographic realities.[5]

In 1830 the Owners of the Middlesbrough Estate purchased just over 500 acres of agricultural land, including the one farm that remained, upon which to develop their new town. Their surveyor, Richard Otley, produced a plan for a town that would occupy a 26 acre site, with 125 building plots organised in a simple grid centred on the church and market-place, and lying to the east of the newly completed Middlesbrough branch railway and immediately adjacent to the wharf and coal staithes of Port Darlington. The majority of the plots were sold freehold but, under the Deeds of Covenant attached to the conveyances, the purchasers were required to pave and sewer the roads and to meet basic building requirements, regarding window and door sizes, for houses that faced on to the main streets. The influx of population could not be accommodated in the original town. The three roads of the original grid running approximately east to west were extended in an easterly direction as far as the dock boundary, and further development took place in the triangle of land lying to the south of the original town, with the dock branch railway line effectively forming the southern border. The Market Place, opened in December 1840, was the focal point of the town and it was there that the old town hall stood from 1846 and in which the original police station was housed until 1852. In that year the police moved to North Street, where they stayed until moving into the new town hall in Albert Road in 1886.

The original town soon became densely populated. The original plots of land were of some 700 square yards that enabled builders to construct cottages – as many as 12 per plot – behind the three or four front houses on each parcel of land. These cottages were commonly built along the sides of a narrow yard with privies in the centre. The yard itself was entered through a tunnel through the front houses. Conditions were worst in places such as Graham's Yard or Chapman's Yard in the north-west corner of the old town, but the situation was only little better in culs-de-sac such as Mason Street which were located in yards behind the row of houses. The situation was further compounded by the juxtaposition of residential and commercial premises, including numerous beerhouses. It was in these narrow streets that some of the worst policing problems were to be found. Living in close proximity and with inadequate facilities, men and women easily fell to blows. Day-to-day tensions fuelled by alcohol gave rise, at times, to more serious communal conflicts. For the police these were dangerous streets to patrol. Violent assaults on the police by the public, singly or collectively, were a common experience. None the less, it remains the case that, unlike the China district of Merthyr, for example, Middlesbrough did not have an unpoliced district that had to be 'conquered'. In its early years the town was undoubtedly under-policed, but there was a continuing presence on which to build.[6]

By the mid-1850s the town's population had spilled over its southern boundary and a new town developed south of the railway line. This too was based on a grid pattern, but the overall process of development was unstructured and unregulated. There were three major north/south links between the old town and the new: Albert Road, Linthorpe Road and Boundary Road. Cutting across these were Wilson Street and Corporation Road, which was effectively the southern limit of the town by the mid-1860s. A decade later the southern boundary had moved to Grange Road (see Map 4). Intensive house-building also took place to the west, notably along Newport Road and Cannon Street. Housing along the main thoroughfares, notably Albert Road, tended to be larger. Behind this façade smaller houses – and many of the houses built in these years were very small – were hidden. The need to house such a rapidly growing population combined with the economic realities of providing working-class houses resulted in the construction of large numbers of tightly-packed, drab houses. The problems associated with the old town were replicated, though it was somewhat later in the century that the Cannon Street district first acquired its reputation for violence and lawlessness.[7]

The rows of functional terraced street houses dominated the new town and contrasted with the larger terraces built on the south of Newport Road for the professional classes. Even sharper was the contrast with the new residential suburbs.[8] Southfield Villas date from 1853 and North Park Road from 1866. Both were quickly swallowed up by the rapidly growing town; but Grove Hill, developed in the 1860s, retained its identity as an area of superior housing for the town's elites. Far less prone to drunkenness and violence, these districts were targets for thieves. Patrolling policemen noted the presence of open or unfastened windows and the police superintendent regularly chastised the middle-class inhabitants for their foolish neglect!

The town's population was characterised by a number of distinctive features. First, from its earliest days there was a significant element of long-distance migration to the town, which stands in contrast to patterns of migration to other towns in the country. Leonard's detailed analysis, based on census enumerators' returns, reveals that in 1841 55 per cent the (male) heads of household were born in either the North Riding of Yorkshire or Durham, and this figure fell to 50 per cent in 1861, and below 40 per cent in 1871 as more long-distance migrants moved into the town.[9] The contrast is even more striking when one considers the evidence relating to the predominantly young, unmarried lodger population of the town. Two-thirds came from outside Yorkshire in 1841 and almost 80 per cent from outside the North Riding of Yorkshire and Durham in 1871. This lodger population was not homogenous. A distinction, which runs throughout the period, should be made between skilled labourers who tended to come from other parts of England and Wales and unskilled labourers who came increasingly from Ireland. Relative to its size, Middlesbrough had a large Irish community but one that was largely cut off from both the predominantly English working classes and also English Catholics. Often viewed in the local press as little more than savages, Irish men and women were involved in frequently spectacular disturbances and,

Table 2.1: Middlesbrough: selected demographic characteristics, 1841–71

	Total households	Average size	Age of head of household	Percentage households with lodgers	Lodgers	
					Ave. number	Ave. age
1841	5,463	5.90	36.6	60	2.6	27.6
1851	7,631	4.54	40.4	13	1.7	29.4
1861	18,992	5.23	39.5	29	2.2	29.8
1871	39,563	5.33	39.2	27	2.1	30.7

Source: Adapted from J W Leonard, Urban and Demographic Change in Middlesbrough, unpublished D. Phil., University of York, 1974.

more generally, were heavily over-represented in the crime statistics. The extent to which this was simply a product of racial and religious prejudice is difficult to establish precisely. While there is evidence to suggest that there were important (and long-lasting) religious tensions in the town that were compounded by a belief in the violent and uncouth behaviour of Irish immigrants, it is also the case that the unskilled, working-class Irish represented the most serious, and perhaps most easily identifiable, threat to order and decorum from 'the dangerous classes' in general.[10]

The second and related characteristic is the youthfulness of the town's population. A sixth of the town's population was under 5 years of age in 1841. More significantly for our purposes, just over 40 per cent of the total population, and 45 per cent of the male population, were aged between 20 and 40, with a further 17 per cent in their teens. By 1871 the age profile of the town had been modified somewhat, but still some 36 per cent of the total population, and 39 per cent of males, were aged between 20 and 40. Middlesbrough was very much a young person's town. Furthermore, especially in the early years, this was a distinctly male population.[11] Males accounted for 54 per cent of the population in 1841, outnumbering females by over 400, with three-quarters of this surplus concentrated in the 15–45 age groups. In 1871 men still accounted for 54 per cent of the town's population. The absolute difference was now almost 3,500, with three-quarters of the surplus in the 20–40 age range. Nowhere was this gender imbalance clearer than among the lodger population. In 1841, 88 per cent of lodgers were male and, although this figure dropped to just over 80 per cent 10 years later, the figures in 1861 and 1871 were 93 and 97 per cent, respectively. A large number of young, unmarried men, often in relatively well-paid occupations but with very few or no familial ties in the town, represented considerable potential for disturbance, as the crime figures amply testify, though drunkenness and violence were not the monopoly of Middlesbrough men.

The very rapid and unexpected rate of population growth outstripped the plans of the town's founding fathers and resulted in considerable overcrowding and the attendant problems of ill-health. The 1841 census recorded labourers dwelling in temporary 'Hutts' near Durham Street as well as a minority of the population living in keels and steamboats and even in tents. The lower rate of population increase in the 1840s somewhat eased the pressure of population on resources, but this did not prevent a deterioration in the standard of health, especially as infill building created back-to-back arrangements and dark, airless courts. The problem of overcrowding was exacerbated by the dampness of the low-lying riverside site and the growing industrial pollution. The 1854 Ranger Report painted a grim picture of defective houses cramped together with inadequate drainage and ventilation. In some of the worst cases, such as the inhabited cellars in Hopper's Yard there was 'liquid refuse oozing through the walls from the ground above'. Not surprisingly, the health of the town gave rise to concern. Outbreaks of cholera were reported in the town in 1849, 1852/3 and again in 1854/5. Smallpox broke out in 1852 but the major and most persistent killer diseases were typhus, diarrhoea and measles. With an estimated mortality rate of 30 per 1,000 in 1852 and 35 per 1,000 in 1853, Middlesbrough was one of the unhealthiest towns in the country. In response, a private act was brought before parliament in 1855 to permit the 1848 Public Health Act to be applied to the town.[12]

These problems were further exacerbated by the upsurge of population in the 1850s and 1860s. The town spilled out beyond its original confines and building commenced 'south of the border'. Despite some larger houses along Albert Road, the main thoroughfare to the railway station, the bulk of the new houses were small and heavily concentrated in a drab development dominated by a gridiron pattern. More importantly, there were few restrictions on the private contractors and builders before the advent of the 1875 Public Health Act. Unsurprisingly, the crude death rate in Middlesbrough in 1871 was well above the national average. Initially the old town, north of the railway line, had been the most overcrowded and unhealthy area, but by the 1870s the western districts of the town had become the sites of the worst health problems. Despite being considered by the Medical Officer of Health as unsuitable for housing because of its low-lying nature and vulnerability to flooding, this was the area which was to absorb most of the incoming population, including the many Irish who were housed in some of the worst accommodation in the town. In addition to the threat to health, the cramped conditions and inadequate facilities created tensions that burst into crime. Fights broke out over access to water taps, 'washing line' quarrels were regularly reported in the local press, and the day-to-day tensions, exacerbated by poverty and drink, brought inter-family and interpersonal violence on a large scale. It also drove an unfortunate few to suicide.

Middlesbrough's emergence as a major industrial town aroused considerable admiration and pride. Gladstone's comment was but the best-known example of the praise that was lavished on the achievements of the town's founding fathers. Success brought congratulations and bred confidence, but there was also a darker, less confident side to popular attitudes. The inadequate facilities and resulting squalor that characterised the narrow, densely packed working-class backstreets contrasted with the splendid housing enjoyed by men such as Bolckow and Vaughan. Spectacular outbreaks of major killer diseases, notably cholera, were a source of considerable local official concern. However, to many contemporary observers, more worrying than the undoubted physical problems facing the town were the moral problems that beset it. The frontier town from the 1830s and 1840s was characterised by an overwhelmingly working-class population with little in the way of beneficial middle- or upper-class guidance. One observer, writing in 1838, spoke in horror of the 'rough set' in Middlesbrough. Particular concern was excited by the fact that there was '*not one gentleman in the place*'.[13] Although he corrected himself to note the presence of one gentleman in the town, there was no disguising the fact that he was convinced that such a social imbalance was a source of trouble. And trouble there most definitely was in the form of large-scale rioting in 1840. The dock riot appeared as the tip of an iceberg of violence in the male-dominated community. Property was threatened, or so it seemed, by a criminal (or criminally inclined) class that found shelter in the over-crowded working-class streets. In addition, the town quickly gained a reputation for drunkenness and prostitution that persisted through subsequent decades. Less than two years after Gladstone's fulsome praise for the industrial strength of the town, the local newspaper, the *Middlesbrough Weekly News*, was more concerned with the 'moral condition' of Middlesbrough.[14] Rapid economic growth, a surging population – dominated by young men, many drawn from all parts of the country – and the youthfulness of the town's institutions posed real problems for the town's paternalistic leaders as they sought to establish social and moral order initially under the provisions of the 1841 Improvement Act and after incorporation in 1853 within the framework of the Municipal Corporations Act.

3

The New Police in Middlesbrough: From the 1841 Improvement Act to the Early Years of the 1856 County and Borough Police Act

For good reason, historians have drawn attention to the flurry of legisla-tion and reform that reshaped policing in England during the second quarter of the nineteenth century.[1] The various pressures that gave rise to the Metropolitan Police Act of 1829 and, perhaps more strikingly, the Whigs' draft Police Bill of 1832 accelerated (and in some respects set in train) processes of change that were to have a fundamental impact on the social development of the nation.[2] However, it is all too easy to lose sight of what did not change in the 1830s and 1840s. The unspectacular, the relatively unchanging all too often does not catch the eye of either the contemporary observer or the later historian. Such is the case with the development of modern policing. In many respects the most striking feature of these decades is the limited impact made by new ideas. The policing provisions of the Municipal Corporation Act (1835) were not adopted with great vigour, especially among medium-sized boroughs, while the 1839 Rural Constabulary Act, significantly a piece of permis-sive legislation, was ignored in many parts of the country, where polic-ing continued along traditional lines. The system that had long centred on parish constables proved both durable and adaptable. More often than not, key figures remained unconvinced that the promised benefits of a new system of policing outweighed the additional financial costs, let alone the possible loss of local control. Local initiatives were to be found: the hiring of Metropolitan policemen in case of emergency, the swearing in of special constables to meet a particular problem, or the creation of an association for the prosecution of felons, including privately paid police in some instances. But, importantly, such development took place within the framework of traditional policing.[3]

Such was the case in the North Riding of Yorkshire. Parochial policing was supplemented by private initiatives such as the Cleveland General Association established in November 1839. Reflecting a more general determination to facilitate prosecutions, its declared aims provide an interesting insight into the priorities of its founders. The Association was, unsurprisingly, committed 'to use every endeavour to detect and prosecute to conviction any person or persons who may be guilty of Felonies [and] Robberies', but also focused on 'Petty Thefts, Assaults, Breaking down fences and gates, Trespassing upon property, cutting down young trees or underwood, breaking windows, or committing any other Malicious Trespass or Misdemeanour.' Poachers, vagrants and 'all persons Encamping upon the Road Sides' were singled out for attention, as were, less obviously, 'all Farmers' Servants, Coachmen and others who may be detected in driving their waggons, carts and carriages furiously or negligently on the Turnpike Roads or Highways, so as to endanger the Lives and Persons of Her Majesty's subjects.'[4]

There was, however, no widespread support for the adoption of the 1839 Rural Constabulary Act in the county. On the contrary, and as in several other parts of the country, the magistrates of the county meeting in 1840 were bombarded with petitions from numerous townships whose inhabitants, like those from Kirby Moorside, had 'learnt with great Alarm, that the Establishment of a Rural Police is intended', despite the fact that in their opinion there were 'no instances of Insubordination or riotous Proceedings . . . but that on the contrary, the Riding is in a state of perfect tranquillity' that rendered a police force 'altogether unnecessary and uncalled for'.[5] There were other considerations. The petitioners noted that they and their property were 'already heavily burthened with rates for Poor, Church, Highway and County': hence their opposition to 'this additional and unnecessary tax'.[6]

Middlesbrough in the early nineteenth century was one of numerous small habitations, to be found throughout the length and breadth of the country, policed in time-honoured fashion by a Head Constable responsible for the hundred. A concern with crimes against property in general and with crimes committed by the inhabitants of Middlesbrough led to the creation of a Society for the Conviction of Felons which appointed 41-year-old James Oliver as the first constable of the new town in 1830. A local man, originally a shoemaker from the nearby village of Linthorpe, he was permitted to combine the post of constable with that of ferryman across the Tees.[7] Oliver was assisted by Richard Swinburne in the day-to-day preservation of order in a town that was soon to expand rapidly. Almost no evidence has survived from these early years, but it is apparent that the life of a constable's assistant was not always easy. On at least two occasions, in 1839 and again in 1840, Swinburne was the victim of an assault that gave rise to prosecution at the Northallerton quarter sessions.[8] Of greater concern to the magistracy of the county was the more general threat to order and the 'inefficiency of the Constabulary force' in the North Riding. Such was their concern that it was felt appropriate to appoint 'a body of Constables disposable at any point of the Shire'.[9] Such action was insufficient to quell fears, and in December of the same year the Cleveland Association agreed to pay for two mounted policemen, to be stationed close to Middlesbrough at Guisborough and Stokesley, to preserve order in Langbaurgh.[10] The impact of these measures cannot easily be gauged. The Association's claim that vagrancy had been almost entirely suppressed is unconvincing, though the arrest and bringing to trial of 20 suspected felons suggests some initial success. The experiment was short-lived. For reasons that are not recorded, membership of the association fell away and it proved impossible to generate enough money to pay the two policemen. In January 1842 the decision was taken to discharge them, though one was immediately dismissed for misconduct. The Association itself continued to struggle on but had ceased to exist by April of the same year.[11]

Police reform in many parts of the country was incremental as the continuing growth of population and new expectations of security gradually overwhelmed older structures. The situation in Middlesbrough was more dramatic. The upsurge of population in the 1830s swamped the original plans for the town and necessitated further action, which was made possible by the adoption in 1841 of an Improvement Act whereby the Commissioners were empowered to 'appoint and employ such Numbers of Constables and other Officers as they shall judge necessary for the proper Protection of the Inhabitants and Property'.[12] The purpose of the act was straightforward: to create a well-ordered and well-regulated town within the powers granted by parliament. Through the introduction of 'better paving, lighting, watching, cleansing and otherwise improving the Streets, Lanes, public Passages and Places' all 'Obstructions, Nuisances and annoyances' within the town were to be removed. This was a recipe for physical and moral improvement. Within the overarching framework specific mention was made of a series of street offences that carried a fine of up to £2.[13] Many of these were concerned with the regulation of daily trade. It was forbidden to 'shoe, bleed or farry any Horse or Animal' or to 'clean, dress, exercise, train, or break, or turn loose any Horse or Animal'. Wagons, carts and cattle had to be driven with care at no more than walking pace. The public thoroughfares were not to be blocked by animals, carts or any goods and so forth. Noxious activities – the burning of cork, the cutting of stone or the transporting of a carcase of a slaughtered animal – were forbidden. Safety was to be assured by ensuring that vaults and cellars were properly covered and flower-pots not placed dangerously on upper windows. In addition, behaviour in public places was subject to strict control, in theory at least. Dangerous activities such as sliding on ice or flying kites to the annoyance of horses were subject to penalty, as were anti-social activities such as wilfully ringing doorbells, letting off fireworks or extinguishing street lamps. Above all decency was to be preserved (or instilled) by forbidding the indecent exposure of the person, or the sale of 'profane, indecent or obscene' material in any form. Abusive and insulting words and behaviour likely to cause a breach of the peace were likewise proscribed.

The use of by-laws to maintain the decorum and respectability of the town increased in the following years. The police were expected to enforce new provisions to deal with general nuisances in the streets (including swearing and the playing of pitch and toss), dog and cock fighting, brawling, urinating in the street and wilfully damaging the pavement.[14] Significantly, when Albert Park was opened in 1868 as an alternative and wholesome site of entertainment for working men and their families, special by-laws not only forbade alcohol, swearing and brawling in the park but also made provision for the removal of persons 'offensively dirty or indecently clad'.[15]

In theory the Improvement Act could have heralded the start of a new era, but in practice policing under the act was characterised by confusion, parsimony and incompetence. Old and new constables, whose status and responsibilities derived from very different legal sources, coexisted for several years. This created tension that was not conducive to effective policing. As late as 1848 the Commissioners found it necessary to instruct that 'the Police constables appointed by the Commissioners . . . confine themselves to discharge their duties by the Act of Parliament and the Bye-laws, and in ordinary cases, interfere as little as possible with the duties of the Parish Constables of Middlesbrough.'[16] The problem appears to have died away after the warning was reissued in sharper form later that year, but whether this was due to a genuine resolution of the problem cannot be determined. However, the Commissioners were happy to see responsibilities shared – not least, one suspects, because it was cheaper than employing more constables in the new police force.

It was not unusual for small police forces to be created in the 1830s and 1840s. Across England as a whole there were more than 50 forces that comprised 5 men or less. Middlesbrough with only two officers for much of the 1840s was on a par with two dozen or more boroughs, such as Congleton, Folkstone, Henley, Richmond, Ripon and Thetford.[17] However, such figures need to be set against the size of population to be policed. The *Police and Constabulary List* of 1844 provides some comparative data. Among the 32 small boroughs or towns listed there were a number of towns of similar size to Middlesbrough. Tavistock and Bridnorth, with populations of 6,000 and 6,500 respectively, both employed 3 policemen, Evesham with 4,245 people employed 7, Pontefract with 4,832 people employed 6, while Stamford employed 11 policemen for a population of 7,828. Middlesbrough, in comparison, with a population of some 6,000 struggled to retain 2 police officers.[18]

A Light, Watching and Police Committee was established by the Improvement Commissions, but it did not meet regularly or frequently in the early years. In 1842 only two meetings are recorded and a mere three in 1843. The number of meetings increased over the first decade but it was still common for there to be meetings in only six or seven months each year. Only from the second half of 1852, as the town approached borough status, did regular monthly meetings take place. From the scant minutes of the committee there is little evidence to suggest that there was any great concern with the levels of crime in the town. Indeed, there was a consistent reluctance to increase police expenditure throughout the 1840s.

The parsimony of the Commissioners was apparent from an early stage. The first police officer appointed under the Improvement Act was Richard Ord, a saddler from another nearby village, Ormesby. He already had some experience of policing, having been sworn in as a special constable during the1840 dock riot, of which more later. Described as 'a big man, well-built, of a genial disposition, and a favourite', he took up post in the autumn of 1841 and was paid £50 for each of his first two years in post, rising to £60 when he took on the additional responsibility of Collector of Rates and Tolls in 1843.[19] The salary was not sufficient to keep him in post. Ord, who also had a butcher's shop in town, resigned in February 1844, well before the termination of his year's contract. The Commissioners expressed concern at the inefficiencies of the police and the difficulties of obtaining and retaining suitable men for the post, but Ord's successor was appointed at an annual salary of only £32. Chief Officer Thomas, unlike his predecessor, also had to agree 'to devote the whole of his time to the duties of his office.'[20] Thomas proved not to be wholly satisfactory. His conduct was subject to enquiry in October 1844, but he remained in post. Indeed, his salary was raised to £40 on his reappointment in July 1845, but this proved insufficient. In October of the same year the Commissioners felt it necessary to advertise in the *Newcastle Courant* and the *Manchester Guardian* for 'an active and efficient Police Officer' with the promise of 'a Liberal salary' for a properly qualified candidate.[21] Significantly, no attempt was made to recruit directly from the most experienced police force of the time, the Metropolitan Police. No details have survived of the applicants for the post, but the outcome suggests that no high-calibre applicant from outside the town was attracted to the post. Richard Ord was re-appointed with a modestly increased salary of £52, out of which he was expected to pay for his own uniform and the annual rent of £10 for the Police House (beneath the Town Hall) in which he lived with his family as a monthly tenant.[22] Ord remained for just over three years, despite having his salary reduced to £50 in June 1847, but finally relinquished his post in May 1849 to take up better-paid employment as a watchman for the town's leading employers, Bolckow and Vaughan.[23] For Ord this was a less demanding job; for his employers he was a man of proven ability. The Commissioners, once again, looked to bring in a new man. Enquiries were made of the Leeds, Manchester and Newcastle forces in the hope that a suitable man would be recommended. However, the Commissioners refused to increase the chief officer's salary when appointing a successor: a fact that may well explain the poor quality of men who subsequently filled the post. James Amos, appointed in June 1849, was dismissed in October 1850 and refused a character reference for unspecified but 'great negligence in the exercise of his Duty' and, despite an attempt at a special meeting of the Commissioners to have the decision rescinded, which was narrowly lost by 5 votes to 4, he was requested to leave immediately.[24] Somewhat surprisingly, Ord was appointed, yet again, as chief police officer, only to resign within two months to become superintendent for the North and East Riding Lock Ups.[25] His successor, William 'Tin-Ribs' Kilvington, had served as second officer under Ord but was in no way his equal. His brief period in office was dogged by controversy. He narrowly escaped dismissal in August 1852 when he was reported for 'entering a beerhouse improperly and being guilty of improper conduct therein', only to be dismissed in May 1853 as a result of being 'entirely unfit for the office he now holds' in light of the 'numerous complaints that are so current in the Town against the First Police Officer'.[26]

Ord was the one man of ability to hold the post of first police officer. His 'meritorious conduct' had been commended as early as September 1842 in a letter from the chairman of Quarter Sessions for the North Riding of Yorkshire, James Pulleine, and his subsequent career was not marred by the criticisms and controversy that surrounded his successors. His commitment to policing was also not in doubt but, significantly, he resigned on two occasions to take better-paid employment. The Commissioners were fortunate that he returned after a brief spell as watchman for Bolckow and Vaughan but still did not deem it necessary or appropriate to pay him the 'Liberal salary' they had promised for a properly qualified man. To that extent they were the authors of their own problems.

The difficulties of finding and retaining a good senior police officer were but one part of a complex and confusing series of personnel changes that characterised the 1840s and early 1850s. Despite demands, particularly from Ord, for additional officers, the Commissioners were reluctant to appoint, and when they did so it was at relatively low salary levels. As early as November 1841 an assistant constable, William Chapman, was appointed for 12 months at a salary of £10 but he was no longer required at the end of the year. No assistant officer was appointed during the next year.[27] In November 1844 James Sigsworth was appointed for a year with an annual salary of £11 and his contract was renewed in the following July. Having served two years, Sigsworth disappeared from the force; but in July 1846 John Thomas returned as second police officer on a salary of £25 per annum. A year later, when Ord was installed as first police officer, Thomas's annual salary was raised to £40. Although this was a significant increase on previous salaries for second officers, it did not ensure stability and efficiency because the police officers sought to supplement their official pay. In August 1847 the commissioners were forced to issue an instruction requiring the police officers 'to give their entire attention to the business of the Commissioners' and forbidding them from 'accepting appointment or employment under any other party'.[28]

The problem of finding men willing to take on the post of police officer is highlighted by an incident later that year. In November 1847 the clerk to the Commissioners was obliged to write to Abraham Saxon of Ashton under Lyme to enquire if he would accept the position of second police constable. There is no record of a negative response but later that month James Burns was appointed second police officer on a salary of £40 per annum, subject to a 3-month probationary period. After this period Burns was confirmed in office until the end of the legal year.[29] None the less, the town's Police Committee was concerned that low-quality men were not giving value for money, and questioned the wisdom of paying for two men. It had two options, one of which was to raise salaries in the hope of attracting better men, the other to reduce expenditure by cutting the police establishment. In May 1849 the Police Committee put financial prudence first and recommended that 'one officer was sufficient'. The Commissioners accepted this proposal but, as it transpired, only briefly. Within a month the folly of false economy was realised to the extent that they felt it necessary to appoint a second police officer. The Commissioners were unwilling to commit large sums of money, and appointed John Graham on a salary of only £10 per annum that was to be supplemented by 'fees in cases relating to the Transfer of Licenses, Summonsing Coroners' Juries and Removing of Paupers'.[30] Graham soon left. Six weeks later John Thomas was appointed (yet again) as assistant police officer, and also town constable, but still on an annual salary of £10.

The magistrates, for reasons that are not recorded, refused to swear in Thomas. Consequently, the position of assistant police officer was taken by Christopher Brown. This was not a wise appointment. In December his conduct was described as 'highly reprehensible' and the Police Committee were asked 'to have an interview with him and to consider what means ought to be adopted for placing this officer under more stringent control.'[31] One month later he was condemned for his 'exceedingly lamentable conduct' in falsely accusing a woman of perjury before the magistrates at Stokesley, while in February 1850 the Police Committee was ordered to 'enquire generally into his conduct as an officer' following a report that Brown had 'been guilty of improper conduct in partaking of drink at the *Rising Sun* Public House on Sunday morning and afterwards giving evidence against the landlord.'[32] Following further 'well founded' complaints against him, including his refusal to obey orders, he was 'forthwith dismissed' on 1 March 1850. Such was the concern of the Improvement Commissioners with the lack of discipline that it was decided that in future 'the Police Officers be placed under the immediate control and superintendence of the Surveyor'. Not all assistant police officers were this bad but none stayed for any length of time.[33]

The earliest policemen in Middlesbrough, as in many other towns, came and went with stunning rapidity. Little is known of the development of small forces in the early Victorian period, but, on the surface at least, there is a sharp contrast between the experience of industrial Middlesbrough and the agricultural market town of Horncastle. The latter had more success in retaining its officers, though periods of service rarely exceeded six years. Part of the explanation may reside simply in the contrast between the socio-economic characteristics of the two towns. A further part probably resides in the levels of remuneration. In Horncastle both police officers were paid around £40 per annum in the early and mid-1840s. Finally, it is of significance that from the outset Horncastle employed at least one (and sometimes two) experienced 'Metropolitan' men.[34] In Middlesbrough, even those who served on more than one occasion rarely served for any length of time. The surviving records do not contain details of why men did not stay, but the fact that Richard Ord, the town's outstanding early police officer, left on one occasion to work as a watchman suggests that financial considerations were not unimportant. Such is the paucity of information relating to the earliest police officers that any conclusions are necessarily tentative. The over-riding impression is of a combination of inexperience and incompetence among the police officers (with the notable exception of Richard Ord) and indifference among the members of the Improvement Commission. Notwithstanding the major disturbance in 1840 and a rapidly expanding town that was reckoned to be such a magnet that it became 'a complete thoroughfare for vagrants of every class travelling between the towns of Newcastle and York', the Commissioners showed a reluctance to pay adequate salaries for two officers and, on at least one occasion, were advised by the Police Committee that two officers were not required. Clearly the perceived threat of disorder was not yet sufficient to bring about a change in spending habits.

The dismissal of William Kilvington, which divided and created tension between the town's commissioners, brought to an end the first and relatively unsuccessful phase of policing under the Improvement Act. 1853 also saw the incorporation of the town and with it responsibilities under the Municipal Corporations Act. Clause 76 of this act required the establishment of a police force under the control of a Watch Committee. For reasons that cannot be explained by the surviving evidence, a new commitment to policing was precisely what emerged in the run-up to incorporation and after. In the 12 months before incorporation the meetings of the Light, Watching and Police committee become more frequent and more regular and there was a growing awareness of the need to improve the security of the town. Unlike some other towns, Middlesbrough witnessed a relatively smooth transition from the old Lighting, Watch and Police Committee to the new Watch Committee. The new committee, which contained some of the town's leading politicians, such as Vaughan and Wilson, met more or less on a monthly basis, though in 1858 and 1859 there were only 6 and 7 meetings respectively. In contrast with the 1840s, the official record for the 1850s and 1860s shows a marked increase in activity. A considerable amount of the Watch Committee's time was given over to the recruitment, remuneration and disciplining of the force. Wilson prided himself on the fact that the committee was 'very strict with its men', but its role was also supportive, responding positively to the requests from successive superintendents of police for increases in the establishment and levels of pay.[35] More generally, the Watch Committee sought to improve police conditions through the establishment of a superannuation scheme, the creation of a police library and the establishment of a police band. There is little to suggest any major tensions within the Watch Committee nor between it and the town's police force. Certainly there was nothing to compared with the pay-related police strike experienced in Hull in 1853.[36] None the less, the Watch Committee made it clear that they expected the police to maintain order and decency in the town. Concerns with Sunday drinking recur throughout the 1850s and 1860s, as do worries about indecent behaviour in the streets, the menace of tramps and vagabonds, and the nuisance of troublesome children playing in the street. In this the Watch Committee spoke a common language with its chief police officers. As a consequence, there was a growing willingness to allow the successive head constables (Hannan and then Saggerson) a considerable degree of independence in operational matters.[37] In these respects there are strong similarities between the approaches adopted in Middlesbrough and Kingston upon Hull. Both towns had watch committees characterised by continuity of membership and long-serving chairs; both towns had a watch committee that responded positively (if paternalistically) to demands for increases in establishment and improvement in conditions; and both watch committees treated their head constables as professionals, deserving of respect.[38]

To all intents and purposes, 'new policing' started in Middlesbrough in April 1853 with the appointment of William Hannan as Superintendent of Police on an annual salary of £75, that is 50 per cent more than that paid to his predecessor. The cumulative evidence of low-quality officers, culminating in the dismissal of Kilvington, brought home to the Commissioners the unpalatable fact that a low salary was a false economy that brought only low-quality men. Indeed such was the willingness to spend more money on the police that John Galloway had been informed in April 1853 that 'on the appointment of the new superintendent' he would be paid £50 per annum as assistant police officer in addition to receiving his share of fees and fines. Unfortunately, Galloway was not the man for the job and was given one month's notice of dismissal at the beginning of July, only two months after the start of the new arrangement.[39]

The Watch Committee had finally succeeded in appointing a man of firm purpose and with some outside police experience, though the difficulties of attracting experienced men to Middlesbrough persisted, with only two applications being made.[40] Fortunately, Hannan proved to be an able man who soon brought new standards of security to the town. The last link with the previous order had been severed with the dismissal of Galloway, and the way was paved for the creation of a new force untainted by previous experience of policing in the town. Hannan informed the Watch Committee within a fortnight of his appointment that 'it is absolutely necessary to the preservation of the peace that the number of Constables be increased to three'.[41] An appointment, John Knox, was made forthwith; and when Galloway was dismissed, a replacement, William Wake, was sworn in immediately to maintain numbers. In the light of 'recent occurrences in the Town', Hannan declared that 'the present police is on some occasions insufficient for preserving the public peace'. Accordingly, he proposed the appointment of 12 special (that is, part-time) constables, to be paid half a crown (12.5 pence) each, for a Saturday night shift from 9 p.m. to 3 a.m.[42] This recommendation was acted upon almost at once and the 12 new men were sworn in on 3 September 1853. Further changes took place in the following year. In June, Hannan's request that the street lamps be lit from 10 p.m. to 1 a.m. was granted. Following assaults on the town's police, he was allowed to order cutlasses for two of his men to supplement the staves they carried routinely.[43] More importantly, the strength of the force was increased from three to four in September 1854 with the appointment of Charles Bowes from the York City force, while in the following October a night patrol, comprising the regular force and 'as many of the auxiliary Constabulary as are necessary', was instituted for Saturday, Sunday and Monday nights of each week, following 'complaints being made that there are frequent riots in the neighbourhood of the Docks and Lower Commercial Street by which the persons and property of ratepayers within that vicinity are often endangered'.[44] An additional 'common constable' was agreed but not appointed. The impact of these changes is difficult to judge. The Watch Committee was aware of the continued rapid turnover of men – both Knox and Wake left within months of appointment – but also for the first time expressed concern about the level of protection enjoyed by the town's inhabitants. For example, in February 1855 they noted that

> having gone very fully into the hours of duty of the several Borough Constables, [it found] that their strength is taxed to the utmost and that in the interval between 3 & 6 o'clock in the morning no watch is kept and that the Town is then left without any protection whatsoever.[45]

The Watch Committee chose not to draw these concerns to a wider audience and took a positive view of the position in the town in the quarterly report to the Secretary of State in March 1855, claiming that 'the Police force of this Borough is at present in a satisfactory state and fully equal to the requirements of the place' and noting that even the additional constables were 'seldom called out save on Saturday nights'.[46] In fact the Watch Committee remained concerned with the level of security in the town and felt that at least one further officer was required. An additional man was added to the permanent force in July 1855 and yet another in the following October.

Preserving order in the town was enhanced by a distinctive, though not unique, aspect of policing in the town, namely the use of constables at local works.[47] From the mid-1840s onwards Bolckow & Vaughan had had their watchman sworn in as a constable under the Improvement Act. Other firms adopted the same policy. In May 1854, for example, Richard Kirk, described as a 'servant' of the firm of Snowden & Hopkins, was appointed a constable. The value of this was explained in the report to the Secretary of State:

> There is also [another] Common Constable attached to the workforce who is paid by Messrs. Bolckow and Vaughan the largest Manufacturer in the place and who employ upwards of 1000 men and the three other Common Constables take their turn with him in attending at their works in order that they may get a knowledge of the workmen.[48]

This practice was of obvious benefit to the major employers in the town, but they were at pains to ensure that 'the public would not take up a false impression with regard to the policemen being employed at the works' but would appreciate the wider good.[49] Close knowledge of the working men of the town undoubtedly helped but it was not a substitute for numbers. The Watch Committee was still concerned that population growth was outstripping the expansion of the police force and, accordingly, ordered the appointment of 12 or 20 additional auxiliary constables. To this end a list of 48 special constables was produced to go before the local magistrates. Also, after the augmentation of 1855, a further body was added to the establishment in early 1856. Thus, by the spring of 1856 – and at a time when new legislation was passing through parliament and coming into force – the Middlesbrough borough police force comprised a total of 7 men: a superintendent (Hannan), a sergeant (Flavell), 4 constables and an inspector of nuisances. In addition, there was another constable, 'but the pay [of this man] is borne by Messrs. Bolckow and Vaughan under an arrangement by which each officer in rotation does duty at their works'.[50]

Major proposals for police reform were under discussion during 1856. The Middlesbrough Watch Committee considered the question of police manning levels in the town during the summer of 1856. The possibility of consolidating the borough force with that of the North Riding was considered but rejected in a display of independence. However, some increase was deemed to be necessary and the decision was finally taken to increase numbers from 7 officers to 10. The local debate was swallowed up in the wider question of the implementation of the County and Borough Police Act. To qualify for financial support the town had to demonstrate that it had an efficient force. Efficiency was measured in terms of the police/population ratio. The proposed expansion to 10 men was dealt a blow by the departure of sergeant Flavell. However, even with a force of 10 men the town would not have met the efficiency standard set by the government. On 16 December 1856 Lieutenant-Colonel Woodford, one of the newly-appointed Inspectors of Police, wrote to the Middlesbrough Watch Committee spelling out the difficulties of their current situation. The proposed increase would now take the strength to 9 men and a total cost for pay and clothing of approximately £575 per annum. With a force of this size the full cost would have to be borne by the town's ratepayers. However, an increase of 6 men, almost doubling the current size of the force, would qualify the town for financial support and the net cost of this larger body would be some £546. In other words, 3 more constables could be obtained for £30 less! The offer was too good to refuse. The decision was taken, and by the late 1850s the town was policed by a force of 13 men, comprising one superintendent of police, two sergeants and ten constables.

The ratio of police to population provides a rough measure of the changing police presence in the town and, in turn, gives some indication of improving levels of security. In the three years since Hannan's appointment there had been a dramatic change in the provision of police in Middlesbrough. Under the Improvement Act the police/ population ratio had deteriorated sharply from an already high figure of 1 to 3,000 in the early 1840s to 1 to 4,000 a decade later. Under Hannan the situation changed dramatically and by 1855 the town already enjoyed a level of policing (1 to 1,375) that put it on a par with Wigan and York, while the expansion of 1856 brought a further reduction to the contemporary benchmark figure of 1 to 1,000. (See Table 3.1.)

The town's force remained unchanged in size for the rest of the decade and was increased to 15 men in 1861. However, the town's population had grown rapidly and, as a consequence the police/ population ratio deteriorated to 1 to 1,266 in 1861. More men were required. In 1861 the new chief officer Edward Saggerson, who had moved from Oldham, adjudged the town force was 'inadequate to the requirements of the inhabitants'. The force was augmented but the problem not solved. In October 1863 Saggerson returned to the argument in a detailed letter to the Watch Committee.

> I have to recommend for your serious consideration the appoint-
> ment of at least two additional Constables; with a population of
> 22,000 and a force of 20 men, three of whom are engaged at the
> Iron Works, one inspecting nuisances, one on reserve during the

Table 3.1: Police/population ratios in selected boroughs in the mid-1850s

City	Year	Size of force	Population	Ratio
Manchester	1853	554	303,000	1:547
Salford	1853	95	85,000	1:895
Bradford	1853	111	104,000	1:937
Wolverhampton	1856	55	55,000	1:1,000
Exeter	1856	30	32,000	1:1,066
Leeds	1853	152	172,000	1:1,132
Middlesbrough	1855	8	11,000	1:1,375
Middlesbrough	1856	13	13,000	1:1,000
Wigan	1853	23	32,000	1:1,391
York	1856	27	38,000	1:1,407
Bolton	1853	26	61,000	1:2,346

Sources: D. Taylor, 'Crime and policing in early Victorian Middlesbrough, 1835–55', *Journal of Regional and Local Studies*, 1991, p. 54; P. Bramham, 'Parish constables or police officers: the development of a county force in the West Riding', *Journal of Regional and Local Studies*, 1987, p. 71; and R. Swift, 'Urban policing in early Victorian England 1853–86: a reappraisal', *History* 1988, p. 227.

day, one –do- at nights, one Sergeant attending foreign Routes, one Constable partly engaged at the Ferry, one –do- at the Theatre, one –do- conveying prisoners to Gaol and deducting one for sickness and leave of absence, the Committee will perceive that I can rely on about nine men for street duty by day and nights. A number in my opinion totally inadequate for the requirements of a Town like Middlesbrough.' [51]

Three more men were appointed but this was still deemed insufficient. In 1866 the force had been expanded to 29 and four years later to 39. This increase in numbers reduced the police/population ratio to 1 to 1,014, that is, a figure comparable to 1856. However, as can be seen from Table 3.2, the number of privately paid police officers, working mainly with local firms, increased markedly in the second half of the 1860s. Although their sphere of activity was necessarily restricted by the nature of their employment, their presence none the less increased the overall police presence in the town. In 1869 the combined total of officers was 49. At the top, the Chief Superintendent was assisted by a detective inspector.[52] Day duty was the responsibility of a second inspector, a sergeant and 10 constables; night duty of a third inspector, 2 sergeants and 15 constables. One officer acted as sanitary and lodging houses inspector. Finally, two sergeants and 14 police constables were located at local ironworks.[53]

Low levels of pay had been a problem since the inception of the new police in Middlesbrough in 1841 and remained a constant source of concern. Pressure from below manifested itself in the summer of 1857 when police constables successfully petitioned the Watch Committee for a pay increase.[54] But the ever cost-conscious Watch Committee faced real problems as industry boomed and wages soared. None the less, various changes were introduced to improve the lot of the policeman. A sickness fund was set up in 1860 and a superannuation scheme started two years later.[55] Saggerson continued the process of improving conditions of work by persuading the Watch Committee to establish a merit class in 1864. Concerned with the high turnover rates, he argued that there was a need 'to reward officers deserving of promotion instead of keep [*sic*] them so long in the lower classes as to create in them a desire to leave for other employment'.[56] Despite increasing weekly pay for men in the merit class to 23s. (£1.15) in November 1865, the loss of men was not checked.[57] Members of the town council openly expressed concern at the high rate of turnover among police constables and recognised that pay was at the root of the problem.

Councillor Lacy complained bitterly that 'no sooner did an officer get to know the bad characters of the town than he left the force'; only to be told somewhat lamely that the situation was 'in consequence of the high rate of wages paid in the town and district that the men were so often leaving the force'. Defending the actions of the Watch Committee, Alderman Richardson explained that 'they had increased the pay of the constables from time to time purposely to meet this difficulty'.[58] Unfortunately, pay increases were too little, too late. Reflecting on those years, when 'trade was very brisk in our district' in the late 1860s and early 1870s, Isaac Wilson, himself a leading local industrialist and long-time chair of the Watch Committee, ruefully noted that despite increased police pay, 'we perhaps hardly kept pace with the rise outside, and the men left us'.[59] The wage data for the Middlesbrough police is summarised in Table 3.3.

The failure to match wage levels in local industries is not surprising given the relatively high level of wages enjoyed in local industries, but it is somewhat perplexing to find that the wage rates for policemen in Middlesbrough often compared unfavourably with other forces.

Table 3.2: The Middlesbrough police force, 1857–70: (*a*) establishment, (*b*) privately paid police

	(*a*)	(*b*)		(*a*)	(*b*)		(*a*)	(*b*)
1857	13	n.k.	1862	19	n.k.	1867	31	16
1858	13	n.k.	1863	20	n.k.	1868	33	16
1859	13	n.k.	1864	23	4	1869	33	16
1860	13	n.k.	1865	23	14	1870	39	14
1861	15	n.k.	1866	29	18			

Source: *HM Inspectors of Police Annual Reports*.

Table 3.3: Middlesbrough police, weekly wage rates, 1857–71 (in shillings)

	1857	*1865*	*1871*
Third class	18	19	21
Second class	19	20	22
First class	21	22	23
Merit class	–	23	24/6
Third class sergeant	–	24	26
Second class sergeant	21	24	27
First class sergeant	23	25	28

Source: Borough of Middlesbrough, Minutes of Watch, Police and Lighting Committee.

Table 3.4: Comparative police wage rates, 1857–70 (s. per week)

	1857	*1861–5*	*1866–70*
Durham			
Minimum	17	17.5	19
Maximum	22	23	23
Mean	19.5	20.25	21
North Riding			
Minimum	17	17	19
Maximum	21	21	24
Mean	19	19	21.5
West Riding			
Minimum	18	18	20
Maximum	22	22	23
Mean	20	20	21.5
Middlesbrough			
Minimum	18	18	20
Maximum	21	21	23
Mean	19.5	19.5	21

Source: Annual Reports of Her Majesty's Inspectors of Constabulary.

Second and third class constables and sergeants received between 1s. (5p) and 3s. (15p) per week less than the national average, and even first-class constables saw their pay fall from 1s. (5p) per week above the national average in 1857 and 1865 to 1s. (5p) below by 1871. More important were local comparisons. Pay in Middlesbrough was not significantly different to that in nearby county forces (see Table 3.4). There was no financial incentive for a policeman, or would-be policeman, to move to a fast-growing town with a reputation for hard living, if not outright violence.

Although the appointment of Hannan represented a major break with the past, not least in his new expectations regarding security and the police, in certain other respects there were important continuities. Policing was still an occupation characterised by rapid turnover. In the three years between his appointment and the advent of the new force under the County and Borough Police Act, Hannan saw 23 men sworn in as constables, of whom at least 6 were employed by local firms. Seven served for less than a year and a further 9 served between 1 and 4 years. In other words, roughly three-quarters of the men recruited were essentially short-term men. Of the remainder, 3 served over 5 but under 10 years, while there were two long-serving men who remained in the force for 14 and 22 years respectively. In addition, 2 men rejoined in the 1860s, one of whom served in all for 30 years. The crucial test, however, was to come in the following years, for the County and Borough Police Act was intended to ensure a comprehensive network of efficient forces, subject to annual inspection.

The subsequent growth in the police establishment was but the end product of a more complex and dynamic process of change. Unfortunately the incompleteness of the early police registers makes it impossible to chart precisely this movement. None the less, some indication of its scale can be obtained. Thus between 1857 and 1870 just under 200 men were sworn in as police constables, and yet the net increase in the total number of policemen in Middlesbrough was less than 40. Full records survive for some 90 per cent of these men and reveal that two-fifths served less than a year and just over half less than two years. Two-thirds served less than 5 years and less than 1 in 10 served for more than 10 years, though of this group of 15 men, 8 served for 25 years or more.

As a result of the rapid turnover of men, the Middlesbrough police force remained an essentially inexperienced body of men, particularly in the 1850s when the proportion of men serving for more than 5 years was significantly lower than in many other forces. None the less, change was taking place, and by the late 1860s Middlesbrough was roughly in line with many other forces. The number of men failing to adapt to the force in the first year fell perceptibly, while at the same time there was a steady increase in the number of men with several years of experience.

Table 3.5: Length of service of Middlesbrough police officers, 1854 to 1869 (as % of total in service in each year)

	1854–9	1860–4	1865–9
Less than 1 year	50	43	42
1 year but less than 2	21	16	13
2–4 years	26	21	25
Total less than 5 years	97	80	80
5–9 years	3	18	14
Total less than 10 years	100	98	94
10–14 years	0	2	5
15–19 years	0	0	1
Total	100	100	100

Source: Constables' Conduct Registers, CB/M/P, 29, 30 and 31.

During the period from 1854 to 1869 large numbers of men (30 per cent of the total) simply resigned, while only a further 4 per cent resigned for health reasons. The level of resignations is a measure of the dissatisfaction felt by these men with the force, its demands and ethos. Unfortunately, the reasons for resignation are rarely, if ever, recorded. The fact that most men who resigned were on the lowest levels of pay and that the most common month for resignation was January, followed by October and November, suggests that there was a feeling that the rewards were not commensurate with the demands of the job. A change in the relative attractiveness of police pay impacted on turnover rates. Giving evidence in 1875, Isaac Wilson, by now a highly experienced, long-serving member and chair of the Watch Committee, noted that 'now a reduction of wages is taking place in other employments, and we have not reduced ours . . . we are keeping our men rather better'.[60]

During this period larger numbers (36 per cent) were dismissed from the force. Like their counterparts who resigned, the men who were dismissed tended to be recent recruits. Two-thirds had served less than 12 months when the police careers were terminated and three-quarters did not reach the end of their second year in the force. However, there were a small number of men who appeared to have settled into the discipline of the job only to be dismissed after 5 or 6 (and in one case 18) years in post. Of these men, two were merit-class constables and two had been promoted to the rank of sergeant.

The authorities within the force were also dissatisfied with many of the individuals recruited to the force and this is reflected in the number of men dismissed. Information about dismissals is more plentiful. The predictable reasons for dismissal were drunkenness, neglect of duty, assault (on fellow policemen as well as members of the public), insubordination and immorality. The demands of policing – especially winter night duty – were considerable and the temptation of hard liquor and a comfortable resting place were too much for some men. William Johnson abandoned his post at Bolckow & Vaughan and sought solace in a local public house only to be dismissed. John Boynton stayed at his post at the ironworks but his drunkenness was his downfall. Thomas Bamford escaped dismissal when found drunk in the same state at the same place, but saw his police career end a year later when he was found drunk on duty in the town at 5 a.m. Likewise, Neil Maccarron and Thomas Storey were both dismissed for being drunk on night duty. John Hammond avoided drink but was found asleep in a cabin at 3.15 a.m., an act of neglect that cost him his job.

Alfred Bailey's resting place is not recorded but once again an inability to keep awake on duty was the sacking offence. Drunkenness was often accompanied by abusive language and physical assault. A second offence of drunkenness and abusive language saw the dismissal of John Kidd. Edward Coulon and Joseph Warters, both in a state of drunkenness, though on different occasions, assaulted prisoners in their charge. Jewitt Hardy's drunken assault was directed at his sergeant. In addition to being dismissed from the force Hardy was prosecuted and received a sentence of one month's hard labour. Edward Markey, on the other hand, simply destroyed his uniform while under the influence. Not every man required the assistance of alcohol. Thomas Taylor, previously dismissed from the Durham City force, lost his job when he assaulted a senior officer. Insubordination led to the dismissal of Ralph Gofton, John Grainger, Edwin Hirst, James Pattison and James Wilkinson. Thomas Cook verbally abused Sergeant Temple when confronted with his neglect of duty, while in separate incidents Henry Mardon, Thomas Ray, Matthew Spenceley, Charles Stewart, John White, William Wright and Samuel Bowes assaulted members of the public and prisoners in their charge. Bowes was a striking example of the wrong man in uniform. He joined the Middlesbrough police in January 1866 and for the first few months appeared to be settling into the job, reaching the rank of first-class constable. However, in September he was reprimanded for being drunk and using threatening language to Inspector Home. A month later he was reduced to the second rank for being drunk and unfit for duty at 11.30 p.m. in Durham Street. Finally, in November an assault on John Hobson led to his dismissal. Other men failed to meet the moral standards expected of the force. George Dawson, despite having acquired an extra merit to go with his promotion to merit class, was dismissed because of irregularity in the collection of tolls. John Thompson, a single man, was cautioned for allowing a female to live with him for a week, while William Alney was dismissed when a Mrs Walvier reported him for 'taking improper liberties'. In a class of his own was Richard Buckle, who left the force to appear at York assize charged with the attempted poisoning of his wife.

Recent police histories have understandably focused on high turnover rates and the reasons behind them. Much less attention has been given to those men who chose to stay. There is no comparable study of career policeman against which to assess the Middlesbrough experience. The dimensions of the change in the town are relatively straightforward. Despite the high turnover rates, a growing number of men made a career out of policing, serving for 10 or more years. Of those who joined in the 1850s, only 4 went on to become career policemen. Of one, Robert Wright, almost nothing is known. Having joined the force in 1855, he served for just under 15 years, but there is no evidence of him gaining even one promotion. Some of his time was spent as the police officer at the works of Bolckow & Vaughan, but beyond that there is no surviving detail about his career. Almost as obscure is Charles Bowes, who joined the Middlesbrough force in 1854 after a brief period of service in the City of York. A married man, his wife was appointed 'female searcher' later the same year. Within two years Bowes had been promoted to the rank of sergeant. In addition, he acted as drill sergeant for the force. Five years later, in 1861, he was promoted to the rank of inspector. In this capacity he also took on responsibility for the collection of rates, and this was to be the pattern for the remaining 12 years of his career.[61] He retired in October 1876 having served 22 years as a policeman in Middlesbrough.

Another stalwart from the early days was John Reed. Reed's career is interesting in a number of respects. He first became a policeman in November 1855 but resigned less than 15 months later. Clearly unable to find satisfactory alternative employment he rejoined the force later in the same year as a first-class constable. A year later he was appointed inspector of nuisances. His career took off dramatically in the early 1860s. In June 1861 he became a sergeant and just over a year later he was promoted to inspector. He distinguished himself in a number of ways, not least in arresting an alleged murderer in 1865 for which he received a gratuity of 20s. (£1). In the early 1870s his career took a different direction. In November 1871, for a salary of £110, he was privately paid by the Sanitary Committee in which capacity he continued to work until the end of his career in May 1887. Although not automatically entitled to a pension, he received, on retirement, a salary of £122 per annum, equivalent to 70 per cent of his final salary. Perhaps unsurprisingly for a man who had completed 30 years' continuous service as a policeman, retirement was brief: in November 1890 John Reed died.

Policing had a number of attractions as a source of employment for working-class men. The job offered short- and medium-term regularity of employment. There was not the seasonal or cyclical unemployment that threatened those working in the building trades or at the ironworks. In addition there was the prospect of promotion, and for those who survived the opening months and years of their police career promotion came quickly. However, the work was physically demanding at all times and dangerous on a number of instances. Furthermore, there was no guaranteed pension and as a consequence men worked until they were physically unable to continue – jokes about flat-footed policemen were grounded in painful reality – or until they died. One such person was Robert Thorpe, who also joined in 1857 and was promoted to sergeant four years later. Despite an increase of 1s. a week for good conduct in 1862, his second promotion did not come until 1864. However, unlike Reed he went on to become a superintendent with an annual salary of £150. Eventually appointed assistant relieving officer, though with no increment to his salary, he continued in service until his death in April 1890 at the age of 58.

The expansion in numbers during the 1860s and the gradual maturation of the town's police force saw a greater number of long-serving policemen beginning their careers in this decade.[62] Of 163 men recruited during the decade, 15 served more than 10 years. Of these, 13 were promoted to the rank of sergeant, taking on average 5 years to do so, but only 7 became inspectors or above. The rate of progress was somewhat slower than for career policemen of the 1850s, with second promotion taking place, on average, seven and a half years after the first promotion.

These career policemen fall into three categories. First, there were the most successful men who gained at least two promotions, i.e. to the rank of inspector. Seven men fell into this category, including the most successful of local nineteenth-century Middlesbrough policemen, William Ashe, who went on to become chief constable. The careers of some men were unspectacular. John Cooper joined in 1860, served for just over 20 years and received a comfortable weekly pension of 26s. 4d. (£1.32). Skilled men in full employment earned little more than this in the 1880s. Like many Middlesbrough policemen he served a spell at Bolckow & Vaughan during which time he became a sergeant. Ten years later he became an inspector until his retirement in 1881. George Mann served over 20 years in Middlesbrough with but a brief break of less than 6 months when he was chief of police at Richmond. He was rewarded with a weekly pension of 20s. (£1) in 1885. Thomas Temple's career was very similar except that ill-health forced him to retire after 12 years' service for which the Watch Committee awarded him a gratuity of £60. Andrew Sample's career was also ended by ill-health. Like the other two men his career was characterised by steady but unspectacular progress. His promotion to inspector came in a slightly different manner, as the result of his appointment as beadle to the School Board in 1872. The School Board also paid for Matthew

Mawer, though he had already achieved the rank of inspector when this happened in 1874. Mawer continued in service until 1891 at which time, after 30 years' service and aged 54, he received a pension of 28s. (£1.40) a week. A more remarkable career in terms of its longevity was that of William Atkinson. With 8 years' service already to his name, he joined the Middlesbrough police force in 1866, aged 29, and served for a further 36 years. When he resigned on a pension in 1902 he was 65 years old and had served as a policeman for a total of 44 years.

The most interesting career of all the recruits of the 1860s is that of William Ashe. Aged 21 and with little more than a hundred days of previous police experience in Leeds, he became a third-class constable in 1866. His early career was not untypical of many recruits. On one occasion in October 1868 he was reprimanded for being drunk and unfit for night duty. On a number of other occasions he was the victim of violent assaults by members of the public. He was duly promoted to the rank of sergeant in 1870 and progressed to the merit class four years later. At this stage there was little at all to set Ashe apart from his fellow officers. However, dramatic events in 1876 were to change this. Following the revelation of a major financial scandal, his dramatic role in arresting an absconding accountant after a manhunt that took him to Australia transformed the reputation and career of William Ashe.

Some years before Ashe's police career had begun, Thomas Cameron Close had been appointed the Borough Accountant for Middlesbrough. A seemingly responsible and respectable young man, though clearly ambitious, he 'enjoyed the confidence and respect of his employers and the esteem of his fellow officials'.[63] Living in one of the smart new suburbs on the edge of town, a man of professional standing with a wife, 'a lady by birth and education', and a growing family, he appeared the epitome of respectability. The reality was somewhat different. Close became involved in a series of fraudulent acts and, when the matter came to light in December 1875, he was accused of embezzling some £2,500 from the town council.[64] Despite press coverage of the alleged crime, both the council and the police were slow to act. Close had sufficient time (and nerve) to sell his house by auction, depart the town and make his way 'somewhere on the Continent'.[65] Finally, on 10 February 1876, the Town Clerk, J. T. Belk, applied to the stipendiary magistrates for two warrants against Close on charges of embezzlement and forgery. Unfortunately for the council it was authoritatively reported that the 'absconding accountant', as the local press had predictably dubbed him, had sailed for Australia.

Cometh the hour, cometh the man! The man of the hour in 1876, in Middlesbrough at least, was William Ashe. Chosen by the Chief Constable, Edward Saggerson, perhaps for his record of doggedness, Ashe set about his task. The people of Middlesbrough were informed that the intrepid Ashe proposed to take a steamer from Liverpool to New York, cross America by train, and then set sail for Australia. On February 13 Ashe left the country, though for reasons that were never explained publicly he took the mail steamer from Southampton, travelling via Venice to Alexandria, where he took a P&O ferry. The excitement of this trans-world chase, eagerly reported in the local press, was heightened by an outbreak of cholera in Ceylon, which forced Ashe to delay for 10 days.

Despite this delay the race went to the righteous and Ashe duly arrived in Melbourne one day before the aptly named *Highflyer*, on which the fleeing Close was travelling under the fictitious but hardly inconspicuous name of Gascoigne. With some help from local detectives, on 19 April Ashe's pursuit reached its climax on the Sandridge Pier, Melbourne. Notwithstanding the rigours of his journey nor the tension of the moment, the unflappable Ashe, with a terse 'Mr Close, I have come for you', arrested his man. Unruffled by success and clearly not a man to waste words (or money), he sent a telegram to England, exemplary in its economy, which read: 'From Ashe, Melbourne to Saggerson, Middlesbrough, Yorkshire. Have got him.'[66] Some doubt surrounded the arrest but it was finally confirmed in the town in June. Ashe's reputation assumed heroic proportions in some quarters. 'Seldom, if ever, in the annals of the Metropolitan Police Force, and perhaps never in the history of a provincial force, has such a feat been performed as the quick capture of a criminal in Australia' – or so the readers of one local journal were told.[67]

Excitement in the town was increased as the returning Ashe and his prisoner were delayed by storms around Cape Horn. By early August Middlesbrough was said to be 'on tip-toe of expectation'.[68] Rumours were rife that a 'lunatic strong room' had been prepared for Close and a large crowd was expected to greet the two men. In the event the local police took elaborate precautions to smuggle their man into town. Taking the overnight train from King's Cross, the party arrived at Darlington at 3 a.m., only to be held up for almost three hours until the 5.45 a.m. train left for Middlesbrough. Chief Constable Saggerson, conscious of the responsibilities resting upon his shoulders, was in no mood to take risks with a local populace that might turn angry. Taking the unusual step of rising at 5 a.m., he took a cab to nearby Stockton station well in time to meet the Darlington train. On its arrival the prisoner was transferred to Saggerson's cab and driven to Middlesbrough via Ayresome, thereby depriving those who had arisen early to greet the train at Middlesbrough station of the opportunity to give vent to their feelings on the return of such a notorious villain and his brave captor. Ashe, in predictably downbeat fashion, eschewed a triumphant homecoming and proceeded immediately to report for duty at the police station. He made no comment to the press.

There was no 'lunatic strong room' awaiting Close. Indeed, the specially fitted cell prepared for him was occupied by another prisoner when he arrived in Middlesbrough. Committed to trial at the Leeds winter assize, he was found guilty and sentenced to five years' penal servitude. Close's career ended in ignominy, but for his captor there was glory and success. While he was promoted to the rank of inspector on his return from Australia, just under 7 years later in 1883, when he was aged 38, William Ashe became chief constable of Middlesbrough. Such success, which must have been beyond his wildest dreams when he joined the force, was the product of an absconding accountant and an antipodean adventure which, even by Middlesbrough standards, were somewhat unusual.

The second category of career policemen, comprising the 6 men who reached only the rank of sergeant, enjoyed neither the fame nor the success achieved by Ashe. On the contrary, for these men there was little prospect of advancement, although they could expect a pension on retirement. They had joined the police force in their late twenties or early thirties, and most had very limited previous experience. Thomas Black, for example, joined at the age of 32. Promoted to sergeant 6 years later, he continued to serve at that rank for 19 years until he was pensioned off in 1894 at the age of 57. Similarly, Charles Hopper, who joined in his late twenties, stayed a sergeant for 16 years, while Thomas Jobson, aged 30 when he joined, had been a sergeant for 24 years when he retired aged 60. The lack of further promotion appears not to have created significant frustration as all of these men had an unblemished disciplinary record. The other three men in this category had relatively minor blemishes to their record of service, though Joseph Tomlin was twice reprimanded for being drunk, once for assaulting a member of the public and was reported to the Watch Committee for using the 'offensive term "Fenian"' by the local magistrates. Only one man, James Metcalf, who was also drill instructor for much of his career, had substantial prior experience, having served 12 years in the army and a year in another police force before signing up in Middlesbrough at the age of 35. Perhaps because of the relatively late age at which they joined, or because of limited ambitions, this group enjoyed security of employment rather than continued upward mobility.

The final and smallest, but in many respects most interesting, category comprises those men who never rose beyond the rank of constable. Here, prefiguring problems for later recruits, there could be a real problem of frustration leading to indiscipline. This is well exemplified by the career of Robert Gatenby who had joined in 1866 and progressed to first-class constable, picking up a merit badge in 1874 for arresting a criminal on a stabbing charge. Thereafter his career suffered a number of setbacks. In the same year he lost his merit badge and had his pay reduced for being drunk on duty at the parliamentary election. This financial loss was made good within 18 months, but Gatenby never gained promotion. After 10 years as a first-class constable his career fell apart. In March 1884 he was reduced to the third class and lost four days' pay for being drunk on duty. Four months later he was ordered to resign following an assault upon a complainant. Despite this inglorious end to his career, Gatenby was awarded a gratuity of £20 by the Watch Committee, perhaps aware of the problems facing such men.

Taking an overview of these years, a number of conclusions can be reached. First, the Middlesbrough force, like most if not all of the new police forces required under the 1856 County and Borough Police Act, was small and inexperienced. Policing was seen, for the most part, as a stop-gap occupation. The demands were considerable, the pay and the status low. Second, over the period of a decade and a half, a gradual transformation can be detected. The high turnover rates begin to diminish and there is a growing stability to the force reflected in the growing number of long-serving, career policemen. For this small group there were good opportunities for promotion, precisely because of the 'young' nature of the force. Almost all could expect to become a sergeant, many could reach the rank of inspector and a few could progress beyond this level. However, even at this stage, one can detect the beginning of a problem for men who did not move upwards. The very fact that a merit class for ordinary constables was introduced in 1864 indicates that the local Watch Committee were not just aware of the problem but prepared to act to alleviate it.

Unsurprisingly, the police took a positive view of developments. Saggerson regularly reassured the Watch Committee of the security brought to the town by its police. The extent to which this opinion was shared is not easy to establish. There is little to suggest that there was widespread dissatisfaction in the town. Furthermore, as was reported in both council minutes and the local press, there was clear evidence that outside authorities – that is, the recently established inspectorate of police – took a positive view of the Middlesbrough force. In 1858 forces of a comparable size and age, such as that in Doncaster, were being criticised for the high level of turnover that rendered 'anything like complete efficiency most difficult of attainment'. Larger and longer-established forces such as that at Leeds were found not to have men 'carefully chosen with regard to their qualifications or physical ability to discharge the arduous and important duties of the office of police constable'. The Wolverhampton force was similarly criticised but, in contrast, the Middlesbrough police were praised for their 'very creditable appearance' and being 'in a very complete and satisfactory state of discipline and efficiency'.[69] Indeed, in the previous year the report had been even more fulsome in praise, referring to a force of men 'all of whom were thoroughly effective and appeared to have been selected with special regard to their qualifications for office'. With the benefit of hindsight it is easy to seize upon the shortcomings of early police forces, but it is important not to overlook the fact that by the standards of the day, the Middlesbrough police force comprised 'a well-chosen and efficient body of men'.[70]

4
The British Ballarat? Crime in Middlesbrough, c. 1840–70

As Britain became increasingly an urban and industrial society, fears of social disorder became more prominent in the educated discourses of the Regency and early Victorian period. Crime became both a symptom and a barometer of wider problems in a society that was experiencing an unprecedented change in values and patterns of behaviour. The reporting of crimes, especially serious crimes against property and person, heightened anxieties particularly in the difficult years following the end of the Napoleonic Wars and again in the strife-torn years of the 1840s. Contemporary fears were fuelled further by the publication of annual crime statistics that showed a dramatic increase in recorded crime and confirmed the fear that there was a real and growing threat to respectable society posed by a growing criminal class. Later historians, rightly, have drawn attention to the fact that these figures do not simply measure changes in criminal behaviour but also reflect important changes in the behaviour of prosecutors.[1] But others have gone further and challenged the notion that property and the person were under increasing threat. Philips' influential study portrays the Black Country as not 'a notably violent society', nor one in which 'very large amounts or ... very important articles' were stolen. Furthermore, by the 1850s there was a sense of safety, because crime had been controlled, or at least contained, at acceptable levels.[2] Similarly, Rudé, discussing London, seeks to dispel 'the lurid picture painted by Dickens in the 1830s and 1840s'.[3] Not all historians have painted such an optimistic picture. Jones draws attention to the high levels of violence in Merthyr and dates the containment of crime to a decade later, that is in the 1860s.[4] The evidence from Middlesbrough supports the latter view. The serious crime rate was very high in the 1850s and did not fall dramatically, notwithstanding the effect of the expansion

of summary justice after 1855, though the 1860s showed a more significant decline. These facts, and the absence of any hard evidence to
suggest that the 1860s figures were the product of any unwillingness or
inability to prosecute, do not sit comfortably with Howard Taylor's
argument.[5] Further, the statistics for summary offences show that
drunkenness and violence were commonplace and a continuing cause
for concern. Fears about the security of the town continued to be
voiced. For many respectable inhabitants crime had not been reduced
to acceptable levels by the end of the 1860s.

Middlesbrough quickly acquired a reputation as a turbulent and
troublesome town. Its dramatic economic growth and its 'frontier-
town' qualities, most notably a distinctive population, unbalanced in
gender and class terms and drawn from all parts of the country,
aroused a mixture of curiosity and fear. Events such as the 1840 riot
made a name for the town as a hard-drinking and violent community,
in Asa Briggs' phrase, on the 'turbulent urban frontier'. As such it
appeared to encapsulate all that was worst in the new social and
economic order that was developing in the country at large.

The validity of this claim for the town's early years cannot easily be
tested in a rigorous manner because the minutes of the Improvement
Commission and its committees contain few references to the state of
crime in the town and no systematic analysis of law-breaking activity;
nor are there any local newspapers. With the creation of an improved
force under Hannan and the advent of the 1856 County and Borough
Police Act the quantity of official records improves significantly.
However, as I noted in an earlier chapter, the official record is not
without problems. Given the limitations of the evidence it is essential
to exercise caution in drawing conclusions. But two general points can
safely be made. First, serious crime (that is, offences tried on indictment) constituted only a small part of the totality of criminal activity.
Second, among these crimes, offences against property, and particularly offences against property that did not involve violence,
predominated. Press coverage with its emphasis on spectacular and
violent crimes such as murder, rape and armed robbery could give a
distorted impression of the nature of crime.

Serious crime

The majority of serious offences committed in Middlesbrough were
tried at quarter session at Northallerton with a smaller number of cases
being tried at assize at York.

Table 4.1: **Prisoners tried at Northallerton quarter sessions, 1815–69**

	All offences	*Middlesbrough offences*	*Middlesbrough as % of all offences*	*Annual Middlesbrough offences*
1835–40	574	59	10.3	9.8
1841–5	651	51	7.8	10.2
1846–50	645	65	10.1	13.0
1851–5	808	122	15.1	24.4
1835–55	2,678	297	11.1	14.1
1856–60	367	94	25.6	18.8
1861–5	509	167	32.8	33.4
1866–70	607	174	28.7	34.8
1856–70	1,483	435	29.3	29.0

Source: Northallerton Calendar of Prisoners, 1830–99, North Yorkshire County Record Office, Northallerton, MIC 1454.

Between 1835 and 1855 roughly one-tenth of the cases dealt with by the magistrates at Northallerton came from Middlesbrough. In total there were 297 cases, or some 14 per annum. The level of recorded serious crime generated by the town increased at a modest rate over the 20-year period with a sharp peak in 1840 – the year of the dock riot – and a marked increase in the last two years which coincides with the enlargement of the police force under Hannan. Whereas in the North Riding of Yorkshire (and indeed the country at large) the incidence of crime fluctuated in a cyclical fashion with peaks in 1842 and 1848 and a steady decrease in the early 1850s, in Middlesbrough there was a much less regular pattern. Recorded serious crime was slightly lower in 1842 than in 1841 and the modest peak of 1848, following the trade depression of the previous year, was dwarfed by the increase in the number of crimes after 1850.

The total number of Middlesbrough cases tried at Northallerton quarter sessions – not a complete record of serious crime in the town, but a useful approximation – was not great. Five-year averages of the number of cases tried, centred on the census years of 1841 and 1851, give an unadjusted serious crime rate that fell over the course of the 1840s from 280 per 100,000 to 189. This comparison is partly invalidated by the exceptional events of 1840 that saw a dramatic increase in the number of people brought to trial from Middlesbrough. However, even if the dock rioters are excluded from the calculation, the serious crime rate averaged around 1841 is 230, which gives a decrease of 18 per cent for the decade. The town's serious crime rate was probably worse than those for other comparable parts of the country, such as Lancashire and the Black Country. The serious crime rate (based only on the Northallerton records) in the early 1840s was 425 per 100,000 for men and 113 for women, whereas in Lancashire the overall serious crime rate was 350 and 99 for men and women respectively. Given the inadequacies of the town's police during these years and the disincentive to prosecution created by the distance between Middlesbrough and Northallerton, where the quarter sessions were held, the extent of unrecorded crime was probably greater here than elsewhere. Thus the lawlessness of Middlesbrough was probably greater than the official figures suggest. The relative standing of the town worsened thereafter, and especially in the early 1850s: when crime rates were falling elsewhere, Middlesbrough saw a sharp increase to such an extent that the figure was 40 per cent higher than that for the Black Country.[6]

The figures for the period after 1855 reveal a different pattern, with the growing town accounting for some 30 per cent of all cases tried at Northallerton. In the 15 years under review there were a total of 435 cases sent from the town, an annual average of 29. In absolute terms, the trend was steadily upwards with short-term peaks in 1858 and 1863 (both coinciding with trade depressions in the town), and 1868. Adjusting for population growth, the serious crime rate as measured by these figures was 157 per 100,000 averaged around 1861, falling to 106 around 1871. Direct comparisons cannot be made with the earlier estimates of the serious crime rate because of the extension of summary justice; but, because of this, the extent of improvement over the course of the 1850s (a 17 per cent fall) was less than the figures suggest. Further, the improvement that took place has to be seen in the context of an above-average level of serious crime in the early 1850s. The figures for the 1860s are somewhat less problematic, though a fall of approximately 30 per cent in the serious crime rate did not mean that contemporaries felt the town had been made entirely safe.

In the country at large serious crime (as measured by the official crime statistics) was overwhelmingly a male activity. Roughly 4 out of every 5 serious crimes brought to court were committed by men. With its distinctive gender and age imbalance, one might have expected Middlesbrough to produce more male offenders than most towns. In fact, of just over 700 people from Middlesbrough who stood trial at Northallerton, only 72 per cent were men. Under-represented in the town, women from Middlesbrough were over-represented at the quarter sessions, though by the late 1860s the gender distribution of crime in the town was becoming less unusual.[7] There was also a clear ethnic bias. Although the town had, relatively speaking, one of the larger Irish communities in the country, Irish men and women were disproportionately represented in the court record. Over the course of the 1860s the percentage of heads of household born in Ireland rose from 12 per cent to 15 per cent.[8] In the same period, 44 per cent of those charged at Northallerton were Irish. This was not unusual. As Swift has demonstrated, not only did nineteenth-century observers commonly associate the Irish poor with crime, but also the courts processed a disproportionate number of Irish men and women, particularly in places such as Bradford and especially Preston.[9] Additionally, there was a class bias: 27 per cent of prisoners were unemployed and a further 32 per cent earned less than £1 a week at the time of arrest. Further, the overwhelming majority (90 per cent) of prisoners were classified as being able neither to read nor write, or as being able to do so imperfectly. Unsurprisingly, a disproportionate number of criminals were drawn from the un(der)-educated and unskilled working classes. However, contrary to popular opinion about suspicious outsiders, known thieves and prostitutes, habitual drunkards, and vagabonds and tramps constituted a relatively small proportion of the criminal population. A clear majority, almost two-thirds, was of good character or had no previously known criminal record.

Serious crime in Middlesbrough, as in the North Riding of Yorkshire and the country at large, was dominated by crimes against property. Some 4 out of every 5 offences tried at Northallerton fell into this category. There were, however, relatively more incidents of the more serious offences of housebreaking and robbery committed in Middlesbrough.

Table 4.2: Distribution of indictable crimes (%) in the North Riding of Yorkshire and Middlesbrough, 1835–55 and 1856–70, and the Black Country, 1835–60

	North Riding, 1835–55	Middlesbrough, 1856–70	Black Country, 1835–60
Larcenies	80	80	79
Housebreaking	2	5	6
Assaults	4	6	6
Riot etc.	1	>1	3
Receiving	3	3	2

Source: As for Table 4.1 and D. Philips, *Crime and Authority in Victorian England*, London, Croom Helm, 1977, Table 16, p. 142.

The situation was well known to the local authorities. The annual returns made by the chief constable to the Home Office provide a detailed picture of the incidence of recorded crime in the late 1850s and 1860s and show clearly the predominance of non-violent offences against property.

Larceny in its various forms accounted for 499 offences, while obtaining goods by fraudulent means accounted for a further 85 cases. In contrast, during these 12 years, of a total of 700 offences committed against property, there were only 35 cases of house-, warehouse- or shop-breaking, 10 cases of robbery on the highway and a mere 3 incidents involving arson or the malicious damage of property. Crimes against the person totalled 67 with only 8 cases of murder or attempted murder and a further 4 cases of manslaughter. To that extent Middlesbrough, like the Black Country, was not 'notably homicidal', but the relative low level of violent crime of this sort masks a grimmer reality in the town.[10]

In the summer of 1870 Saggerson provided the Watch Committee with a summary of the criminals proceeded against for indictable

Table 4.3: Serious crime in Middlesbrough, 1858–69

	Total offences	As % of all offences
Larceny	499	59
Burglary etc.	45	5
Receiving	31	4
Fraud etc.	122	14
Crimes against property	700	83
Murder/attempted murder	8	1
Manslaughter	4	>1
GBH/wounding	30	3
Assault	6	>1
Rape/attempted rape	15	2
Sodomy	4	>1
Crimes against the person	69	8
Riot etc.	1	>1
Breach of the peace	1	>1
Disorderly house	4	>1
Miscellaneous	69	8
All others	74	9
Total	843	

Source: Chief Constable's Annual Reports.

offences during the past decade which throws more light onto the criminal state of the town. A total of 1,615 people had been charged with indictable offences but only 3 per cent were charged with offences against the person and less than 2 per cent for offences against property with violence.[11] Nine out of every 10 people were charged with larceny in one form or another. Larceny of goods below the value of 5s. (25p) accounted for just over one-third of these cases, while thefts of goods valued above 5s. where the accused pleaded guilty accounted for a further 30 per cent. In contrast, the more serious offence of theft from a dwelling house of goods valued at more than £5 accounted for a mere 1 per cent of the total. Larcenies by juveniles was the third largest category (23 per cent), followed by thefts on the river, thefts from the person and larceny by servants (7, 3.5 and 3 per cent respectively).[12]

The items stolen or obtained by fraudulent means were of a predictable character, such as clothing, food, household goods, tools, jewellery, watches and money.[13] Most were portable and easily disposed of or turned into cash. Items of clothing were most likely to be stolen. Consistently throughout the period approximately 40 per cent of larceny cases from Middlesbrough tried at Northallerton involved the theft of items such as trousers, waistcoats, jackets, handkerchiefs, coats and shawls as well as boots and shoes. Usually only one or two items were taken, though the value of these to the victim should not be minimized. In a small number of cases more audacious and large-scale thefts were attempted. George Thompson, a sailor, was found guilty in 1842 of stealing 7 shirts, 2 coats, a pair of trousers, a waistcoat, a pair of drawers, a pair of stockings, 2 silk handkerchiefs, a hat and a canvas bag as well as a chest from the house of William Stephenson. Ann Walker, a young married woman, was found guilty in 1854 of stealing numerous items from her employer John Whitehouse, including a cotton dress, a linen shirt, an apron, a fur victorine, a woollen blanket and several pieces of material. In hindsight, these do not appear very important items, but their significance in the context of mid-nineteenth-century Middlesbrough society was somewhat greater.

Employers were obvious targets. Jane Wilson was robbed on two separate occasions by women she employed. In 1839 Isabella Emmerson, the wife of a labourer, was taken to court for the theft of a shawl, three years later Wilson prosecuted Harriet Atkinson, an unmarried woman, for the theft of a veil, an apron, a cloth bag and a pair of curlers. Also vulnerable were local shopkeepers. Dolly Reed Leach, for example, went to court twice in 1842 to prosecute two single women: Ann Northern for the theft of a piece of printed calico and

20 yards of calico and Margaret Coughlin for the theft of two aprons.[14] Shopkeepers were victims of deceit as well as theft. John Gribbin had a web of cotton print stolen in 1853 by John Johnson whom he took to court, but many years earlier in 1837 he had gone to court to charge another labourer, James Byers, with obtaining by false pretences a coat, a waistcoat and a piece of cloth. In contrast, trousers, waistcoats and jackets made of moleskin and shawls and linen shifts were stolen from neighbours, fellow lodgers or fellow workers. For instance, James Hazel, after a less than fraternal gesture, was found guilty in 1834 of stealing a pair of trousers, a waistcoat, a jacket and two handkerchiefs from John Botton on-board the ship *Brothers of London* when docked in Middlesbrough.

Closely linked to this type of offence was the theft of household goods, though somewhat surprisingly, such offences accounted for only some 5 per cent of the total. Sheets and blankets, cups, teaspoons, an earthenware teapot, a pewter pot, pails, sacks and even spittoons figure on the charge sheets. This was a crime commonly linked with servants and lodgers. Sarah Hunter, a singlewoman employed by Joseph Pease Jnr and Isaac Wilson, two of the town's leading citizens, stole 6 plates and 4 cups. Margaret Coyle, a labourer's wife, stole a teapot from John Potter, while Robert Allick stole 5 towels from his landlord.

The second largest category of stolen items comprised money and jewellery, which taken together accounted for 35 per cent of the total. Watches (usually silver but occasionally gold) and watch-chains were the most commonly stolen items for which court action was taken. Women were commonly accused of this crime, often in circumstances of some ambiguity. In a typical case, Elizabeth Oliver, a 19-year-old single woman, was accused of stealing a watch from the person of John Brown, with whom she was keeping company, but there was no doubt about the fate of Robert Lennard. Having spent several hours in the company of a prostitute, some of which was given over to drinking, he fell asleep in the street and was robbed by his companion.[15] The sums of money stolen varied considerably, reflecting the different types of victims. At one extreme were the relatively large-scale thefts involving sums ranging from £5 to over £70 that accounted for as much as 16 per cent of this category of crime. The victims were commonly middle-class gentlemen of the town, but 'labour aristocrats' also found themselves targeted. John Gribbin, as well as being a victim of theft from his shop, was also robbed at home when in 1853 William Baker stole £5 and 17s. In the same year James Cole was found guilty of breaking and entering the house of Robert Morrow and stealing a cash-box containing the

large sum of £35 in gold. Servants also succumbed to temptation, at
times on a large scale. Alice Lamb stole 30 sovereigns, 30 half-sovereigns
and a further 20 shillings from the house of John Coyle. Large sums of
money were also taken from the person, albeit in exceptional cases.
John Hardwick, who had been in the company of Hannah Leyburn and
Richard Bames, was robbed of 3 sovereigns and £70 in banknotes from
his person. By the standards of the day these were clearly very large
sums of money.

Over half the cases involved lesser but not insubstantial sums
ranging between 1 and 5 sovereigns. Men in the company of women
were not uncommon victims. Catherine Hughes stole 3 half-sovereigns
from William Wright, while Michael Dorking had £1 and 15s stolen by
Elizabeth and John Dawson. Finally, just over a quarter of the cases
involved sums of less than a sovereign. The most common of these
cases involved theft, usually of an opportunistic nature, from a fellow
working man or from an innkeeper or beerhouse keeper. For instance,
Stephen Moody, a labourer, who had been involved in the notorious
dock riot, stole a sixpence and 8 one-penny pieces from fellow-labourer
James Stewart.

The third largest category was industrial thefts that accounted for
15 per cent of the total. Again, such crimes were a common occurrence
in many parts of the country. In part this was a reflection of a change in
practice whereby traditional perks of a trade had been criminalised as
attitudes towards private property hardened; in part it was a reflection
of low living standards and the insecurities of life for many working-
class people.[16] Both large and small employers found themselves victim
of theft, though responses were varied. Some of these offences were relatively mundane incidents involving small quantities of wood or the
theft of tools (most commonly shovels) by workmen from employers
or other workers.[17] In other cases, apprentices stole from their masters,
as in the case of Robert Alder who, in 1847, stole 4 irons and 2 shoemaker's tools from his master Eutychus Walton. Not all cases of thefts
from local employers were small-scale. Thus, for example, Thomas
Appleby and Thomas Jewison were found guilty in 1849 of having
stolen one ton and two hundredweight of chalk and a ton of flint from
Thomas Richardson. However, the most common items stolen were
more portable quantities of rope, chain and other metal items, and
coal. Small employers sought redress in the courts. William Burdon
prosecuted John Wayland for stealing 9 chisels, while Richard Wilson
and Robert Walker prosecuted Peter Robinson for the theft of seven
and a half yards of iron chain. However, over half the cases in this

category were brought by the bigger employers in the town. Bolckow &
Vaughan prosecuted on four occasions for the theft of tools (three
dozen rasps and two dozen files in the case of William Kilburn) and of
metal. The scale of petty industrial theft is unknown (and unknow-
able), and there is no statement of the firm's policy regarding such
action, but it would appear that court action was taken only in serious
cases involving relatively large quantities of metal. Barnard Hughes was
prosecuted for the theft of two brass bushes and 4 pounds of brass;
Michael Daley for taking 15 pounds of brass; William Haw for the theft
of 5 pieces of sheet metal and a further 52 pounds of iron; and George
Cockburn for purloining 16 pounds of chain and 100 pounds of iron.
The Stockton & Darlington Railway Company brought the largest
number of prosecutions (a third of the total in this category). The bulk
of these cases involved the purloining of coal in quantities ranging
from 5 pounds to 18 stone. Although this offence was commonly seen
as a woman's crime, men were as likely to be prosecuted.[18] As with
Bolckow & Vaughan, the Stockton & Darlington Railway Company
prosecuted in instances when large quantities of metal had been taken.
Michael Burke found himself in court charged with the theft of three
copper pipes, 9 pounds of copper and 9 pounds of brass, while John
Bell was charged with stealing a coupling chain and 14 pounds of iron.
In addition, the company prosecuted on separate occasions for the
theft of a wheelbarrow and a piece of wood of unspecified dimensions.

In comparison with other parts of the country, there is little
evidence of an employers' offensive against industrial larcenies. In
both the east and west midlands as well as in Staffordshire and the
Black Country there is clear evidence of factory owners and other
employers using the law as a means of disciplining the workforce.[19]
The most recent study of workplace theft highlights the wide range of
measures, both informal and formal, used by West Riding textile
employers, but stresses the importance of the law, notably the Worsted
Acts, and the existence of judicial bias.[20] In contrast, the levels of prosecution by large employers in Middlesbrough are consistently low
throughout this period despite the rapid expansion in their enterprise.
It is difficult to believe that industrial larceny was not seen to be a
problem, but clearly Bolckow & Vaughan and other large employers
did not find it necessary to make great use of the courts.[21] The difference in approach may reflect different values, but it is more likely that
the economic dominance of the big employers made sacking (and
blacklisting) a cheaper and more effective way of dealing with the
problem.

Also surprisingly, the theft of food and drink accounted for little more than 10 per cent of all larcenies. The quantities stolen varied considerably. Harriet Hobson was charged with stealing 13 ounces of butter in 1840, while Thomas Sanderson stole 7 pounds of beef as well as a beast's heart and an ounce of suet, but Barnard Nelson stole 14 pounds of beef. Shopkeepers were usually the victims of larger-scale thefts of food. Twice in 1852 John Garbutt, for example, took local labourers to court for thefts from his butcher's shop. William Wood prosecuted Mary Clarke for obtaining a stone of flour and half a pound of butter by false pretences. Fellow shopkeepers could also commit offences. Patrick Marron, a young draper, was charged with fraudulently obtaining 4 stone of flour from John Close and a further 3 stone of flour from Eliza Wilson in 1854. In other cases, a cheese, a ham, a pound of mutton, a loaf, 10 biscuits and 3 pounds of cheese were the items, often snatched from a shop, for which people were charged. In a few cases live animals were taken. William Maccane stole 6 chickens, 3 geese and 2 hens, while John Todd's crime of the theft of 4 rabbits was made worse by the fact that two of them were tame!

Less common were the more serious offences of robbery and burglary which were tried at assize, though these crimes were rarely if ever dramatically different in scale. For example, when James Doherty, John Burke and Catherine McGrall stood trial for robbery at York assize in 1855; the items that they were alleged to have taken were a silver watch and half a sovereign. Philip Marron, charged with burglary in the following year, was accused and found guilty of taking an overcoat, a cloak and a pair of boots. In other cases of the same time the stolen items included 18 silver teaspoons, a set of joiner's tools, a watch, a brooch and ear-ring, a coat and cap, and a pair of boots and some butter. Only in two cases was the sum of money involved considerable. William Smith was accused of appropriating £17 and, in a league of his own, Thomas Brockett was accused of embezzling the sums of £170 and £300 from his employer, one of the founding fathers of the town, Lothian Bell. Only in one case, that of Ignatez Incender, charged on four separate counts of burglary, was there evidence of a career criminal at work.

Overall, most thefts were relatively mundane but not necessarily unimportant. Some were undoubtedly acquisitive and involved a degree of planning and even daring. Some were quite unusual – the occasional concertina or accordion was stolen, as was one copy of Brown's *Accordance to the Holy Scriptures* (*sic*) – but many were neither. Small quantities of food snatched from a butcher or a baker, single items stolen from a haberdashery, coppers taken from a bar and so forth suggest necessity had an important part to play in a town which, while noted for its relatively high level of wages, still experienced considerable poverty, especially amongst its less well paid and irregularly employed workers and their families.

Larcenies dominated the crime figures of Middlesbrough, but there were other offences committed in the town. Receiving, embezzlement and the uttering (or possession) of false coin were closely linked to the crimes already discussed. Women were more likely to be prosecuted for receiving than men, masters were commonly the victims of embezzlement, and men more commonly prosecuted for uttering false coin, usually of small value, as in the cases of John Moniken and Peter Rortch who were charged with uttering a single false 6d. piece.

Crimes against the person were but a small part of the incidence of serious crime, though (as will become clear later) this did not mean that Middlesbrough was not a violent town. Its reputation for turbulence arose in large measure from the spectacular events of 1840. In that year work was underway on the new dock. As a result of labour shortages, in part reflecting an unwillingness to undertake arduous work for relatively low pay, the contractor, Mr Briggs, brought in Irish labourers who were immediately unpopular with the other men, mainly from Lancashire, already excavating the dock. Such was the open hostility to the Irish contingent that they had to be escorted from the railway station to the dock site by the police of the Stockton & Darlington Railway Company. They were 'followed by a crowd of about 400 who hooted and pelted them'. The arrest of one of the 'mob' failed to calm the situation. Indeed, so great was the level of anger that the local 'kitty' was broken into and the man freed by the crowd. Further police protection was required when the newcomers came to work the following day. The police left once work had commenced, but a mass attack ensued almost immediately, forcing the Irishmen to flee for their lives. Several men were severely beaten before order was restored through the combined actions of the railway police, the Stockton borough police and 50 special constables (including the future town constable, Richard Ord) who had been sworn in by the North Riding justices of the Peace. The ringleaders, 18 in total, were arrested and sent for trial at Northallerton. The town acquired a reputation for violence overnight, but there was to be no repetition of riotous behaviour on this scale.

Nor, at the individual level, was violence common in the quarter session record. As the figures in Table 4.3 clearly show, few cases of interpersonal violence were tried on indictment. Equally infrequent were cases of murder or attempted murder, but when they occurred they were capable of shocking. Francis Coates, for instance, met a singularly unpleasant death when a knife-wielding Henry Hughes disemboweled him in the street. Coates, who had been drinking with Hughes earlier in the evening, was attacked after jeering Hughes, who was trying to make the acquaintance of a young woman. Although he claimed provocation, Hughes was sentenced to death at the York summer assize of 1865.[22] Such cases of murder gained much publicity – not least in the case of Richard Buckle, who was a serving policeman found guilty of attempting to poison his wife – but they were rare if shocking occurrences.[23] This was also true of other violent crimes. In several cases the fact that a gang was involved in the crime added to local concern. Although only one was eventually found guilty, four people – two young men and two young women – were tried at York for an assault on and theft from Thomas Westwood in 1861. Even greater concern was aroused by the two separate gang rapes of young women in 1862. In the first case 6 young men, aged from 15 to 20, were found guilty and sentenced to periods of 6 and 10 years' penal servitude; in the second, only one man was found guilty (and sentenced to penal servitude for life), but it was reported that the wretched victim had been raped by 11 men and then thrown in a stream on her return from Stockton Races.[24] Most crimes of violence were drink-related fights between labourers in the town. Most simply involved fists, though a minority involved bottles or a knife. Conley, in her study of Kent, notes that the authorities made little attempt to halt working-class brawls, especially if they took the form of 'acceptable' violence, such as a fight between equals in a public house.[25] It is not clear that opinion-formers and the authorities in Middlesbrough shared this approach. The close-packed nature of the town, especially the old-town district, and the social tensions and associated high level of routine violence made it less easy to turn a blind eye to trouble. An unexceptional incident in 1865 led the leader writer in the local paper to bemoan the fact that there had been 'another serious case of stabbing, or cutting and wounding, arising out of these beerhouse frays' which had become 'so common' in the town.[26] Saggerson likewise took a firm line on public fights. Unsurprisingly, the local police were also victims of attack, though few cases were actually taken to quarter sessions.[27] Finally, there were a small number of attempted suicides that resulted in unfortunate individuals facing criminal charges.[28] Generalisations cannot easily be made and all too often the precise circumstances and state of mind of the individual are difficult to establish. However, in some cases it is possible to discern the pressures that drove some people to attempt to take – and indeed to succeed in taking – their life. Agnes Burns killed herself in 1864. At the time of her death she was 26 years old, married with 4 young children, heavily in debt and the victim of violence from her husband Richard Hildreth, a labourer. He was also driven (in part at least) by his poverty. However, he failed to drown himself and received a 14-day prison sentence to compound his problems.[29]

Petty crime

Unfortunately it is not possible to analyse the incidence of petty crime in early Middlesbrough in the same detail. The provisions of the Improvement Act and subsequent by-laws give an indication of the activities that were to fall under the control of the newly-appointed police, but the minute books of the Improvement Commissioners contain only scattered references rather than a systematic analysis of petty offences. Consequently, the extent to which the founding fathers were able to regulate the work and play of the inhabitants of Middlesbrough in the 1840s and early 1850s cannot be firmly established. On different occasions, specific mention is made of the driving of 'a beast in an infuriated state' through the streets of the town, the 'dangerous practice of stone throwing', the disturbance caused by a shooting gallery, the nuisance caused by dogs owned by working men not to mention the problem of 'footpaths being blocked up by groups of lads' and 'noises in the street' that brought a complaint from one J. Crookes, but there is little indication of any great concern with serious or petty crime despite the fact that the town continued to grow rapidly and had attracted a relatively young and shallow-rooted population. However, this silence is at odds with the evidence of the 1850s and 1860s as well as with later recollections of the 'uncivilised' early days of the town when the stocks in the Market Place were used to punish 'recalcitrant drunkards' and when pitched battles broke out between advocates of temperance and their opponents.[30]

The first detailed evidence relating to petty crime in the town comes in the chief constable's annual return for 1855. In that year 46 people (of whom 35 or 76 per cent were men) were committed for trial for a serious (i.e. indictable) offence. In comparison a total of 851 people, of whom the vast majority (88 per cent) were men, were charged with a range of petty offences. Of these 546 (64 per cent) were summarily

Table 4.4: Percentage distribution of petty crime in Middlesbrough, 1855

Offence	All offences	All convictions	Female offences	Female convictions	Male offences	Male convictions
Drunkenness	32	39	39	43	31	39
Assault	20	14	10	11	21	14
Assault on PCs*	5	5	4	6	5	5
Felonies*	9	4	26	9	7	4
Breach of contract	5	4	0	0	6	5
Wilful damage	5	5	0	0	5	5
Obstruction	4	5	1	2	4	6
Vagrancy	3	2	7	9	2	2
Common lodgings	3	3	4	9	2	3
Foul language	3	2	6	6	2	1
Others	13	17	3	6	14	20

*Not including offences committed for trial.
Source: Borough of Middlesbrough, Minutes of the Watch, Police and Lighting Committee. CB/M/C, 2/100, pp. 84–5.

convicted. Two offences accounted for just over half the prosecutions and convictions. Drunkenness and drunk and disorderly behaviour accounted for 32 per cent of offences and 39 per cent of convictions. Assaults, including assaults on police officers, accounted for a further quarter of all offences, though fewer than 20 per cent of convictions. (See Table 4.4.)

A number of gender differences emerge from Table 4.4. Drunkenness accounted for a higher percentage of female offences and convictions than of male. The same was true of petty larceny and such 'moral' offences as vagrancy and the use of foul language. In contrast, men were more likely to be prosecuted and convicted for 'physical' offences such as assault, obstruction and wilful damage. Hannan's report for 1855 makes no mention of any exceptional features or circumstances appertaining to the year, but it would not be wholly unwise to assume that these figures reflect the state of crime in the early Victorian years. A more accurate picture emerges from the surviving annual returns of the chief constable, which cover the period from 1858 to 1869. It is clear that drunkenness was the most common petty crime, accounting for 29 per cent of all recorded offences. Assaults account for a further 20 per cent and the catch-all category 'by-law offences' accounting for a further 15 per cent.

While the recorded serious crime rate for the town was high, the recorded crime rate for petty offences was staggeringly so. (See Table 4.5.) At a time when the national rate for drunkenness was around

Table 4.5: Petty crime in Middlesbrough, 1858–69

	Total offences	*As % all offences*
Assaults	3,377	20
of which:		
common	2,514	15
of PCs	600	4
on women/children	263	2
Breach of the peace	298	2
Drunkenness etc.	4,902	29
By-law offences	2,629	16
Malicious damage	706	4
Petty larcenies	1,233	7
Vagrancy (all)	827	5
Master & Servants Act	452	3
Total	16,724	

Source: As for Table 4.3.

400 per 100,000 (and was to peak in 1875 at around 850), the corresponding rate for Middlesbrough, averaged over the period 1859 to 1863, was 1,991. Prosecutions for drunkenness are notoriously unreliable as an indicator of the extent of drunkenness. The attitude of the local authorities could have a dramatic effect on the recorded crime rate. The concern of the town's founding fathers with the problem of working-class excess (not wholly shared by the police, who appear to have taken a more pragmatic approach) may have resulted in greater vigilance than in other towns, but it is unlikely that the high levels of drunkenness prosecuted in Middlesbrough can be totally explained away in this fashion. The town's reputation for hard drinking was grounded in fact. Similarly, the town's reputation for violence and lawlessness also receives support from the statistics relating to petty offences. The national average figure for assaults on police officers in the late 1850s was approximately 70 per 100,000. In Middlesbrough the figure was just over 200. However, policemen were not necessarily singled out for rougher treatment than the rest of the population. The rate of assaults in the town was in excess of 1,300 per 100,000 compared with a national average of some 400. Mid-nineteenth-century Middlesbrough was a violent town even by the standards of the day. Ordinary citizens as well as members of the town's police force were more liable to be attacked than in other towns and cities. These statistics paint a much grimmer picture than that depicted by Philips. No doubt the mid-Victorians, and especially mid-Victorian

working men, tolerated (even applauded) a degree of interpersonal violence that would be unacceptable a generation later, but it is difficult to believe that many people in the town felt that their personal safety was guaranteed.

The stark statistics of the chief constable's annual returns provide the bare bones. Information in the chief constables' reports and the minutes of the watch committee coupled with the accounts in the local press, undoubtedly exaggerated at times, add some flesh to these bones and, in so doing, lend strength to the argument that concern for safety remained a pressing issues.

The town's newspapers had little doubt about the distinctiveness and scale of the problems facing the town, quoting critical local councillors and other correspondents with approval as well as editorialising on the subject. Drunkenness was seen as the root cause of petty crime in general and crimes of violence in particular.[31] A local councillor stressed the scale of the problem in 1860:

> A fortnight last Sunday [there were] three drunken rows in the town. One took place in West-street. Some men were fighting and there was no less than sixty or eighty persons gathered round. Another row took place in Cross-street . . . [and] there was a regular riot commenced in Stockton Street.[32]

The local press did not simply echo the concerns of others. It played an active role both reporting incidents and amplifying fears. An editorial in January 1859 painted colourful, if nauseous, picture of the town during Christmas week:

> Men in a 'beastly state of beer' were perambulating the streets . . . half-puddled walking about in their every-day toggery and black faces . . . half-idiotic imbeciles, as they reeled along – 'all in their glory' . . . On New Year's Eve . . . there were assembled as vile a crew of 'roughs' as ever escaped the inside of Deptford hulks . . . Daylight showed the street and vicinity bespattered with filthy ejections from overburdened stomachs; bestial refuse met the eyes at every turn, bearing the distinct testimony to the dregs of humanity which had been thereabouts.[33]

Another editorial in July 1864 lamented the fact that 'the moral progress of the town does not keep pace with the development of its material resources and its growth in affluence', and drew attention to 'something rotten in the state of the community which weekly gives out such a crop of moral excrescencies in the shape of drunkenness and immorality'.[34] Puck, a regular contributor in the late 1860s, was amongst the most vociferous critics, and felt it 'most sickening' to see the town, particularly at holiday time, 'desecrated by rolling and sottish bipeds cursing and maundering in almost every street'. He was also critical of the fact that 'the police are instructed to be a little lenient with offenders of this class at holiday times'.[35]

But few critics matched the prose of the Dominie, who waxed eloquent on the moral failings of certain parts of the town:

> Middlesbrough has its land of Cockayne and according to all accounts it appears to be geographically no further removed than Newport. Here the people seem to revel in every kind of worldly and carnal enjoyment – drinking and feasting, with music and dancing, and every accompaniment to a sensual and conspiratorial life.

Unsurprisingly, the immigrant Irish community was singled out for criticism:

> [T]he Hiberian portion of the settlers in this new Eutopia are noted in ordinary times for their high carousing and their unspiritual language . . . On Sunday, what is termed in places outside Cockayne, fuddling and lewdness [occur], but always after mass. Bacchus seems to be the principal deity in this new realm of pleasure, and he is worshipped not at the local shrine but at his numerous temples in our thriving borough.[36]

For many opinion formers in the town there was little doubt that Middlesbrough was 'a place which had attained an unenviable notoriety for crime'.[37] With no surviving petty session records the local press is the major source of evidence but press reporting of the specific crimes tried at the town's petty sessions was characterised as much by its brevity as by its formulaic approach both of which obscure the underlying realities. None the less, it is possible to piece together a picture of petty crime in the middle decades of the nineteenth century.

Bearing in mind that not all acts of violence were reported as crimes, the pervasiveness and seriousness of (overwhelmingly) male violence in everyday life comes over strongly from the pages of the press. Men of varying ages appear with chilling regularity before the local magistrates charged with assaulting their wives, children, mothers and mothers-in-law. In one well-publicised incident Patrick McIntyre, described as 'a ferocious looking Hibernian', was arrested for assaulting his wife by Inspector Bowes, who had seen McIntyre's wife, child in arms, crying for help from an upstairs window.[38] A brutal attack by Peter Fall left his wife in 'a most sickly spectacle. Both her eyes were blackened in a frightful manner and her face was so cut and smashed with blows in every direction that it was almost impossible to distinguish the features.'[39] In another, a drunken Robert Long attacked his mother described as 'a feeble old woman'.[40] These were not isolated incidents, though in a number of cases prosecutions were not pursued, while in others 'provocation' was seen as an extenuating circumstance.[41] It has been well-documented by a number of feminist historians in particular that it was widely accepted that a man had the right to chastise his wife (and children) and that intervention by members of the public and the police tended to take place only when a man exceeded community norms: in Nancy Tomes' memorable phrase, 'the community drew the line at murder'.[42] Clearly in Middlesbrough there were a number of incidents that offended community norms, incidents in which the blatant inequality of power made them demonstrations of unacceptable violence.[43]

Other tensions brought conflict between various groups in the town. Men, commonly seeking to demonstrate their masculinity, fought with each other throughout the years, in exceptional circumstances the contests being organised as a prize fight.[44] The vast majority of fights were more spontaneous, often happening in the streets or near the public houses of the old town. Certain venues – the Globe Inn or the Whitby Abbey Inn, for example – crop up time and again. After a drinking session in a private house, Patrick Garland kicked Edward Freeman about the head and body that it was feared he was dead. Daniel M'Quillan, 'a tall and able-bodied young fellow', knocked an old man to the ground in an unprovoked attack.[45] Some fights were more organized and on a larger scale. For instance, Connaught men fought Cork men, English men fought Irish men and working-class men (English and especially Irish) fought the police.[46] And many of the attacks, although dealt with at petty session, involved considerable violence. Michael Callaghan, for example, was fined £1 (plus 9s. (45p) costs) for cutting and wounding Peter Flinn, while David Richardson assaulted Samuel Crompton with such viciousness that the latter lost an eye. A fine of 17s. 6d. plus costs of 22s. 6d. (i.e. a total of £2) was the outcome![47] Male violence was largely, though not exclusively, drink-related. Many incidents involved only two or three men, often known to each other, but there was an element of group conflict and domestic violence that shocked some local observers by its barbarity.

But physical violence was not the sole monopoly of Middlesbrough males. The tensions of day-to-day life led many women to blows. Some wives attacked their husbands. George Graham, a grocer in Dacre Street, complained that his wife, Eleanor, 'has threatened to stab me many a times and to take away my life when she is in drink', while Margaret Cane not only slashed her husband's face with a bottle but also bit the arm of an innkeeper who had refused to serve her. Described as a 'female cannibal' she was sentenced to five weeks' imprisonment with hard labour.[48] The relative severity of the sentence confirms the argument that women who were seen not to be 'respectable' forfeited the protection that might otherwise be afforded them as women.[49] More commonly, women fought each other. Catherine Quinn was accused of assaulting Rebecca Butler, but it transpired that the incident had been triggered by Butler's refusal to allow Quinn her rightful access to a water tap.[50] The simple facts of poverty, overcrowding and poor amenities created tensions that erupted into violence between women struggling to eke out an existence. When Mary Meggison was charged with assaulting Mary Ann Wheatley in 1859 the magistrates found the two women equally to blame and the local press dismissed the issue as just another 'clothes line quarrel'.[51] Two well-known repeat offenders, Hannah Hobson and Mary Ann Thompson, fought in Durham Street later in the same year. The former, with 9 previous convictions to her name, was sentenced to one month's imprisonment at Northallerton, but the latter, with a mere 4 previous convictions, was discharged on promising to leave the town. Proximity could also give rise to other causes of conflict. Mary Charlton and Jane Ann Johnson fought over the same man but, in a case where the evidence was deemed to be 'of so disgusting a nature as to be unfit for publication', it transpired that Johnson's husband was the father of Charlton's illegitimate child.[52] In a more spectacular case three women subjected Catherine Duffy to an aggravated assault.[53] Indeed, it was a courtroom brawl between women that led to editorial condemnation of the propensity of the men and women of Middlesbrough to resort to violence so frequently.[54] Assumptions about the nature of women colour newspaper comments, but one cannot escape the conclusion that a significant minority of women in Middlesbrough had few qualms about resorting to violence when provoked.

Concern with 'scenes of drunkenness and fighting almost every Sabbath' were compounded by the behaviour of the police, who either tolerated the fighting or joined in the fray to enjoy a 'good stand up fight'![55] Such violence was commonly (and rightly) linked with drunkenness. In a town that prided itself on being both hard working and hard living, the consumption of alcohol was a central part of working-class male culture in particular. However, it was also the case that the problems associated with a drink-centred culture were a product of the limited range of alternative leisure activities. Although they were commonly associated with unacceptable behaviour, itinerant shows could have a positive impact, as was seen early in 1864 when Newsome's Circus visited the town. A leading article published in April noted that

> The police reports testify that during the last three months – the time the circus has been open – cases of drunkenness and kindred excesses have greatly lessened, and indeed, in numerous ways we have seen the tendency of the innocent amusement provided within the walls of . . . Mr. Newsome's establishment has been to promote public order and propriety of conduct.[56]

The combined effect of the theatre and the circus was, to the editor at least, dramatic, as he concluded that 'Bacchanalianism has gone out of fashion'. Such optimism soon disappeared but so too had the circus.

Unsurprisingly, the town experienced high levels of drunk and disorderly behaviour recorded, albeit imperfectly, in the official statistics. The court reports carried by the local papers contained a seemingly endless list of men and women variously charged with drunk and disorderly behaviour, drunkenness and assault or simply drunkenness to the point of incapacity. It is also very clear that there was a hard core of persistent re-offenders. When John Cassidy came before the petty session on 21 March 1861 it was his sixteenth conviction for drunk and disorderly behaviour; Philip Shean received his fifteenth conviction for drunkenness and riotous behaviour in 1867. But some of the most persistent re-offenders were women, such as Margaret Davison and Ellen Murray who had 12 and 16 convictions respectively to their names.[57]

Many of the offenders were residents of the town but not all. Middlesbrough not only had a steady flow of sailors coming to the town but also attracted large numbers of vagrants and other transient visitors from the surrounding region. The local magistrates tried to counter this by adopting a lenient policy, that is, discharging prisoners, especially but not exclusively women, charged with drunk and disorderly behaviour providing they left town. Peter Little and Ann McCann, who had been charged with being drunk and incapable, were discharged on promising to leave town, as were the mother and son, Sophia and James McCoy.[58] Such a policy appears to have been used in the case of recent arrivals to the town such as Ann Shipley, described as a prostitute from Birmingham, and that of the travelling hawker, Michael Rogers, who was ordered back to his home-town of Sunderland.[59] The success of such an approach is difficult to assess, but the presence in court of repeat offenders such as Ellen Murray is a warning against an optimistic interpretation. When she was charged for the sixteenth time with a drink-related offence, the magistrates decided to sentence her to a month's hard labour at Northallerton, but their expressed wish that 'she would not come back again to Middlesbrough any more' reflected a small triumph of optimism over experience.[60]

Drink was also linked with other forms of immorality, especially prostitution. The peculiar demographic structure of the town, especially in its early years, coupled with the fact that Middlesbrough was an important port, led unsurprisingly to a persistent trade in commercial sex. There were, however, relatively few prosecutions for brothel-keeping. Clause 102 of the borough's Extension and Improvement Act of 1866 made it an offence to 'keep or act to assist in the management of any brothel or other disorderly house', but this was not followed by an upsurge of prosecutions.[61]

The police appear not to have been interested in closing down brothels, and there were few complaints from the public. None the less the *Middlesbrough Weekly News* felt it necessary to warn its readers not to be complacent, as the town was 'less free from brothels and lewd characters than is generally supposed'.[62] For those who ventured onto the streets, especially of the old town, at night the problem was all too visible and all too offensive for respectable townsfolk. The sight of a half-naked sailor running from one of the town's brothels or of women openly soliciting on the streets at night did not endear itself to the moral guardians of the town. Sensibilities were shocked by scandalous examples of brazen behaviour in public places. Mary Ann Brownless and Joseph Brierly were arrested after being found lying on a footpath at 2 a.m. The magistrates were not convinced by the explanation proffered, namely that Brownless had fallen to the ground and Brierly was simply helping her to regain her feet![63] Both were found guilty of disorderly behaviour. Brownless was imprisoned for 14 days, Brierly only fined 10s. (50p). Prosecutions for drunken or disorderly behaviour were the most common response by the authorities but, as noted earlier, in a number of cases prosecutions were dropped in return for a promise to leave town.

The persistence with which some women appeared before the courts suggests that the deterrent effect of a fine and/or imprisonment (or even banishment to Birmingham!) was not sufficient to offset the economic imperatives that drove much of mid-Victorian prostitution.

Unsurprisingly, there were other moral offences that came to the attention of the town's magistrates. Gambling, although a source of great concern later in the century, provoked worry and complaint, especially when it took place on the Sabbath. An indignant correspondent to the *Middlesbrough Weekly News* in 1860 was appalled by the fact that

> on Sundays our borough and its immediate vicinity is infected with gangs of dissolute and disorderly characters who in defiance of the law, choose the open daylight in which to conduct their schools.[64]

Some members of card-playing schools found themselves in court, though the infrequency with which they appear does not suggest that the police saw this as a high priority. Similarly, prosecutions for the playing of pitch-and-toss were concentrated on a small number of young offenders. The magistrates received somewhat tongue-in-cheek praise for 'very ardently taking the morals of the juvenile population under their care and fining young lads for playing pitch and toss on Sunday'.[65] Similarly, racing in the streets provoked only occasional spurts of prosecution. Racing was not the only activity that disrupted the streets. A large amount of police time was spent on ensuring order and decorum in the streets. Those who obstructed pavements and streets or acted inappropriately – using 'disgusting and foul' language, acting indecently, throwing stones and breaking windows, ringing doorbells, begging or even crying wares on a Sunday or selling goods in breach of the by-laws – could find themselves facing a fine.

Though not dominant to the extent that they were at quarter sessions, crimes against property were still an important part of the work of the petty sessions, especially as the extension of summary justice increased the number of offences that could be tried in this manner. The property offences tried summarily were less serious than those tried at quarter session or assize. None the less, the pattern of crime largely mirrored that found in the higher courts. There was a predictability about the items that were stolen and the manner in which they were taken. Servants took money and jewellery from their employers.[66] Clothes were stolen from washing lines.[67] Men were often robbed by women with whom they had been drinking. Jackson Lavender, for example, a labourer in the town, had spent some time with Jemima McNally whom he had bought several whiskeys at the *Extension Hotel* in North Ormesby Road. Unfortunately, the drink affected Lavender who

> by this time had got rather fresh [drunk] and laid down and fell asleep. When he awoke he found his purse and his money gone and [McNally] had been seen by two or three witnesses sitting on prosecutor's [Lavender'sl knee and feeling in his pockets. she had then left the room and search was made for her, when she was found in a water-closet in Fidler-street'.[68]

The circumstances of the offence might lead to the case being dropped. In a typical case, Eleanor Duffield, a prostitute, was charged with stealing 2s. (10p) and a handkerchief from Bernard Rogers, a labourer, on 14 September 1861. When the case came to court two days later Rogers did not appear to press the charge.[69]

A large number of cases involved the theft of clothing or bedding which was then pawned for cash.[70] Small quantities of coal were stolen from the Stockton & Darlington Railway Company and other local firms.[71] Small quantities of food – including single turnips – were also stolen.[72] The nature of the items stolen suggests that these were necessitous rather than acquisitive crimes – a judgement confirmed by the details of several cases. Caroline Williams, who was sentenced to 6 weeks' hard labour for stealing bedclothes from a rented bedroom and pawning them, was a deserted wife who had followed her absconding husband to Middlesbrough.[73] The turnip thief, John Carter, gave the court a simple explanation, saying that 'he had nothing to eat that day and was hungry'. It was not sufficient to save him from a prison sentence of 14 days. David Samuel was more fortunate. The local butcher from whom he had stolen 9 pounds of beef did not press the case in view of the size of Samuel's family and his (Samuel's) willingness to pay for the meat.[74] Discretion was a central feature of nineteenth-century trials. Several cases were not pursued because of the circumstances surrounding the case. The Stockton & Darlington Railway Company was one of the more determined prosecutors of coal thieves, but chose not to press the case of Alice Hays, who was about to give birth, though her mother with whom she was co-charged was prosecuted and sentenced to 7 days at Northallerton.[75] Erestina Feuring stole clothes valued at 15s. (75p) from Thomas Garnett, a tailor and draper, and pawned them. Her circumstances were 'so distressing' – her husband was ill and out of work and she had a small child – that

Garnett took no further action. The bench was somewhat less sympathetic and as a result she was merely confined in the town lock-up for 24 hours, rather than being sent to prison.[76]

The press reports provide insights into the nature and circumstances surrounding petty crime and the response of 'educated opinion' to the state of crime. For much of the time the coverage is low-key – a catalogue of rather mundane and petty offences – and often patronising, poking fun at the clothes-line quarrels of working-class women. However, this confident attitude is periodically punctured by recurring concerns with the declining moral state of the town. In contrast, the impression that emerges from the comments of the police and the watch committee is that there was no great sense of alarm, notwithstanding an awareness that the rapid growth of the town and the nature of the immigrants attracted to the town necessitated a continuing augmentation of the local police force. Thus, in May 1856 superintendent Hannan spent some time informing the Watch Committee of his failure to cope adequately with

> a series of nuisances committed in the Borough by boys from 14 years and downwards. Hardly a day passes over but I have complaints made to me of boys throwing stones, bowling hoops, and in many cases destroying property.[77]

Despite the concern frequently expressed about the moral state of the town, there is no sense in the reports of Hannan or Saggerson of the town being under serious threat. Police concern was expressed occasionally, as in late 1868 when several robberies took place on the outskirts of town, and was linked in a number of instances to a demand for more men. However, for the most part there was a confidence among its senior officers (regularly transmitted to their masters on the Watch Committee) that the police force, notwithstanding the rapid turnover in personnel, was doing a good job in protecting the town's honest citizens. There was, for instance, satisfaction expressed at an attempt to control prostitution. In 1858 Hannan reported

> great expense has been incurred in prosecuting Ann Ferguson and Henry Clark at the Quarter sessions for keeping Common Brothels. I am decidedly of the opinion that the money was well spent and the severe punishment that they received has been a terror to others.[78]

Hannan's successor was of a similar opinion, expressing satisfaction at the decrease in serious crime in the late 1850s and reassuring his masters on a number of occasions that the town 'remained free from offences of a serious nature' in the 1860s.[79] Furthermore, such reassurances appear to have been accepted. But such confidence appears to be contradicted by our knowledge of the level of crime in the town. However, the contradiction may be more apparent than real. There had been a fall of some 30 per cent in the serious crime rate during the 1860s, and the problems of drunkenness and associated violence were clearly concentrated in the working-class districts in the old town. There, 'over the border', in the overwhelmingly working-class quarter, English and Irish, men and women got drunk and fought with each other, especially at the weekend.[80] However, as long as the problem was confined geographically it could be met with a policy that combined a degree of benign neglect (most drunks capable of doing so were allowed to go home, and a few were assisted on their way by the police) and firm action when the situation threatened to get out of hand. As long as there were few outbreaks of disorderly behaviour in Grove Hill and no burglaries in Southfield Villas, Hannan and Saggerson could confidently tell their middle-class employers, the members of the Watch Committee, that the town (or at least their part of town) was free from serious crime.

5
The Police and the Public c.1840–70: The Limits of Policing by Consent

New policing was fundamentally concerned with the regulation of everyday life in town and country. Its impact was as varied as the settings and the duties that faced the new forces. In rural areas the police were more likely to adopt a watching role. In market towns such as Horncastle, Exeter or York, relatively lightly touched by industrialisation, the introduction of the new police was achieved with little friction. Even in smaller industrialising towns such as Huddersfield and Halifax there was relatively little conflict.[1] However, in other parts of the country the introduction of the new police was met with considerable hostility. In cities such as London or Leeds and in smaller communities such as Colne and Middleton there were violent conflicts between the recently introduced forces and members of the community they were meant to police. Opposition was not restricted to those most directly affected by police action, but most, predictably, came from the working classes who made most use of the streets for work or leisure. The situation was further complicated by ethnic considerations, notably the presence of poor Irish, popularly seen to be the cause of many of the problems besetting society. Middle-class critics, in contrast, were concerned more with than the additional burden on the local rates and the value-for-money that the police represented, though they did on occasion question the constitutionality of police behaviour. Opposition was not confined to the period in which the new police were first established. While middle-class opposition diminished over time, notably but not exclusively in London, working-class opposition remained, albeit in modified form.

The growing volume of research on police history has led to major revisions of the way in which the advent of the new police has been viewed. From the earliest police history, written at the beginning of the twentieth century, through Reith's influential writings, to Critchley's major study that first appeared in the 1960s, the emphasis was upon consensus and crime fighting rather than upon conflict and social control. Opinion shifted markedly in the following decade as Storch's work (and a more general interest in the concept of social control) drew attention to the scale and persistence of working-class opposition in northern industrial towns. More recently, the balance has swung back and Emsley in particular has argued for a neo-Reithian synthesis that returns the emphasis to the police's responsibility for preserving law and order.[2] Although the simple generalisations of the earliest police histories are no longer tenable, there remain differences of emphasis depending upon the wider model – consensual or conflict – of Victorian society subscribed to by the individual historian. The evidence from Middlesbrough, in no small measure because of its distinctive development, lends support to a more conflict-based inter-pretation that emphasises the tensions between the police and import-ant subsections of the policed, subsections that were themselves a product of deeper divides in society in the town.

Policing in Middlesbrough from the very outset was concerned with the regulation of quotidian work and leisure as the provisions of the Improvement Act and subsequent by-laws make clear. Furthermore, there were powerful groups (notably the temperance movement) that, through local newspapers, for example, pressed for the enforcement of the law as a central element in the improvement of the moral state of the town. This moral campaign was unambiguously directed at those seen not to be respectable. Predictably, 'moral policing' in Middlesbrough, as in other towns, was felt most directly by the working classes of the town and dis-proportionately by the newly-arrived Irish community. Not surprisingly the worst incidents of anti-police hostility and the most persistent oppo-sition came from this group for whom the police were 'the peregrinating embodiment of tyranny and oppression'.[3]

In the absence of direct evidence – and the voice of the policed is rarely heard in the historical record – the statistics of assaults upon policeman have been used as an approximate measure of the attitude of the public (or at least, certain sections of the public) towards the police. There are problems with this approach. It cannot always be pre-sumed that the incident provides an insight into the motives of the perpetrator. Assaults on the police arising out of cases of domestic viol-ence, for example, may reflect hostility to any form of intervention rather than opposition to the police *per se*. Again, an assault upon a police officer may reflect the unpopularity of the policeman as an individual rather than hostility to the police in a more general sense. This situation is further complicated by the variable difference between the recorded crime rate and the real incidence of (in this case) assaults on the police. Firstly, there was a problem of definition or perception. At what point in arresting an obstreperous individual for 'drunken and riotous behaviour' did the flailing of arms become an assault? Secondly, there was the problem of appropriate action in the circumstances. Was it worthwhile to prosecute a first-time offender or someone from out of town if he (or she) promised to leave forthwith? How should one deal with more hardened locals? While there is some plausibility in the argument that the new police, especially in the early days, were determined to prosecute wherever possible as a means of asserting their authority, it is also the case that there was a reluctance (among some if not all policemen) to prosecute partly because such action might be counter-productive and partly because it could be construed as a sign of male weakness.[4] Finally, changes in the law, which increased the financial penalty for assaulting a police officer, are likely to have had an impact on the statistics.

The paucity of records makes it almost impossible to establish in detail the nature of the relationship between the newly-appointed police and the rapidly expanding population of the town. There is no evidence of large-scale opposition to the introduction of the police in the manner experienced in Colne, nor of sustained anti-police rioting like that experienced in Leeds in 1844.[5] However, there are a number of references in the Northallerton quarter sessions records to prosecution for assaults on policemen in Middlesbrough. The most striking fact is the infrequency with which assaults on the police appeared in the court record: between 1835 and 1855 there were only 8 such cases, of which 4 took place in a single year. Although some of these involved serious incidents, in one case arising out of an attempted murder, only one involved a gang attack, when in 1855 four Irish labourers were found guilty of assaulting two police officers, Bowes and Ogle.[6] However, it is evident from other evidence that all was not peaceable. The town was certainly boisterous and often riotous, although the nature of the disturbances is not made clear. Frequent riots in the neighbourhood of the docks – notably those in 1854, which necessitated both the appointment of auxiliary constables and the acquisition of staves, and for two men cutlasses – indicate the problems to be found. Nor were these problems confined to a single year. In the winter of 1857 constables on certain beats were empowered to wear cutlasses to defend themselves.[7] It is impossible to say with what frequency policemen were attacked. Nor is it possible to say what level of violence triggered an arrest (nor if the police changed their stance towards assailants) but the details of offences for 1855 clearly show that cases tried at quarter session were but the tip of an iceberg of recorded violence against the police. In that year a total of 43 people (of whom 39 were men) were charged with assaulting a police officer. Thirty-nine of these (including all four women) were dealt with summarily by the magistrates of Middlesbrough.[8]

The figures for 1855 may well understate the situation. Between 1856 and 1869 there were 17 cases tried at Northallerton; but in the same period, 633 assaults on police officers were tried summarily. The number of cases rose sharply in the early 1860s, peaking in 1864 when over 100 cases were recorded, and only falling back to the early-1860s level at the very end of the decade. This was after five years during which the town's magistrates had sought to deter assailants by sending offenders to prison without giving them the option of paying a fine.[9]

The question of violence towards the police could not (and cannot) be separated from a consideration of the peculiar relationship between the police and the Irish. As Swift has argued, the Irish men and women who came to mainland Britain, especially from the late 1840s onwards, were an obvious (and often large) target group for the newly-formed police forces.[10] In many towns and cities across England, south Wales and southern Scotland, the Irish were to be found in some of the worst districts, living in conditions of appalling squalor. Ignoring distinctions between the honest and industrious and those who were less so (and the distinction might often be one between good and bad fortune), it was easy for an indigenous population, especially its self-appointed spokesmen of respectability, to blame these people for the conditions in which they found themselves. Furthermore, it was easy to link their dwelling places (especially lodging houses) and their customs (especially where they centred on drink) with crime and immorality. For a police force charged with maintaining order and decorum in public places, but having to target its limited resources on certain groups and districts, it was easy to take a 'common-sense' approach and focus attention on the recently arrived Irish as the most dangerous segment of the dangerous classes. While it is true that in some parts of the country – Jennings Building in London, for example – it was possible for the police to turn a blind eye to what went on behind the streets, as it were; this was a luxury that could less easily be afforded in Middlesbrough.[11] But other factors could exacerbate these tensions. Religious prejudice, strengthened by fear of 'Fenian' terrorism, could stoke up more specific anti-Irish prejudice. In Middlesbrough the former undoubtedly existed, though the latter appears not to have been a major factor. Finally, the presence of Irishmen in the ranks of the police added a further complication. There were a disproportionate number of Irishmen recruited into the ranks of the police in Victorian England.[12] Unfortunately, it is not possible to say what percentage of the Middlesbrough police force were Irish. The police conduct registers do not contain the places of birth of all recruits and the record is particularly poor for the early years. Of the 309 men for whom a place of birth is recorded only 6 come from Ireland. It is obvious, if only from the names, that several men either came from Ireland or were of Irish descent, but the precise number remains unknown.

The class and ethnic dimension to anti-police violence was well-known in the town. The *Middlesbrough Weekly News* published a long editorial in May 1864 bemoaning a long-standing problem that suggested 'some undefinable organisation amongst the more incorrigible individuals in the lower strata of our society':

> Almost weekly cases come under our notice which bear the surface indication of pecuniary assistance being offered to criminals by their brother rowdies and those cases in which their sympathy takes a more active and reprehensible shape are certainly not few and far between. Assaults on the police, attempts to rescue prisoners, and other similar interferences placed in the way of the due execution of the law are so frequently taking place that they almost cease to be matters for comment.[13]

The editor had no doubt that the offenders were 'principally Irishmen of the lowest class'. Nor could this be dismissed as isolated press prejudice, for, writing in his annual report for 1864, superintendent Saggerson drew attention to the sharp increase in the number of assaults on the police in the town which he saw 'arising out of opposition [by the lowest form of Irish people] to the Constables when endeavouring in the execution of their duty to check disorderly conduct and preserve the peace'.[14]

In ill-lit or unlit streets a policeman was very vulnerable to attack. Saggerson complained bitterly about the failure to light Mary Street where 'Irish Rows are of a frequent occurrence ... and only a few weeks ago one of my officers was assaulted there'.[15] Most attacks were one on one, but there were a number of more spectacular attacks involving large crowds seeking to prevent the arrest of one of their number. The

nature of such incidents is captured in the description of two disturbances in January 1865. The first involved an Irish labourer, Michael
Lougheran, and PC Stainsby in a Saturday night brawl in which

> [the] prisoner commenced kicking the officer and striking him,
> [another] four or five men came up and assisted him in committing
> a most brutal assault. The officer was knocked down and the men
> attacked him in the most savage manner, kicking him with their
> feet, striking him with sticks which they carried with them and
> biting him. Two severe wounds were inflicted on the top of his head
> and the officer was rendered well-nigh insensible.[16]

In the second, 'an Emeralder', as the *Middlesbrough Weekly News* chose
to describe Patrick Evans, had been arrested by PC Wilkinson

> when the prisoner called on the crowd to liberate him. Several of his
> comrades and the prisoner commenced to beat and kick the officer
> who was presently surrounded by a crowd of 500 to 600 people.[17]

Family celebrations could also give rise to large-scale disturbances. The
wedding day of Thomas Vaughan, in December 1858, was celebrated
by some 250 people drinking in an inn kept by Sarah Spawforth in
nearby Eston Junction. For reasons not given, police constable Hardy
entered and

> was instantly rushed upon and violently assaulted by some 15 or 20
> persons. The noise, and his cries, having brought another officer to
> his assistance, the men left him and rushed *en* masse on the new-
> comer; got him down and kicked him and abused him very much ...[18]

The situation could have been worse but the assailants were frightened
away by 'two very respectable women'. However, the seriousness of the
incident should not be minimised, as Hardy was unfit for work for
19 days as a result of his injuries.

Despite the animosity of certain sections of the Irish community
towards the police in the town, there is little or no evidence of the relationship being further complicated and embittered by political considerations. Unlike nearby Stockton, there were no Fenian disturbances in
the town.[19] Indeed, the authorities appear to have gone out of their
way at times to cool political passions. Constables were disciplined for
insulting Irish prisoners with the word 'Fenian' and, in 1867 in an

intriguing display of tactful surveillance, a mass meeting of between two and three hundred Fenians, held in Green Lane, Acklam, passed off without incident, assisted by the fact that 'Superintendent Saggerson and Sergeant Thorpe held the gate at the end of the lane open for them as they passed through on the way back.'[20] However, the Watch Committee was not totally unprepared for trouble. Days after the mass meeting in Acklam 'over 200 special constables were sworn in before the Bench [at the police court] ... as a precautionary measure in case of any disturbances arising in the town.'[21] In addition, Saggerson had been instructed to procure an extra supply of cutlasses and to ensure that there were sufficient staves for the newly sworn-in specials. There was an unexceptional number of assaults on policemen in the town in the following weeks, but no large-scale disturbance. The cutlasses, which were finally acquired in mid-November, and the staves were not put to use. Despite the absence of conflict this time, there was little love lost between the town's police and its Irish community and, unsurprisingly, the Irish were over-represented in the official crime statistics for the town and were prominent in their violent and mass opposition to the police: but it was not Irishmen alone who attacked Middlesbrough policemen.

Police officers attempting to arrest drunk and disorderly men and women often became involved in small-scale brawls in which fists, boots and teeth were the most common weapons used. Daniel Morrison, arrested for being drunk and riotous in 1865 was said by the arresting officer to have 'behaved more like a madman than anything else ... kicking, scuffling and biting ... and behaving in a very wild manner'.[22] But some policemen were attacked with pokers, hammers and clubs; others had stones thrown at them and even had bull-dogs set upon them. One of the worst cases led to a prosecution for attempted murder. Johnson Robinson, a brickyard labourer and well-known criminal with several previous convictions for assault including one for malicious wounding, attacked PC Garbutt in a pig-house. Garbutt was attacked with a knife and in the struggle his thumb was bitten to the bone.[23]

Domestic disputes also precipitated anti-police violence. In one such incident Nathan Fothergill returned home drunk, verbally abused his mother and smashed some furniture. PC Frost, who came to investigate the incident, was attacked with a poker. Although Frost left the scene of the incident, Fothergill followed the policeman into the town market where he was arrested.[24] Patrick Hackey, sentenced to two months' imprisonment with hard labour in 1868, inflicted a 'gross assault' on PC Tomlin when the latter intervened to rescue Mrs. Hackey from her husband's violent attack; while PC Wilkinson like-wise suffered an attack when he attempted to protect Sarah Newcombe from James Ryan, an associate of the notorious Keogan brothers with several previous convictions to his name, who had set about her with a poker. As noted earlier, police intervention usually came when male viol-ence reached an unacceptable level, with the possibility of death as an outcome. However, communal condemnation was no guarantee of pro-tection for the officer seeking to make an arrest. Occasionally police intervention led to assaults by both parties, as PC Horsefield found when he set upon by both John and Bridget McCarthy.[25] In this case the assault upon the police was, to a large degree, the outcome of what was seen as an unwarranted intervention by a third party in a domestic matter, i.e. the chastisement of a wife or partner. However, the very fact that the police were charged with the responsibility of intervening in such disputes meant that there was hostility to the police *per se* for attempting to impose an alien code of behaviour.

Incidents such as these were exacerbated by alcohol consumption. Drink also contributed to other assaults. Heavy drinking, especially at weekends or holidays, led to disorderly behaviour much of which was directed at or involved the police. The marked increase in the number of beerhouses in the town during the 1860s added to the problem.[26] As Saggerson ruefully noted to the Watch Committee early in 1870

> during Christmas and New Year's Evenings there was a great amount of drunkenness and a number of persons whilst in that state violently assaulted the Police, seven of whom were committed to Gaol without the option of paying a fine.[27]

The situation in Middlesbrough was also complicated by its 'mixed and floating population', especially on market days when

> the working classes of the surrounding villages come into the Town in large numbers and being as it were removed from the constraints of their friends, give way to their evil passions and create disturbances.[28]

Although reported in the local press as routine events, the circum-stances and nature of these assaults varied considerably. Ordinary police constables were more at risk, but no member of the force escaped attack. While walking down Linthorpe Road in December 1869 the Superintendent of Police himself was attacked when he went to arrest a drunken and violent sailor whom he had found lying in the road. Nor was this the first time that Saggerson had been attacked in Middlesbrough. Two years earlier he had been involved with a drunk in Durham Street who, having been given the option of going quietly, not only refused the offer but proceeded to bite and head-butt Saggerson and 'kicked about in a very wild manner'. The arrival of Sergeant Sample tipped the balance in favour of law and order and the drunk was thrown onto the floor whence he was dragged to the police station.[29]

Most incidents were relatively minor affairs and many involved drink and took place in or near public houses or other places of entertainment such as music halls, though at least one incident took place in the town post office. Two labourers, John Codey and William Clark, for example, having been refused service in Mrs Horner's beerhouse, created a disturbance which attracted the attention of PC Ashe (as yet making his way in the lower ranks of the force he was later to lead) and PC Sample. Codey attempted to stab Sample with a knife, while Clark punched and kicked Ashe on his arms and legs.[30] PC Robson was attacked by Hannah Robson, a well-known prostitute in the town, when he tried to stop her working at a local theatre. The town's Oxford Music Hall saw a number of incidents in which members of the audience, in various states of inebriation, gave expression to their exuberance by attacking the police on duty there.[31]

More serious though less common were those assaults that involved several members of the public. Such incidents were more common in the early and mid-1860s and bore eloquent testimony to the thinly veiled hostility that existed between the police and much of the working-class community. The majority of incidents were associated with attempts by the police to arrest people for drunken and disorderly behaviour in the streets. Three men attacked sergeant Bowes and PC Johnson in September 1859; five set about PC Thorpe in the following year, while PC Stainsby attracted the unwanted attention of seven men after he had intervened to assist a member of the public in September 1864.[32] In some cases large crowds gathered to attack the police and to rescue a prisoner. In early 1860 PCs Byworth, Heyburn and Thorpe were set upon by crowds in separate incidents but with the common purpose of aiding the escape of a prisoner.[33] The harder line adopted by the magistrates in the face of concerted prisoner resistance to the police appears to have had some impact, but large-scale assaults did not entirely cease. PCs Burton and Robinson were faced with 'a great mob of people', some of whom threw 'a great many stones' in the

Table 5.1: Assaults on the Middlesbrough Police in the 1860s

	Indictable offences	Summary offences	Summary convictions	Fined	Imprisoned
1860	2	19	18	17	1
1861	3	26	26	26	0
1862	2	56	54	54	0
1863	0	62	58	50	8
1864	2	109	106	85	21
1865	0	75	71	49	22
1866	0	77	72	43	29
1867	0	74	70	52	18
1868	0	55	51	35	16
1869	0	23	21	15	6

Source: Chief Constable's annual returns.

summer of 1867; and PC Nixon was similarly threatened by some forty people in an attempted prisoner rescue in November 1869.[34]

Policing Middlesbrough was a dangerous activity As the figures in Table 5.1 show, recorded assaults on the police averaged almost 60 a year during a period when the size of the town force averaged 30 men. Put simply, a Middlesbrough policeman could expect, on average, to be assaulted twice a year. Unfortunately, neither the local press nor the Watch Committee minutes recorded all assaults on policemen. However, the partial evidence that survives provides some indication of the incidence of violence on the police. The minutes of the Watch Committee record details of over 55 constables who had been assaulted while on duty during the 1860s. For a quarter of these men there was but one attack, though this could be a serious crowd assault. However, a further 50 per cent (i.e. 27 men) were attacked on two or three occasions. Of the remaining 25 per cent, 5 were attacked on four separate occasions, 4 on five occasions, 5 on six and 1 on nine. Furthermore, many of the attacks were concentrated in a relatively short period of time. PC Gatenby was attacked three times in the six months between March and September 1868. PC Ashe was attacked five times between December 1866 and July 1869. PC Richardson was unfortunate enough to be attacked five times in November and December 1869, while the long-serving Robert Thorpe was assaulted on nine occasions between April 1859 and November 1869, with four incidents happening in the one year of 1860.[35] Further interpretation of these figures is problematic. Was the incidence of attacks related to particularly dangerous beats? Were the individual officers particularly unpopular men? Were the individual officers more fool-hardy or less tactful? It is not possible to answer these questions directly because of the absence of evidence. Undoubtedly some beats were more dangerous than others, but officers did not spend all their time on one beat. More likely the incidence of assaults had more to do with the way in which the individual carried out his duty but whether over-zealousness was more important than insensitivity will never be known.[36]

The pages of the local press carry numerous examples of assaults upon policemen, but not all working men and women responded in this manner. There was no concerted attempt to drive the police from the streets of the town, though this would have been relatively easy to achieve in the 1840s. For the most part the police were accepted, not necessarily loved but not automatically hated. Most people probably conducted their lives in such a way as to avoid the police. Some viewed them more positively as a force to help out in time of trouble. Some were even more positive and were prepared to go to the aid of the police. In October 1864 Inspector Thorpe and PC Stainsby were called to a disturbance at the Zetland Inn caused by Thomas Mitford and some friends. They attacked the two officers and 'dragged them to the ground'. However, other bystanders intervened and rescued the officers, who 'otherwise ... would have received considerable injuries'.[37]

The police were not always the victims of violence. Police could be perpetrators, but as one noted police historian has observed, 'the "dark figure" of less spectacular police violence is, perhaps, even more obscure than that of crime'.[38] In theory, the police were not intended to be an aggressive body of men and even when armed were supposed to act only in self-defence. However, it quickly became clear that policemen throughout the country adopted a more positive approach and not only when faced with crowds. While there can be little doubt that varying degrees of 'tolerated' violence were part and parcel of routine policing, it will never be known to what extent the judicious shove, the clip with a rolled cape or the blow with a truncheon was part of police practice. Living in a predominantly masculine, working-class culture that prized physical strength and bravery, and facing certain members of the public who, collectively or singly, were more than willing to take them on, it is not surprising that the police 'got their retaliation in first'. However, as the same historian has warned, it is all too easy to replace the misleading 'Whig model of the respectable, considerate "bobby" with another, equally fallacious model of the policeman as the simple and brutal enforcer of the inequality inherent in the state.'[39]

The evidence relating to Middlesbrough in the 1850s and 1860s reveals several instances of enthusiastic police involvement that brought a critical response from opinion-formers in town. An editorial in the *Middlesbrough Weekly News* of 13 August 1859 bemoaned the fact that 'our streets are the scenes of drunkenness and fighting almost every Sabbath' in which 'the delinquents' responsible for such reprehensible behaviour were very frequently 'abetted in their demoralizing practices by the aid of persons who ought to be conservators of the peace, instead of exulting in what they [the police] are pleased to term 'a good stand up fight'.[40] It was quite clear that the police not only encouraged fighting but also took part with enthusiasm.

Given the general violence of the town and the degree of violence directed at the police it is not surprising to find that the Middlesbrough force was prepared to 'look after itself'. But if assaults on the police by members of the public are incompletely recorded, even more so are assaults by the police on members of the public. Some incidents were sufficiently serious, or sufficiently public, to make an appearance in the official record. The watch committee minutes and constables' conduct books contain, every now and again, terse references to policemen dismissed for 'ill-treating John Hobson this day' or for 'assaulting two men while on duty'.[41] Others were disciplined for actions that took place when a prisoner had been brought into custody. In January 1866, for example, James Campbell, by now a sergeant, was demoted to the rank of merit constable for having assaulted a prisoner in the town's Police Office. PCs Warters and Coulon were dismissed from the force following 'a serious complaint ... [of] seriously ill-using a person named William Morton taken into custody by them at 2.30 in the morning of Sunday last as being in a state of helpless drunkenness'.[42] It transpired that both constables were also under the influence of alcohol. Even more serious was the assault by PC Samuel Bowes on John Hobson, variously described as a confectioner and a builder's labourer, which led to the dismissal of the former and (as will emerge later) resulted in widespread concern with and condemnation of police brutality in the town.[43]

Despite the opacity of some of the evidence, there is little doubt that in the mid-1860s, a time of rapid turnover in the town's police force, there was a major problem of police indiscipline that was eroding confidence. The situation was compounded by the suspicion of bias on the part of the police in their treatment of certain individuals. This was revealed in a series of incidents involving a well-known trouble-maker, a local blacksmith, Robert Brown. The relationship between Brown and the police was complex and much remains shrouded in mystery. However, the lengths to which the police were prepared to go in not bringing prosecutions themselves and then, when a private prosecution had been taken out, offering character references from two senior men to a man with a reputation for violence, suggests that either he was a police informer or he had knowledge of police practice that would have been highly embarrassing if made public. The incident started in August 1865, when Brown was charged with assaulting PC Stainsby and using insulting language to PC Horsefield. The *Middlesbrough Weekly News* tantalizingly noted that 'great interest was attached to the case, on account of recent proceedings before the Town Council with respect to the conduct of the police'.[44] Reporting on the court case, the paper quoted the following exchange between Brown and the local magistrate, Mr F. Atkinson, who was also the mayor of Middlesbrough:

> Mr. Brown: I am charged ... with having assaulted Stainsby without just cause and provocation. Now I contend I have a reason for what I did. Now, gentlemen, at a meeting of the Town Council last week he [Stainsby] was reported for being drunk. It so happens that I was at the police station on Saturday night on business. Whilst I was there two prisoners were brought in by two officers, P.C. Stainsby came in in plain clothes.
> *The Mayor*: You had better not go into that. It will do no good.

With no further explanation Atkinson continued:

> We are of the opinion that the assault was committed under considerable provocation and therefore that the case will be met by your paying the expenses of 12s. You put yourself in the wrong by taking the law into your own hands.

Somewhat ominously Brown concluded that 'him and I will square accounts some of these days'.[45] The Watch Committee minutes simply record that Stainsby resigned, having been reported as being drunk.[46] There was an air of mystery surrounding the affair that gave rise to 'a great deal of dissatisfaction abroad in the town'.[47] In fact little further happened for over four months. Then, in January 1866, Timothy Brown was accused of assaulting PC Eland. His father – none other than Robert Brown – was also accused of attacking the constable and of using threatening and insulting language. Doubts, never made fully explicit in the press coverage, surrounded the case, and it was dropped. Just over a year later (and less than three months after the Bowes/Hobson incident) the *Middlesbrough Weekly News* carried a letter complaining about further violence perpetrated by the blacksmith Robert Brown and, more importantly, the repeated failure of the police to take action against him. A week later the paper ran an editorial that drew attention to yet another violent incident in which Brown had broken the ribs of his servant girl. Describing Brown as a 'notorious and brutal transgressor of the law', the paper condemned the Watch Committee for conducting 'a well-nigh private hearing' in which Brown was 'screened from the penalties which his conduct merited'. A week later the Mayor, Mr Atkinson, wrote to the paper admitting that a charge of assault should have been brought against Brown but arguing (rather lamely) that the full information was not available at the time of the original decision and, therefore, Superintendent Saggerson was exonerated of any charge of bias in favour of Brown.[48] The Watch Committee minutes are silent on the matter, but the situation came to a climax two months later, when Brown (along with a coal merchant named James Hedley) was charged by James Francis, a local chemist and dentist, with conspiracy to assault him [Francis] or to have him assaulted. Brown and Hedley were committed for trial at Northallerton quarter session where they were found guilty of conspiring to inflict grievous bodily harm. There was one final twist to the tale. Inspector Thorpe and ex-detective sergeant Hopper gave Brown a character reference at the trial which provoked the chairman of the bench to publicly criticise Thorpe for his action: 'it was hardly creditable to him as a policeman to come there [i.e. to court] and give a man a character when in his heart of hearts he knew he was keeping back something ... which was important to forming the right estimate of a man's character'.[49] The details of the relationship between Brown, Saggerson and Thorpe will never be known, nor will the wider political context, but the fact that Saggerson had to be publicly defended by the mayor against charges of bias and that Thorpe was criticised for his unprofessional behaviour at the quarter sessions suggests that some form of cover-up had taken place. Whatever the precise details of these incidents, Saggerson's report to the Watch Committee in early April 1867, in which he commended his men for their satisfactory behaviour, has a hollow ring, coming as it did only days before the very public criticism of the unprofessional behaviour of one of the town's most senior and longest-serving officers. The Brown affair throws a dark shadow over the Middlesbrough police force in the 1860s, and despite its seeming atypicality, creates an element of doubt about the integrity of the force at the highest levels, and also gives an indication of the limitations of that 'well-chosen and efficient body of men' so fulsomely praised by Her Majesty's Inspector in the following year.

The Brown incident was not an isolated instance and the local press carried several accounts of other incidents, albeit less dramatic. Indeed, it is through the letters and editorials that appeared in the local press that one can obtain some insight into 'middle-class' attitudes towards the police. In most police histories these people are seen as supporters of the new police, benefiting from the improved levels of protection for both property and person and viewing the police essentially as servants, to be hired and fired by their elected representatives on the Watch Committee. However, it would be misleading to suggest that middle-class attitudes, as reflected in the local press, were uniformly supportive of the police.

In the early 1860s the *Stockton Gazette and Middlesbrough Times* took a positive view of the town's police. The paper put a positive gloss on the recent increase in recorded crime, believing this to be the product of the 'active conduct of Superintendent Saggerson and his staff', and noted with approval 'a great decrease in the number of beggars and vagrants [following] a vigorous effort' by the town's police. In an editorial commenting on the annual police report for 1862 it noted how 'they discharge their difficult duties in a highly creditable manner' and praised them for being 'much above the average in intelligence, discipline and good conduct'.[50] The clearest expressions of sympathy and support for the police came in 1864 with the growing awareness of the problem of policing 'Irishmen of the lowest class'. In a long editorial in May 1864 the *Middlesbrough Weekly News* praised the police as the embodiment of the law and sympathised with the difficulties they faced from drunken assailants who then escaped the full force of the law through the practice of rescuing prisoners and of collective payment of fines.[51] Thus the police were represented as defenders of decent society against the threat of the drunken and uncivilized outsiders. It is no coincidence that the paper ran an editorial less than two months later which lamented the failure of 'the moral progress of the town ... [to] keep pace with the development of its material resources and its growth in affluence'.[52]

However, not all readers were satisfied with the service they received from the police. There was oft-repeated concern that too little was being done to clear the streets of drunks, beggars, gamblers and other unsavoury characters who offended the sensibilities of the town's middle classes. A correspondent to the *Middlesbrough Weekly News* clearly felt he was speaking for a larger constituency when he asked 'is nothing to be done to check the spread of this crime' of gambling? The police had failed to deal with the 'gangs of dissolute and disorderly characters' who flagrantly breached the law, especially in and around Nile Street, Marton Lane and the second Sailors' Trod.[53] 'Why,' bemoaned Puck some years later, 'do the police allow so many beggars to infest our streets?' A regular critic of police inactivity, he returned to his theme to fulminate against scenes of public drunkenness and to condemn the fact that 'the police are instructed to be a little lenient with offenders of this class at holiday times'.[54] The extent to which Puck's concerns were shared by others cannot be determined precisely, but while he was the most frequent he was not alone in expressing dissatisfaction with the 'moral policing' of the town.

The police were expected to maintain an effective presence in the streets. The maintenance of order and decorum was their responsibility, and failure to do so aroused the ire of local ratepayers. But the police were also expected to conduct themselves properly in their treatment of all inhabitants irrespective of class. Police treatment of working-class members of the public during and after arrest came in for a steady stream of criticism over the years. Councillor Baxter informed the town council that he 'had seen men very roughly handled in the police yard' and was less than happy with the fact that in some cases they had been 'dragged in by the heels'.[55] The ever-vitriolic Puck was highly critical of the increased incidence of drunken behaviour among policemen and was particularly scathing about the mistreatment of working-class suspects struck. In November 1866 he highlighted the case of a Mr Hobson; this was not seen as an isolated incident and Puck waxed eloquent on his concerns as to

> what might happen to me were I to walk the streets of Middlesbrough in anything but a black coat, clean collar, shining boots and a conventional 'tile' to complete my outer man there is no doubt about the risk, as witness the brutal way in which Mr., Hobson was dragged through the streets like a felon, in spite of the remonstrances of several tradesmen.

The Middlesbrough police, he concluded were 'dominated by bullies'.[56] Here was further evidence, for Puck at least, that the local force was degenerating from its earlier higher standards and that the policeman of the day was not the 'thorough moral purist' that he should be.[57] The credibility of his deteriorationist argument is undermined somewhat by the claim (not borne out by the evidence of the police conduct books) that Middlesbrough once had a teetotaller police force. None the less, the fact remains that a regular contributor to the local newspaper was convinced that policing standards were falling and told readers so on a number of occasions. Nor is the allegation of discrimination and bullying implausible, as evidence from other parts of the country suggests. Although he was writing of police attitudes in London a generation later, Hugh Gamon, as a result of his research for the Toynbee Trust, concluded that the Metropolitan police were

> sad respecters of person; they distinguish at once between the silk hat and the battered bowler. The silk hat is presumptively devoid of iniquity; the battered bowler covers a potential criminal, and is to be regarded at least with suspicion.[58]

Puck was not a lone voice in criticising the police. The Brown incident, noted above, attracted critical editorial comment, as did police actions in the latter part of the decade. Following a series of allegations about illegal entry and assaults by members of the force, the *Middlesbrough Weekly News* came out with an unequivocal condemnation:

> They [the police] were doing an illegal thing in entering the man's house [at midnight] ... It reveals a systematic contempt and disregard for the rights and feelings of poor people simply because they are poor.[59]

Indeed such was the unsatisfactory response to the affair that the newspaper published a further highly critical editorial a month later.[60]

Any attempt to assess the nature of the relationship between the police and the public during the first generation of new policing in Middlesbrough is constrained by the limitations of the surviving evidence. There is little or no direct evidence of how the majority of people viewed the police, and there are doubts surrounding the typicality of those witnesses – be it the local gossip columnist Puck or the blacksmith Robert Brown, for example – whose testimony is heard. Similarly, the incidents, both large and small, of anti-police violence are far from unambiguous. Conclusions are necessarily tentative.

Policing bore most directly and most heavily on the working classes. Police work was not simply about fighting crime but involved the preservation of order and decorum in public places. Those for whom the streets were the major sites of work and recreation found many of their activities circumscribed, criminalised and subject to regular surveillance. Unsurprisingly, the policing of routine work and leisure activities created friction, particularly among certain sections of the population. There seems little doubt that working-class Irish immigrants, despite not living in clearly defined districts as in other parts of the country, were seen by the police as a particular problem group and received a disproportionate share of police attention. In part this was a product of overt anti-Irish prejudice. Official reprimands for the use of insulting language in public revealed (almost certainly) but the tip of an iceberg. In part it was a product of a more general class bias in police thinking. Police resources were limited and the demands made upon them considerable. Priorities had to be determined and strategic decisions made. Protecting Grove Hill by patrolling 'over the border' was Middlesbrough's equivalent of protecting St James by patrolling Aldgate.

That said, there were other considerations that came into play. Under Superintendent Saggerson, policing was often highly pragmatic. Drunks were given the opportunity to go home of their own accord, and in some cases were given assistance; but when they chose to stay (and often to stay and fight) they could and did on occasion feel the full force of the law. None the less, faced with perceived and real police hostility, it is not surprising to find that many working-class Irish people (not all men) viewed the police antagonistically. The mass rescues and collective payment of fines betokens a clear sense of conflict between the police and this section of the policed community. For these people the policeman, far from being the embodiment of the law, was the living symbol of injustice. Such attitudes, however, were not simply to be found among the Irish (and there will have been Irish men and women who were less hostile in their views and actions), but existed more widely among those who fell foul of the law. There is only limited and indirect evidence to suggest that there was hostility to the police *per se* (and the very newness of the town is significant here), but there was a dislike of certain police activities (including over-exuberance) and of the actions of certain policemen.

However, the vast majority of working men and women stayed clear of the law. One can only speculate about their attitudes. Pragmatism appears to be the predominant feature. Most people appear to have accepted the police and used them when needed to interfere in a fight, to arrest a thief and so forth, but this did not mean that there was necessarily any great affection for them. The willingness to offer assistance, not a common or frequently reported occurrence, likewise was more likely to reflect a pragmatic recognition that supporting the police in upholding the law was in the interest of generally law-abiding working-class members of society.

For the middle classes of Middlesbrough the police were more obviously allies in the fight against criminality and immorality. To that extent they supported the police, praising them for arresting criminals and driving out tramps, but also criticising them for failing to deal effectively with drunks and gamblers, especially on the Sabbath. However, middle-class criticism went beyond concern with value for money. There was a genuine (and recurring) concern with the liberties of 'the poor'. It is easy to dismiss the hyperbolic outpourings of Puck as little more than froth, but his observation about the impact of dress on police perceptions and actions indicates the class bias of much police activity. Saggerson was at pains to warn over-zealous officers, ensuring clear passage through the streets of town, not to move on 'ladies' who were window shopping. Unwarranted violence and unjustified intrusions into the privacy of homes aroused anger and condemnation, albeit somewhat paternalistic, from middle-class champions of the poor. There is also some evidence of more positive responses to the police: a willingness to give assistance and words of praise for a job seen to be well done. Recognition of the worth of individual policemen is also to be seen in the response of the Watch Committee. Again, praise for brave action in the apprehension of a dangerous criminal, the awarding of gratuities or the praise bestowed at retirement or on death indicates an awareness of worth that went beyond the merely ritualistic.[61] However, for many middle-class people the police were simply part of the normal order of things, peripheral figures patrolling the streets, and as such largely taken for granted and viewed with indifference.

As for the police themselves, their attitudes remain heavily shrouded. The transient nature of the job also makes it difficult to arrive at firm conclusions. In their official statements – annual reports, monthly reports to the Watch Committee – the image presented was of a responsive force that did a good job in maintaining law and order.[62] Criminals and criminal activities were seen as exceptional and there was little sense of fundamental conflict between police and policed. Indeed, on more than one occasion there was praise for the law-abiding behaviour of the poor, particularly in times of economic hardship. This positive image was punctured by periodic references to the persistent and larger-scale problems of drunkenness and violence, and a less rosy, more hard-nosed attitude emerges when the practicalities of routine policing are considered. As noted above, prejudice was to be found in parts of the force and there was a more general realisation that the job carried a high risk of accident or injury. At the level of street policing, the police (following the example of their superintendent) adopted a pragmatic approach, turning a blind eye wherever possible to relatively harmless drunkenness to minimize the risk of conflict. This was not universally popular. A disgruntled correspondent to the *Middlesbrough Weekly News* complained that 'a drunken man was allowed to disturb the peace of the locality from ten o'clock in the evening until four in the morning with[out] receiving any notification to "move on"'.[63] The police were prepared when necessary to take firm action, as John Thomas found to his cost. Having 'refused to go home when the officers gave him the chance to do so, he met all entreaties with defiance, and was therefore locked up'.[64] Others were even less fortunate and were literally hauled in to the station. Dragging a prisoner by his feet across the cobbles of the police yard may have disquieted some middle-class observers, but it also sent out a very clear message to those who might chance their arm with the police. However, while senior officers and the few long-serving men may have subscribed to this style of policing, the attitudes of the ordinary constables (many of whom served for very brief periods at this time) are very largely unrecorded. Some it would seem were very little different from the people they policed: there was a willingness to drink and fight that exacerbated the troubles of the town on a Saturday night. Others one suspects had little sympathy with the moral order they were supposed to enforce and had little inclination to take positive action. Why risk serious injury when one could snatch a few moments sleep in a warm cabin? Why indeed when all one wanted was a proper job 'at the works'?

****

The great boom of the late 1860s and early 1870s experienced by the town marked the end of the first major phase in its growth and development. Originally conceived as a small planned community at the far end of the Stockton & Darlington extension line, Middlesbrough had dramatically outgrown the economic and social boundaries envisaged by its founding fathers. The coal export trade had expanded well beyond expectations and the economy had diversified to a degree that could not have been envisaged in 1830 or even 1840. From an economic and technological viewpoint Middlesbrough's history to 1870 was an almost unqualified success story. Though it was lacking in the glamour that surrounded the discovery and exploitation of gold or silver, iron provided the basis for considerable wealth creation. Economic expansion drew in men and (to a lesser extent) women from all parts of the United Kingdom. Scots, Irish and Welsh mixed with people from Cornwall, south Wales and Staffordshire as well as from nearby Durham and the north riding of Yorkshire. The influx of population made the original Otley Plan inoperable, as first the original town layout was infilled and later the town spilled out to the south and west of its original boundaries. Densely packed housing and limited facilities created threats to the physical and moral well-being of the town. Disease and disturbance were enduring features of the town's early history. Middlesbrough had many of the qualities of the frontier towns to be found in America or Australia, and many of the problems. The men who were responsible for the laying out of the original town in 1830, the men who had sought an Improvement Act in 1841, had a vision of an ordered society. And yet the very success of the town they had created threatened to undermine the order they sought to establish.

The prospects for law and order in the early years were not good. With a newly arrived and shallow-rooted population, and dominated by a high-wage economy and an overwhelmingly working-class, young-male society, Middlesbrough had all the ingredients for a turbulent, if not lawless community. The parish constable, still effective in many rural parts of England, was inappropriate and inadequate in the conditions that obtained in Middlesbrough. But so too were the constables appointed under the Improvement Act. Middlesbrough, before the advent of William Hannan in 1853, was under-policed, if not unpoliced. The paucity of evidence for the 1840s makes it impossible to assess the ways in which and the extent to which its was a self-policed community. The mid-1850s were a critical transition period. The advent of a new police superintendent, bringing experience and new standards of security to the town, and the passing of the County and Borough Police Act three years later, put policing in Middlesbrough on a qualitatively and quantitatively new footing. The transition was neither smooth nor complete. The borough force was characterised by high levels of turnover and varying levels of incompetence and indiscipline. A determined Watch Committee, led by Isaac Wilson, took a firm line in establishing a disciplined force, but only gradually did the core of a stable and proficient force emerge in these years. At the same time, there was continuing physical hostility towards the police, most notably but not exclusively from the Irish community, and this hostility increased during the decade from the mid-1850s. The police were also under attack from the pens of their critics among the town's middle classes. However, there were signs that the period of transition was coming to an end as the balance began to shift, hesitantly and almost imperceptibly, in favour of the police. The number of physical attacks slowly diminished, more (though never many) members of the public were prepared to come to the aid of their constables, and the voices of the critics became less strident. At the same time, there were men in post for whom policing, out of choice or necessity, was to become a career. With an experienced man at the helm (Saggerson), the town's force was acquiring the skills and experiences that would enable Middlesbrough to become a fully-fledged policed town by the end of the century.

6
The Years of Maturation: Urban and Industrial Growth, *c.* 1870–1914

Within little more than a generation before 1870 a new town and a new police force had come into being.[1] The dramatic growth and distinctive character of the town created particular problems that compounded the difficulties faced by all new police forces. However, the 'frontier stage' in the town's development came to an end and a more mature economy and society gradually emerged in the late-Victorian and Edwardian years. None the less, as in the early years, the economic and characteristics of the town impacted on the development of policing.

Economic developments

Not for nothing was Middlesbrough known as Ironopolis. The iron and steel industry continued to play a major role in the development of the town in the last quarter of the nineteenth century, though the development of new technologies, the emergence of new and powerful competitors abroad and the vicissitudes of world trade resulted in mixed economic fortunes for the staple industries. With its heavy dependence upon exports the iron and steel trade was subject to trade cycle fluctuations. The operation of the sliding scale meant that workers in the iron and steel trades (and indirectly others in the town) felt the direct impact of variations in prices. But employment opportunities and earnings fluctuated markedly on a week to week basis. Uncertainty and the threat of poverty were ever-present for those 'at the works'.

However, there was (and always had been) more to the town's economy than iron and steel production, and in the latter part of the nineteenth century one can see a distinct maturing of the local economy (Table 6.1). The dominance of manufacturing industry throughout the period is beyond dispute, but a majority of the workforce were employed

Table 6.1: Principal occupations in Middlesbrough, 1871–1911 (as % of all occupied persons)

Sector	1871	1881	1891	1901	1911
Manufacture	49	46	43	46	45
Transport	9	10	11	12	14
Dealing	7	8	8	10	12
Industrial service	17	14	15	9	6
Public service & professional	3	4	5	6	6
Domestic service	5	11	10	8	9

Source: Census.

elsewhere. The occupational structure of the town remained heavily biased towards male employment. Engineering, shipbuilding and the iron and steel industries were bastions of male supremacy. Unsurprisingly, in a predominantly working class community dependent upon heavy industry, among towns with a population of 50,000 or more in England and Wales, Middlesbrough had the lowest proportion of women in employment. Most women found themselves in poorly paid jobs such as bottle washing. Nor was there great demand for domestic servants. Although there were informal sources of earnings, the absence of employment opportunities for women on any large scale increased the dependence upon a narrow range of industries (Table 6.2).

For the town's staple industries the last quarter of the nineteenth century was to prove problematic. In mid-1873 there began a trade depression that had a severe impact on local industries. Worst hit was the malleable iron production. In July, Fox, Head & Co. were forced to close down the Newport Rolling Mill because of the complete absence of orders. Other closures in the region took place in the following year.

Table 6.2: Middlesbrough's industrial structure, 1871–1911 (as % of all occupied persons)

Sector	1871	1881	1891	1901	1911
Iron & steel	31	25	18	14	18
Engineering and machine	5	4	5	11	9
Shipbuilding & vehicles	3	3	6	7	5
Textiles etc.	7	7	7	4	4
General labouring	17	12	15	13	8

Source: As for Table 6.1.

Then, in 1875, the town's largest employer, Bolckow & Vaughan, announced the closure of all their puddling furnaces in Middlesbrough, and only months later the massive Britannia Ironworks met the same fate. Finally, in 1879, both the Teesside Ironworks and the Ayrton Ironworks (owned by Jones Brothers & Co.) suspended payments while the Imperial Ironworks of Jackson, Gill & Company went into liquidation. The trade never fully recovered from these hammer blows. Some local firms, such as Bell Brothers, suffered less since they specialised in the production of iron plates, bars and angles for the iron shipbuilding industry whose continued growth partly offset the collapse of the rail trade in the face of competition from steel. Production picked up briefly in the 1880s but thereafter there was a steady decline in production in the town that reflected in starker form a more general national decline in the production of puddled iron.

Pig-iron production was also badly hit by the collapse of prices after the ending of the Franco-Prussian war. In 1873, at its peak, the price of pig-iron had been 122s. 6d. (£6.13) per ton, but by 1879 it had fallen by a staggering 80 per cent to 32s. 6d. (£1.63). None the less, output continued to grow – perversely adding to the problem – but stagnation set in after the early 1880s. Although the production of pig-iron did not collapse to the same extent as that of malleable iron, the future lay with steel production. The development of cheap steel dated from the development of the Bessemer process in the 1850s and the Martin-Siemens open-hearth process in the 1860s. The problem for Middlesbrough iron-producers was compounded by the fact that the local iron-ore had a high level of phosphorous that resulted in poor quality steel. This was overcome by using ore imported from Spain. However, the technological problem remained and was not solved until 1879 when the Thomas and Gilchrist process enabled the unwanted phosphorous to be removed during the refining of iron to bulk steel. Unfortunately, a technological advance that benefited local producers also proved highly beneficial to European competitors who could now exploit their abundant supplies of phosphoric ores. Competition in steel production intensified and brought new pressures onto Middlesbrough firms.

The 1880s were critical years in the transition from iron to steel production. Bolckow & Vaughan introduced four Bessemer converters at their Cleveland Works at Eston Junction that were to continue in production until 1911. In 1883 the newly formed North-Eastern Co. joined them in basic Bessemer production, but it was the firm of Dorman Long that emerged as the second major steel producer on Teesside.[2] Widespread adoption was limited, not least because of the reputation for unreliability that the resultant steel products gained. Faced with fierce, often subsidized, competition from abroad, where the extensive reserves of haematite were more easily and economically exploited, the steel industry in Middlesbrough never enjoyed the prosperity to compare with the heyday of iron production. In particular, the early twentieth century saw a clear slackening of growth.

Despite these problems the local iron and steel industry experienced long-term growth that was reflected in the substantially increased exports of manufactured iron and steel products from Middlesbrough. In 1870 the figure was approximately 167,700 tons, rising by a factor of four to 682,000 tons in 1910. This long-term trend, however, was overlain by marked medium-term fluctuations determined by the trade cycle and also by sharp year-to-year variations. Equally volatile was the local shipbuilding industry. Raylton Dixon opened a new yard in 1873 while Smith's Dock was opened at South Bank in 1908. Between the late 1870s and 1890 there was a 50 per cent increase in the tonnage of new ships launched on the Tees and by the early twentieth century there were six shipbuilding firms on the river. Engineering, in contrast, was less subject to sharp fluctuations. Although it was closely linked with other local heavy industries, there was a diversity of activity that gave greater flexibility that in turn minimized the traumas of trade-cycle fluctuations. Nevertheless, the closely inter-related heavy industries, with their characteristic cyclical pattern of boom and slump, accounted for such a large percentage of the local work force that they exerted a wider and profound influence on the economic and social life of the town.

The preoccupation with manufacturing in general and heavy industry in particular is understandable but misleading. The growth of retailing and leisure industries, albeit on a modest scale, were important to the economic well being of the town. Equally they reflect an important underlying social phenomenon, namely rising real incomes and increased consumption. A mass working-class market emerged in Middlesbrough in the mid and late nineteenth century. As in other parts of the country, the sale of uniform-quality, low-priced mass-produced goods brought revolutionary change to the grocery trade led by the new multiple stores.[3] Indeed, it was from the ranks of the new 'shopocracy' that the next generation of Middlesbrough's political leaders emerged.

As early as the 1860s a growing number of local tradesmen were developing small-scale chains of shops. In 1861 the grocers T. Appleton & Co. had shops in South Street, Corporation Road, Gurney Street and

Durham Street. In 1867 George Watson had shops in East Street, Wilson Street and Wellington Street. However, the most successful local entrepreneur was 'the Alderman', Amos Hinton.[4] This family firm enjoyed two periods of expansion. The first in the 1870s and 1880s saw the opening of six shops; the second came in the 1900s, by which time Amos Hinton & Sons employed some 230 staff in their various shops. Other local multiples, such as William Woffenden & Son, Charles Ephgrave and Pybus Brothers, challenged but never matched the achievement of Hinton's.

It was not only in the grocery trade that changes took place. Butchers such as Eastman's and Nelson's had a dozen or more shops in and around the early twentieth century. What is more, the introduction of cheap imported meat into the country from the 1880s onwards was reflected in the presence of such firms as the British and Colonial Meat Company that boasted fourteen shops in the district by the eve of the Great War. Elsewhere, in the bakery trade, for example, Forbes and Sparks emerged as the leading local multiples, while Sutton Brothers took the lead in the greengrocery trade.

The growth of multiples has to be set in the wider context of more traditional patterns of retailing centred on the corner shop. Food retailing was a highly volatile sector of the economy with firms appearing and disappearing with bewildering rapidity from year to year as the local economy moved from periodic slump to boom. For the most part the number of retail outlets kept pace with overall population growth although this was less true of the bakers, fishmongers and especially fried fish dealers where the position improved over time. However, three qualifications need to be made. First, the simple total of retail outlets does not take into account increases in the size of shops. As the history of Hinton's amply demonstrates, there were important developments in the scale of operations of certain food retailers. Second, the figures do not capture the qualitative changes that took place in the late-nineteenth century. The presence of regional and national multiples, such as Maypole Dairies, Home and Colonial and the Co-op, resulted in a wider range of foodstuffs, improved and more consistent quality and also lower prices. Finally, Middlesbrough had more food retail outlets per head of population than Darlington, Durham, Stockton and Sunderland. In the north-east of England only Newcastle was better provided.

Multiple stores catering for a mass market were also to be found, albeit on a smaller scale in other sectors of the market. The first multiples in the men's clothing trade emerged in the 1880s but the major development of the early twentieth century was the emergence of the wholesale bespoke multiple shop retailer. Although overshadowed in the historical record by the better-known name of Montagu Burton, Stewart's the 'King Tailors' of Middlesbrough was the leading firm by size and scale before the Great War with its speciality, the 20s. (£1) suit, that was aimed at a market between the very cheap off-the-peg ware and the expensive product of the bespoke tailor. Multiples in the town also catered for boots and shoes as well as clothing with nationals such as Freeman, Hardy and Willis and the London Boot Co. (as well as less well-known concerns such as the Public Benefit Boot Co.) and Hepworth's and Dunn. Again, Middlesbrough was well provided in comparison with other towns in the region.

Finally, mention should be made not simply of the development of the professions – another indication of economic maturity – but also the emergence of the commercial leisure industries that spoke of working-class demand for entertainment. Theatres, music-halls and the early cinema had a small but important role to play in the economic and the social life of the town. The significance of the growth of retailing and leisure must not be overstated. None the less, the very fact that such change took place bears witness to improvement in overall working-class living standards. Necessity might still drive the desperate to steal but not to the same extent as a generation before. A drink-centred culture was still to be found in the late-nineteenth century but there were alternative and permanent forms of entertainment for the men, women and children of Middlesbrough, as Lady Bell, the wife of local industrialist Sir Hugh Bell, noted.[5]

Demographic and social developments

The very rapid growth in population which had characterised the early town slowed somewhat after 1871, and yet by 1911 the town's population had grown by a factor of three to reach 120,000 as the relative prosperity of Middlesbrough continued to attract people. New housing sprang up in the west, centred on Cannon Street. The southern boundary of the town was now marked by Union Street and Borough Road (see Map 5), but to the south lay the impressive Albert Park. The land had been purchased from the Borough Council by Henry Bolckow in 1867 and opened by Prince Arthur in the summer of the following year. Further south the old agricultural village of Linthorpe was being transformed into a smart middle-class suburb as the wealthier middle classes moved to the edge of town or to outlying villages.

The oldest and predominantly working-class district of the northern part of the town had a prolonged history of speculative and largely unrestricted building which gave rise to a complex network of narrow, ill-lit and ill-ventilated courts and alleyways. By the end of the nine-teenth century the sheer age of much of this property meant it was in very poor structural condition. In contrast, housing in the western part of the town, which bore the brunt of population growth in the years after 1870, was influenced by building regulations. The adoption in 1855 of the Public Health Act was followed by the introduction of wider-ranging building regulations under the 1856 Middlesbrough Extension and Improvement Act and the 1858 Local Government Act that prevented the building of further culs-de-sac and alleyways. The most important change stemmed from the introduction of by-laws in 1875 that prevented the worst excesses of poor construction and con-gestion. Utility and uniformity was the order of the day but, notwith-standing the monotony of 'by-law housing', there was a perceptible improvement in the quality of working-class housing in the new streets of the 1890s, such as the 'jewels' – Pearl, Emerald, Ruby and Amber streets. Furthermore, there were not the physical barriers to expansion that had compounded the problems in the northern district. This was also true of the east of the town, though here a different social mix, combining both working-class and middle-class residences, resulted in a more generous spacing of houses than elsewhere in the town. Aspiring labour aristocrats and members of the lower middle classes purchased bay-windowed street houses in Angle Street, while those slightly higher up the social scale moved to Parliament Road or Ayresome Street.

From 1871 to 1911 the number of inhabited houses more than kept pace with the overall growth in population. As a consequence, average household size fell from 5.78 to 4.29 in these 40 years. In relative terms Middlesbrough's improvement was in line with other towns locally and nationally. However, the above-average family sizes and large number of lodgers that had long characterised the town ensured that overcrowding remained a problem. More detailed information in and after 1891 provides a more sensitive indicator of the adequacy of the housing stock. In 1891 some 13,412 people, or almost 20 per cent of the town's population, lived in conditions that were defined as over-crowded, that is having more than two persons per room in a house. By 1901 this number had been reduced to some 10,000 or 12 per cent of the population, but in the next decade the situation deteriorated to the extent that in 1911 13,513 people, equivalent to 13 per cent of the population, were living in overcrowded accommodation. Financial hardship rather than a shortage of housing *per se* was at the root of the problem in the most acutely affected places such as the Marsh and Cannon wards. Predictably those with large families and the single casual labourers were those most at risk. And, as earlier in the century, the social tensions created by the limitations of the built environment, the uncertainty of employment and exacerbated by the ready availability of alcohol led to outbreaks of violence. For the police in the late nineteenth century the district centred on Cannon Street was as great a source of concern as 'over the border' in the old town.

Especially in the old town, insanitation compounded the problem of overcrowding. The appalling sanitary condition of Oliver Street and Princess Street was the product of densely-packed housing and the location of sanitary facilities close to doors and windows. The sanitary and medical officers were so concerned that they sought to alleviate the situation by a policy of 'loopholing' whereby congestion was relieved by the demolition of properties at regular intervals throughout the most badly affected areas. More generally, the poor sanitary condition of the town was the result of rapid population growth outstripping facilities and swamping good intentions. The main drainage system of the borough was planned in 1869 and implemented in 1873 for an estimated population of 40,000. By the turn of the century the population was in excess of 100,000 but the drainage system was largely unchanged. Sewage flooding, exacerbated by the low-lying location of the town, was a recurrent problem. In the older parts of the town catchpits were the major form of sewage disposal. These were cesspools, as much as 6 feet in diameter, sunk about 10 inches below the road surface. High tides and heavy rainfall led to the constant flooding of streets and basements in parts of the Marsh, Newport, Cannon and Vulcan wards. The situation was compounded by the fact that catchpits in the back streets were not regularly emptied. Only when they became an obvious nuisance was action taken. The persistence of the problem is illustrated by the fact that between November 1878 and August 1895 there were 22 instances in which houses in the Marsh Road area were flooded by sewage. At its worst, as in November 1901, 400 houses and over 2,000 people were affected.

Domestic sanitary arrangements were also problematic. Water-closets were relatively few in number and largely confined to middle-class districts. Conservancy methods of excrement disposal (the privy midden and pan closet) predominated. Theoretically emptied once a fortnight, in practice less often, the custom was to throw the contents of the privy midden, often located close to back doors and pantry windows, onto the street to allow the liquid residue to soak away before scavengers removed the solid remains. The attendant fouling of the air added to the air pollution from local industries. Not surprisingly, areas of poor sanitary provision and poor health were coterminous. Diarrhoea, dysentery and enteric fever and the highest rates of infant mortality were the distinctive features of districts such as Newport and Marsh.

Water supply was another source of concern. In quantitative terms Middlesbrough was inadequately supplied. In many courts and yards there was but one tap for a dozen houses and the same supply of water was used for a variety of washing and cleaning purposes. In qualitative terms there were further problems. The Tees had been explicitly and directly linked with the typhoid epidemic of 1890/1 and there was a continuing concern that this supply was always impure.

To some extent the problems were tackled by local government action but there was never the same sense of urgency about sanitary issues in Middlesbrough as was to be found in Sheffield or even Leeds. The appointment of a full-time medical officer of health in 1893 was a step forward but in itself insufficient to guarantee positive action. Finance was the crucial stumbling block and the situation was made worse by the fact that from 1866 to 1918 the so-called Ironmasters' District, which had the greatest concentration of property and of sanitary problems, enjoyed a differential rate, paying only three-quarters of the full rate. There was a sharp contrast between the advice of the town's medical officer of health and the action of the council. An investigation in 1900 into conditions in St Hilda's ward identified 671 houses as injurious to health and recommended the destruction of at least 150 and as many as 299. The recommendation was never acted upon. Nowhere was this failure to act coherently and systematically more starkly seen than in the notorious Nile Street area. In 1900 the density of persons per acre was 429 compared with an average of 34; the death rate per 1000 was 30 compared with a figure of 20 for the rest of the borough. Despite pressure from the medical officer of health, Nile Street remained unchanged until the 1930s.

From 1871 onwards the general mortality rate for the town fell, notably in the early twentieth century. However, when allowance is made for the sex and age structure of the town, it is more accurate to talk in terms of stabilisation. Furthermore, a number of important qualifications have to be made. First, the rate of decline was not as great as in other towns. Locally, the contrast between Stockton and Middlesbrough, which had been clear in 1871, was even starker by

1911. Middlesbrough was an unhealthy place in which to live, with respiratory diseases more prevalent than elsewhere in the country. Indeed, such was the scale of the problem that a special enquiry was held and report made to the Local government Board in 1908. It transpired that the greater part of the difference between Middlesbrough's mortality rate and that of other Great Towns could be explained in terms of Middlesbrough Pneumonia, a particularly virulent and widespread local affliction. Second, for certain age groups (that is, children under 5 and adults over 45) mortality rates rose in the years before 1900. Third, in certain districts, notably in the north of the town, mortality rates for all age groups increased between 1870 and 1900. The combination of a heavily concentrated population, many of whom were poorly and irregularly paid labourers living next to, if not actually within, industrial sites, led to a long-term increase in mortality. Infant mortality rates were particularly high 'over the border'. The starkness of the contrast between different areas of the town is illustrated by figures compiled for the years 1911–14. In that period the average death rate per 1,000 births in the town was 251. In the Newport ward the figure stood at 303, in Cannon ward 329 and in St Hilda's 369. In contrast the figures for the wards of Ayresome and Grove Hill were 146 and 147 respectively.

Overall, in many respects the housing and sanitary conditions of the town had scarcely improved between 1870 and 1914. Indeed, in some districts conditions had deteriorated. Structurally unsound and congested housing, antiquated and unhealthy sanitary arrangements and poor health were a continuing feature of the lives of at least a third and possibly as much as a half of the town's population. Improvements in real wages and diet, noted below, only partly offset the health-threatening environment in which working class men and women in Middlesbrough lived and worked. It is no coincidence that the most vulnerable members of society lived in the most overcrowded and unsanitary districts of town and suffered the worst standards of health. Furthermore, there was a polarisation of working-class experience. For those unable to move out of the vicious cycle of irregular and/or inadequate pay, poor housing and poor health, there was both an absolute and relative deterioration. It is, once again, no coincidence that these districts tended to be seen as the problem areas by the town police.

In broad terms working-class living standards rose both quantitatively and qualitatively in the period between *c.* 1870 and 1914. Estimates of real wages for the town's major industries suggest a steady long-term improvement.[6] The iron and steel trades suffered considerable cyclical fluctuations and some branches of the industry, notably puddling, never recovered the prosperity of the early 1870s boom years but even in this shrinking sector real wages increased in the long run after 1880. In other industries, notably engineering and building, the Victorian years were a period of steady improvement in real earnings rarely punctuated by the sharp rises and falls experienced by those in the iron and steel trades. The early twentieth century saw a check to this long-term trend and it was only after 1908 that real wages resumed their upward trend.

Unsurprisingly, evidence relating to skilled workers is more abundant than that for the unskilled and often irregularly employed labourer. The latter not only earned less than the former and, in all probability, enjoyed lower rates of improvement, but were also more likely to be made unemployed. The iron and steel industry provides some indication of the differential circumstances experienced in this period. In the Cleveland blastfurnaces, for example, there were at least 26 different types of worker to be found and each was paid a different rate depending upon his place in the industrial hierarchy. Keepers, who accounted for less than 10 per cent of the total workforce, were the best paid. In 1905 their wage rate was 60s. (£3) a week. Metal carriers were paid 50s. (£2.50), while mine fillers received 42s. (£2.10). Lower down the scale, slaggers received 37s. (£1.85), keepers' helpers and enginemen 35s. (£1.75) and coke fillers 31s. 6d. (£1.58). Less well-off were weighmen whose weekly wage rate was 24s. 6d. (£1.23), while ordinary labourers received only 19s. (95p). In percent terms each of these occupational categories had experienced a similar increase since 1870. However, in absolute terms the gap between the best paid and the worst increased and with it had increased relative deprivation.

The social and economic development of Middlesbrough after 1870 cannot be summarised easily. For the middle classes and the skilled working classes there were undoubted improvements in accommodation and the standard of living. For the unskilled the situation was much bleaker. Living in deteriorating environments and rarely able to benefit from the rise in real wages, such people were faced with bleak prospects. The link between crime and the wider social environment is complex. None the less, the persistence of poverty, the economic insecurity of many working men and their families, the overcrowded and the squalid conditions in which many Middlesbrough people continued to live was not conducive to a diminution in crimes against property or the person. Indeed, the emergence of relative wealth in such close proximity to such abject squalor may well have provided both motive and opportunity for theft. Contemporary observers linked the harsh, brutalising environment with intemperance, immorality and crime. Women were seen to be particularly at risk. The *North-Eastern Daily Gazette* in 1894 wrote in shocked tone of the growth of female drinking and gambling in the town: 'Sweeter to them [working-class women] is the hum of the betting ring and the clink of the glasses in the dram-shop, than the cooing of innocent babies.'[7] There were, however, changes operating in the opposite direction. As working-class living standards slowly rose, as consumerism gradually took off, so more working-class people had a stake in society. The desire for security was not confined to the middle classes of Grove Hill or Linthorpe. For aspiring and respectable working class people the law and its uniformed upholder, the policeman, were there to be used, even to be welcomed.

7
Expansion and Professionalisation: The Middlesbrough Police, *c.* 1870–1914

Historical interest has, for the most part, focused on the formative years of the new police forces.[1] The general histories, with varying degrees of emphasis, chart the creation of a policed society and the establishment of police legitimacy in late-Victorian England.[2] The extent to which the old image of the 'crusher' had been replaced by that of the 'handyman of the streets' is debatable, but it is noticeable that, with the exception of Shpayer-Makov's work on the Metropolitan Police, there is no published study that looks in detail at the second and third generations of new police.[3] It is, therefore, more difficult to put the development of the Middlesbrough police force after 1870 into a comparative perspective.

The continued growth in the population, the geographical expansion of the town, especially the burgeoning working-class areas in the west of the town, the continuing problem of over-crowding and social tension, and the growing differences in income and lifestyles between the old town and the more prosperous upper working-class and middle-class districts all required continuing augmentation of the local police force. Between 1871 and 1911 the size of the force more than tripled from 41 men to 134 with a 45 per cent increase in numbers in the 1880s and a 40 per cent increase in the first decade of the twentieth century. [4] With the exception of Dewsbury (whose force was less than half the size), no Yorkshire borough force grew to such an extent (see the appendix at the end of this chapter: Table A7.1).

This rapid growth presented managerial problems for all concerned, from the Watch Committee through the chief constable and his senior men to the sergeants. Further, these difficulties were compounded by the fact that the town's population grew more rapidly in the 1870s and 1880s thereby worsening the ratio of population to police (see the appendix – Table A7.2). This ratio worsened by almost 10 per cent over the 1870s and this was not made good until the beginning of the new century. However, even at this time the prevailing ratio (one police-man to approximately 950 people) was appreciably higher than in 18 towns 'somewhat similar to Middlesbrough' where the figure was approximately one to 790.[5] It was only later in the first decade of the twentieth century that significant improvement was achieved as the new chief constable, Henry Riches, pushed for more men. The poten-tially deleterious effects of a declining police/population ratio were offset, in part by declining crime rates – of which more later – and in part by the emergence of a more stable and experienced force.

The Watch Committee continued to play a major role, not least as employer; but the positive relationship that had evolved in the middle decades continued in the latter part of the century. Successive chief constables – Saggerson, Ashe and Riches – enjoyed a considerable degree of independence and there was never the conflict experienced notably in Liverpool in 1890.[6] It continued to meet, except in a few years, on a regular monthly basis and, as before, involved itself in a predictable range of concerns: the appointment, disciplining and dis-missal of men; the level of wages and various disturbances in the town. However, the overwhelming impression is of a committee that kept interventions to a minimum and that was prepared to allow its chief constable to get on with the job.[7]

The 1870s emerge as the transitional decade in which the character of the force changed. Recruits of the 1850s and 1860s were much more likely to treat policing as a short-term expedient than a long-term career.[8] In contrast, their counterparts of the 1880s and 1890s were more likely to make policing their career. Less than 10 per cent of mid-Victorian recruits served for 10 years or more compared with almost 50 per cent of late-Victorian recruits. (See Table 7.1.) The situation in Middlesbrough was not dissimilar to that experienced in other parts of the country such as the Black Country, Staffordshire and Buckinghamshire.[9] Unfortunately, the surviving records do not allow a detailed analysis of the background of recruits. The majority were men in their early to mid twenties and (of those for whom a place of birth is recorded) came from the North Riding of Yorkshire or Durham.[10]

The process of maturation is further illustrated by the figures in Table 7.2, which confirm the transitional nature of the 1870s and the steady improvement in the last quarter of the nineteenth century, with the percentage of men with more than 10 years' experience steadily increasing and the percentage with less than five years' service declin-ing. The trends were partially reversed after 1900, though the experi-

Table 7.1: Length of service of Middlesbrough police recruits by decades

	1856–69	*1870s*	*1880s*	*1890s*
Mean (years)	>0.0	2.0	4.0	11.0
Median (years)	4.0	6.4	10.0	11.6
Less than 1 year (%)	41	25	7	6
1–4 years (%)	23	34	41	27
5–9 years (%)	8	13	9	8
10–19 years (%)	2	5	14	38
20 years & more (%)	6	13	25	19
Not known	20	11	4	2

Source: Police Conduct Registers.

ence of the force was still significantly greater than in the 1870s. The higher rate of turnover among newly recruited men reflected the tougher line adopted by Henry Riches. His judgements could be scathing – one recruit whose appointment was not confirmed was dismissed as having 'little aptitude for Police Work and [of having] not endeavoured to improve his education, or seriously tried to be efficient' – and he was noticeably less tolerant of misconduct than his predecessor.[11] This approach and a vigorous recruiting campaign in the northeast by the Metropolitan police and other large city forces in the immediate pre-war years led to real problems when extensions to the borough in 1913 necessitated an increase in the town's force. There was, Riches ruefully noted, 'a dearth of suitable candidates for employment in the Police Forces. Fully 60% of the applicants during the past year were not physically or otherwise fitted for the Service.'[12] The extent to which these problems could have been solved in normal circumstances will never be known as the outbreak of war in the following year fundamentally altered the staffing situation.

A more detailed picture of the late nineteenth-century force emerges from two surviving nominal rolls that detail the structure of the force. Men of considerable experience held the senior positions. In 1882 the Chief Constable was the 53-year-old Edward Saggerson. In total he had served 34 years as a policemen, the last 21 as chief constable of Middlesbrough. He was supported by Superintendent Robert Thorpe, who had served just under 25 years in the borough force, and by three inspectors (Andrew Sample, William Ashe and George Mann), all of whom had just under 20 years' police experience. Two more inspectors, both privately paid (John Reed and Matthew Mawer), had over 20 years' service. (See Table 7.3.)

Table 7.2: Range of experience (as measured by length of service) of Middlesbrough police officers, 1870 to 1914 (as % of total in service in each year)

	Less than 1 year	1 year but less than 2	2 to 4 years	Total less than 5 years	5 to 9 years	Total less than 10 years	10 to 14 years	15 to 19 years	20+	Total 10+
1870–4	30	16	29	75	15	90	7	3	>1	10
1875–9	10	10	32	52	28	80	11	7	2	20
1880–4	18	13	15	46	21	67	18	10	6	34
1885–9	8	8	26	42	20	62	15	14	8	37
1890–4	9	9	18	36	23	59	16	10	15	41
1895–9	10	9	17	36	21	57	18	11	14	43
1900–4	13	8	22	43	20	63	16	12	9	37
1905–9	17	8	15	40	21	61	16	12	10	38
1910–14	20	8	17	45	16	61	16	11	12	39

Source: Constables' Conduct Registers, CB/M/P, 29, 30 and 31.

Table 7.3: Rank and age structure of the Middlesbrough borough police force, 1882 and 1889

Rank	Number	1882 % of force	Average age	Number	1889 % of force	Average age
Chief Constable	1			1		
Superintendent	1			1		
Inspectors	5			4		
All senior officers	7	11	46	6	8	47
Sergeants	10	16	39	9	13	47
PC 1st Class	25		36	41		37
2nd Class	7		34	5		32
3rd Class	7		30	7		27
4th Class	3		25	2		26
5th Class	2		22	1		21
6th Class	1		67	1		40
All PCs	45	73	34	57	79	34
All	62	100	36	72	100	37

Source: Nominal Roll of the Police Force of the County Borough of Middlesbrough, Sept. 1882 and May 1889; Printed Council Minutes, 25 July 1882, CB/M/C, 1/42, pp. 169–70, and 28 May 1889. CB/M/C, 1/49, pp. 234–5.

By 1889 Ashe had replaced Saggerson as chief constable. Thorpe, now 59 and with over 30 years' service, remained superintendent, while Mawer, now over 50 years old, was still paid by the School Board. There were now three new inspectors (William Atkinson, Frederick Knowlson and William Peacock) with comparable experience to the men they had replaced. More importantly, the maturity of the force was further reflected in the fact that in 1882 all but one of the town's police sergeants had 10 years' experience or more while in 1889 all but two had 15. Even more striking, over 80 per cent of first-class constables in 1882 had more than 5 years' experience, 25 per cent more than 10 and 8 per cent over 15. The corresponding figures for 1889 were 78 per cent, 37 per cent and 22 per cent. These men provided the backbone of the force.

One element of the town's force is difficult to establish with certainty. Detective work appears not to have been very important until the late nineteenth century. The first detective officer was appointed as early as 1859; and this level was maintained, with the exception of 1866, until the late 1880s. Frederick Knowlson, who was to become a Detective Superintendent in 1894, was the longest serving and most distinguished of the town's early detectives. Between 1890 and 1914 only 9 men are recorded in the conduct registers as being detectives, including 2 high-fliers, Matthew Hodgson and John Stones. Even in the immediate pre-war years, when there had been an expansion of detective work, in part a result of the utilisation of photography and fingerprints, the total number was no more than 6 or 7 in a force of over 130 men.[13] The retirement of Knowlson was the occasion for fulsome praise in the local press. The Middlesbrough detective force under Knowlson was described as 'working unostentatiously but very assiduously' and seen (somewhat exaggeratedly) as 'a terror to evil-doers'. Predictably Knowlson was singled out for praise but so too was his successor, the recently-promoted Stones.[14]

The move to a more stable and more experienced force – a development of major significance both for the force itself and for the wider community it policed – is to be explained more in terms of a sharp reduction in the percentage of recruits who demonstrated themselves unfit for police-work and were dismissed than in terms of declining dissatisfaction with police-work, as evidenced by the level of resignations.

Levels of resignation remained high and only dropped below 30 per cent in the last decade of the century, though there were year-on-year fluctuations that reflected changes in the local economy.[15] Although the police conduct registers are an incomplete source of information, it is possible to identify certain key characteristics of the men who chose to leave the force. The men who resigned were less likely to be locally born and therefore less likely to have a local network of family and friends, and correspondingly more likely to have loyalties to and responsibilities in other and not easily accessible parts of the country. Frederick Cole, who had been born in Leicestershire, resigned after just over a year's service because 'Middlesbrough does not agree with him and he is anxious to return to Nottingham'. Walter Gould resigned after one year because he 'does not like Middlesbrough and is anxious to join the Metropolitan Police as he has so many relatives there'. William Jones resigned 'to return home [to Byker, Newcastle] to support his widowed mother', as did a local man, Arthur Silversides, born in Ormseby, who resigned because of his wife's ill-health.[16] Those who resigned were also more likely to be young men. Three-quarters were under 25 years old and 1 in 5 was only 21. It follows from this that most of these men were new to policing. Almost 40 per cent had served less than a year when they resigned and a further 20 per cent resigned within their second year. The reasons for resigning are not recorded consistently. Several men simply returned to their former occupations,[17] while others found other situations including work as a

Table 7.4: Career Outcomes of Middlesbrough police recruits as % of total
recruited by decade

	1856–69	*1870s*	*1880s*	*1890s*	*1900–14*
Resignation	32	38	36	27	29
Resignation (ill-health)	5	11	8	4	2
Death in service	2	4	11	5	1
Dismissal	35	27	16	17	14
Not confirmed	0	0	0	0	9
Pensioned	6	13	21	5	1
In service 1914	0	0	5	41	43
Not known	20	6	4	2	0

Source: Constables' Conduct Registers, CB/M/P 29, 30 and 31.

clerk, or as an attendant at the local asylum, or as a gardener in Albert
Park, or employment with Bolckow & Vaughan as a timekeeper – and,
in one instance, employment with HM Customs.[18] A few sought their
fortunes abroad in America and Canada.[19]

There is an interesting subset of this group, that is men who had
settled into the job but resigned before becoming long-serving policemen in Middlesbrough. These men fall into two distinct and unequal
groups. The larger group comprised men who abandoned policing. Of
42 such men, 34 had failed to gain promotion and 6 had been promoted once. Although their reasons for resigning are not recorded, it is
not unreasonable to suggest that frustration with limited or non-
existent promotion prospects, and the implications that this had for
income played an important part in the decision. For the second
group, resignation from the Middlesbrough force was part of an
upwardly mobile career pattern. After 9 years' local service, Inspector
Bellamy became Head Constable of Boston, Lincolnshire while
Inspector Moore left Middlesbrough also after 9 years to become chief
constable of nearby Beverley. Albert Hargreaves, who had been
appointed as an inspector, resigned to become chief inspector and
deputy chief constable of the Borough of Cambridge police force, while
Christopher Taylor, who rose from first-class constable to inspector in
only 3 years in the early 1880s, moved on to become chief constable at
Walsall. Less dramatically, Sergeant Farndale became a superintendent
in the Chesterfield police, though PCs Frost and Morris simply moved
to other local forces.[20]

Finally, for some men there was little choice but to resign because of
their physical infirmities. Somewhat surprisingly, in view of the demands

of the job, the number who left for this reason is relatively small. It is no coincidence that retirement through ill-health (and death while in service) was more common for earlier recruits. In all, 36 men's careers ended in this way but, again somewhat surprisingly, the bulk of these (over 70 per cent) had served less than 5 years and a quarter proved to be physically inadequate for the job within their first year. The loyal veteran – such as Inspector Cooper, broken by 15 or 20 years' of service – was a real but relatively rare figure, in Middlesbrough at least.[21]

There is more evidence relating to dismissals from the force.[22] Like those who resigned, the men who were dismissed tended to be young constables in their early twenties. Over half were dismissed within a year of joining and 90 per cent of dismissals took place within the first five years of service. Unlike those who resigned these men were more likely to have been born locally. Reasons for dismissal are not always recorded but the pattern was largely unchanged from mid-century. Drunkenness and drink-related offences (assault, insubordination or simple neglect of duty) account for 3 out of every 5 dismissals.[23] Neglect of duty alone accounted for just over 1 in 10 of dismissals, though in some cases drunkenness was also involved.[24] The remaining reasons for dismissal were almost evenly divided between assault (either on a member of the public or another police officer), insubordination and what might be termed as acts of immorality.[25]

The latter category, though small, was important not least because of the example expected of the police but also because of the danger of corruption. Submitting a false report or lying about an incident led to the dismissal of PC Barrow and PC Williams, for example. Sexual improprieties led to the dismissal of several men. PC Blakeborough was dismissed for passing himself off as single and carrying on 'an intrigue with a widow', an offence he persistently denied. PCs Caddy, Metcalf and Robinson were dismissed in 1908 for having been found in a brothel at 2 a.m. on a Sunday morning, though it is not clear which was viewed as the more serious element of the offence. PC Basham was another brothel visitor to be dismissed in 1908. PC McEvoy lost his job for 'highly improper conduct in entering the house of a woman without permission and in the company of a strange man', while PC Wilson managed to combine drunkenness and threatening behaviour with frequent consorting with prostitutes that contributed both to his indebtedness to local tradesmen and his eventual dismissal.

The danger of corruption or blackmail following indebtedness and consorting with known convicts was something that exercised the collective mind of the Watch Committee on a number of occasions.

PC Morgan's indebtedness to local publicans led to his dismissal in 1888; PC Wilson was disciplined for being indebted to local tradesmen, while PC Hutchinson's career came to the same ignominious end in 1896 as a result of his frequenting and drinking with known thieves and accepting money for unspecified but 'dishonourable' purposes. The most consistent source of concern was gambling. Repeated warnings were given to constables by the chief constable and the mayor from the 1880s onwards and the occasional, exemplary dismissal took place in the late nineteenth century.[26] The problem assumed more serious proportions immediately before the Great War. In 1910 the Watch Committee was concerned that a concerted effort was being made to corrupt certain policemen.[27] Four men were given severe reprimands for visiting gaming houses and for their over-familiarity with local bookmakers. After a quiet year the problem flared up again in 1912. Two constables were warned for visiting gaming houses. One, PC Nash, was dismissed for compounding his offence with 'improper conduct' in keeping the company of a young woman when he was married. Two more men were dismissed for gambling while in uniform on the train to the York assize in the same year.

Not all offences fitted neatly into these categories. Some men, while clearly not acting as policemen should, were more foolish than anything else. PC Castle's use of 'obscene and offensive language' while on special duty at the town's football ground was one such instance. Likewise PC Melber's dismissal in 1896 owed more to exuberance that spilled over into stupidity when, while on a special round trip by steamboat from Middlesbrough to Scarborough organised for the police, he leapt from the SS India into the sea, thereby endangering the lives of passengers – and presumably himself. In exceptional cases dismissal was the result of a serious criminal offence. This was seen most starkly in the case of Inspector Grey, whose successful career was terminated in 1902 when he was charged with stealing monies (£1 1s. and £1 5s.) from prisoners in his charge.

None the less, during and after the 1870s a growing number of men served for 10 years or more in the town force, making policing their long-term career. The number of career policemen increased in absolute terms and as a percentage of all recruits. Experiences varied considerably but three broad categories of men can be identified and their experiences are summarized in Table 7.5.[28]

The first and most successful category comprised those who gained two (or more) promotions within the Middlesbrough force. Eleven men fell into this category: 3 joining in the 1870s, 5 in the 1880s and

Table 7.5: Career outcomes of long-term policemen

	1860s	1870s	1880s	1890s
Total recruits		134	91	86
Total long-term	15	25	34	50
% total recruits	9	19	37	58
1. One promotion: sergeant				
No.	13	10	15	14
% long-term	87	40	44	28
2. Two or more promotions: inspector (or above)				
No.	7	3	5	3
% long-term	47	12	15	6
3. No promotion beyond constable: long-service PC				
No.	0	9	16	36
% long-term	0	36	47	72
No promotion				
No.	2	6	3	0
% long-term	13	24	9	0

Source: Constables' Conduct Registers.

3 in the 1890s.[29] For the 1870s recruits promotion was relatively slow, taking an average of 18 to 20 years to become an inspector as they waited for the successful men from previous cohorts to reach the end of their careers. Of these three men, one – Frederick Knowlson (appointed 1872) – became a detective inspector when 43 and made superintendent aged 47 in 1894. In comparison the most successful men recruited in the 1880s rose more rapidly, and were still in their mid to late thirties when they gained their second promotion. The one exception was John Stone. Joining at the age of 21 in 1889, he became a sergeant within 8 years and a detective inspector (following Knowlson) just before his thirtieth birthday. Five years later he became a chief inspector and at the age of 38 he was promoted to Detective Superintendent. Two other men recruited in the 1880s went on to become chief inspectors and one a superintendent. No one from the 1890s cohort matched Stone's progress, but both Robert Hird (appointed 1890) and Matthew Hodgson (also appointed 1890) were quickly promoted from sergeant to inspector.

The second category contained those men whose progress stopped at the rank of sergeant. The percentage of career policemen who achieved one promotion dropped sharply between the 1860s and 1870s and fell again in the 1890s. Furthermore, it took longer to become a sergeant.

In the 1870s first promotion took an average of 10 years. This was twice as long as it had taken in the 1860s and was double the national average for the country at large.[30] The position deteriorated for recruits in the 1880s: it now took 12 years. There was a slight improvement thereafter but it still took the men recruited in the 1890s an average of 11 years to gain a first promotion. The average figures conceal two distinct career trajectories. The first – exemplified by Joseph Lancaster, Hugh Neill or William Taylor – was characterised by relative late age of joining (mid-30s) and promotion near the end of an already long career of 15 or even 20 years. Promotion was the reward for loyalty and good conduct. The second – exemplified by Thomas Raisbeck or William Wilkinson – was characterised by enlistment at a relatively early age (early twenties) and quick promotion to sergeant within as little as 3 to 5 years.[31] Despite the absence of further promotion for these men, there is no evidence to suggest any major disciplinary problems ensued, though there were demands for pay increases.

The final category comprised the rank-and-file officer who never achieved promotion except to a long-service class. The bulk of career policemen fell into this category. Despite the failure to gain promotion these men provided loyal service of many years and were the often-unrecognised workhorses of the late Victorian force. Elias Blackburn was one such man. His police career started in Norwich in 1856 and continued in the Durham County Constabulary in 1859. He then joined the North Riding Constabulary before returning briefly to Durham. In 1871, aged 33, he joined the Middlesbrough force and served for a further 22 years with no promotion and but one small blemish to his disciplinary record (a caution for riding a bicycle on a footpath in Linthorpe). The men in this category were, with few exceptions before the 1890s, older men who had become policemen in their late twenties or early thirties and, like Blackburn, had good disciplinary records. Henry Parkin was another such man. Aged 30 when he joined up in 1884 he served for 21 years before resigning because of ill-health, while Alfred Bell who joined in 1891 was still an ordinary constable 23 years later at the outbreak of war. Less fortunate were Frederick Hobson (appointed 1881) and Mason Dobson (appointed 1891) who served 19 and 16 years as constables before dying in service in 1900 and 1907 respectively.

The recruits of the 1870s, notwithstanding their good disciplinary records, were not entirely satisfied with their position. The expectation of promotion, which was held before all recruits should they become long-serving officers, had not been fulfilled. The introduction of a merit badge scheme in 1890 (bringing an additional 1s. (5p) per week) was important in giving formal recognition and reward for gallantry or good work but it did nothing to solve the wider problem of loss of motivation and dissatisfaction among men trapped at the top of the first stage of the career ladder. Following representations to the Watch Committee a number of these men (as well as some long-serving sergeants) were the first beneficiaries from the introduction of the long-service class in 1894. The average age of the 10 first-class constables thus promoted was just under 50 years. Moreover, they had spent between 13 and 19 years trapped as first-class constables prior to this promotion. The 1894 reform provided a short-term solution to an enduring problem posed by the (understandable) frustrations of long-serving constables (and to a lesser extent sergeants) who had not been promoted. The situation became acute for recruits of the 1890s. Of the 50 men who became long-term policemen, 36 remained constables. Half of them were fined or reprimanded for disciplinary offences and 15 committed offences of sufficient seriousness to warrant demotion. In 1905 a new service class was introduced for which men were eligible after 7 years' service and a long-service class was introduced in 1914 for those with 20 years' service.

For a small number of men, less than 10 per cent of all long-term policemen recruited in the last three decades of the nineteenth century, the difficulties were sufficient to bring resignation (in the case of four men all recruited in the 1890s) or dismissal (in the case of five others). Robert Sparks and James Waller, both recruited in the 1880s, had been promoted to sergeant but were reduced to the rank of constable for drunkenness before being ordered to resign for further disciplinary offences after careers that had lasted 18 and 13 years. James Scott, a detective sergeant with 5 commendations and a special promotion in less than 8 years, saw a promising career come to a juddering halt. Found guilty of 'improper conduct with a woman extending over a long period [that was] likely to bring discredit on the reputation of the force', he was demoted to the rank of constable. George Dixon's career was more prolonged and hardly less dramatic. Four years after his appointment aged 30, he became a sergeant in 1875. He further added to his reputation in 1882 when he arrested two shop-breakers for which he was given a reward. Problems set in after 10 years. In June 1885 he was cautioned for neglecting to work his beat properly and further reprimanded for drinking in the Bridge public house while on duty. In March 1886 he was found guilty of two similar offences and reduced to the third class with the loss of 2s. (10p) a week. Five months later he was found to be absent from his beat and was given a further demotion and a final warning. This appears to have had some short-term success as he worked his way back to second-class constable by early 1889. However, the improvement was not sustained and in May of that year he was found guilty of being drunk in uniform and was dismissed. Here was a good example of a man in his forties finding the strains and frustration of the job too much after 15 years in service.[32]

John Gladstone Tate suffered a similar fate. He joined the borough force in 1894 at the age of 28. Within four years he had become a first-class constable but troubles set in two years later. In 1900 he was found drunk on duty and reduced to the rank of third-class constable. Within six months he was back at the top of the constable scale but, in 1904 came further demotion for drunkenness on parade. Despite the faith of his superiors – he was specially promoted to the long-service class – drunkenness led yet again to demotion in 1909. The Watch Committee was less sympathetic but still gave him one last chance. In 1912 he was found drunk on duty and dismissed from the force. Clearly Dixon and Tate had problems with drink (and they were not alone in this), but their failings need to be seen in a broader context. Along with several others, they appear to have found the pressures of work as a constable and the failure to gain promotion after several years' service increasingly irksome, if not downright intolerable. The Watch Committee was aware of the problems and, on a number of occasions, showed considerable leniency towards men with poor disciplinary records even though these were not years in which it was difficult to recruit men to the force.[33] This is most clearly seen in the chequered career of Robert Spark, who served, in all, for 18 years. He had been promoted to sergeant only to be demoted because of drunkenness. Notwithstanding long absences from work, some of which time was spent drying out, the Watch Committee persevered with him. Eventually he was dismissed but with a weekly pension of 9s. 6d. (47.5p). Spark was not alone. Both Joseph Place and Francis Hudson had poor disciplinary records but were not dismissed. The latter had assaulted a member of the public and been found guilty of being 'too familiar with Bookmakers and their Touts', but this may have been offset by his success as a policeman which included one commendation for the 'difficult and dangerous' arrest of a burglar.

Such then were the career paths followed by the long-serving policemen who formed the backbone of the more stable and mature Middlesbrough force.[34] In absolute and relative terms a core of long-serving policemen emerged over the course of the last quarter of the nineteenth century. Somewhat paradoxically, this critical change took place at a time when promotion prospects diminished. For the recruits of the 1850s and 1860s the promotion ladder was relatively uncluttered. Indeed, the rapid expansion of the force created more opportunities. However, for later recruits it increasingly became a matter of waiting for dead (or more commonly, retired) men's shoes. The stabilization of the borough force around a core of long-serving policemen was the product of a number of inter-related factors of which improvements in wages, changes in the condition of work and the development of an *esprit de corps* were the most important.

Isaac Wilson, the longtime chairman of the Middlesbrough Watch Committee, had no doubt that police recruitment was 'simply a matter of wages'. This was clearly an oversimplification, but Wilson had correctly identified one of the most important single issues influencing men's decisions to make a career of policing. Determining the pecuniary well-being of the police is not straightforward. Wages were clearly central, though they were reduced by superannuation deductions. There could also be restrictions on the jobs that policemen's wives could undertake. On the other hand, there could be perks, offical and unofficial, to the job. The situation varied across the country but it was not uncommon to find police benefiting from subsidised housing, free fuel, free or subsidised work clothing and boots, and so forth.[35] The situation in Middlesbrough is not clear-cut. Some police wives, for example, were allowed to run a shop, but not all. Further, even where perks can be identified (men being permitted to keep their old uniforms and boots, for example) it is almost impossible to quantify them. Consequently the following analysis has focused on wages alone while recognising that this is a simplification.

A perusal of the Watch Committee minutes reveals a variety of petitions and appeals from individuals but also groups (notably sergeants and unpromoted first-class policemen) for an increase in wages. As already noted the Watch Committee responded positively on a number of occasions by introducing new wages scales and new service classes. The impact of these changes can be seen from the figures in Table 7.6. Certain points are worthy of note. First, after a sharp increase in the pay in the mid-1870s, wage levels for ordinary constables stayed largely unchanged through to 1914. This provides a measure of the problem of recruitment during the boom of the early 1870s. Further, the ladder of advancement was extended by the introduction of a fourth and fifth (probationary) class in the 1880s and service and long-service classes in the 1890s and 1900s. The latter were a response to problems of dissatisfaction among established men. Second, the mid-1870s pay increase

Table 7.6: Wage rates (s./week) in the Middlesbrough police force: selected years, 1871–1912 (1876 = 100)

	1857	1871	1876	1880	1889	1907	1912
Constables							
On appointment	18	21	26	25/8	25/8	27	27
Index	*69*	*81*	*100*	*99*	*99*	*104*	*104*
First class	21	26	29	30	30	30	30
Index	*72*	*90*	*100*	*103*	*103*	*103*	*103*
Third-service class	–	–	30*	–	–	33	34
Index			*100*			*110*	*113*
Sergeants							
On appointment	23	27	31	31	31	34	35
Index	*74*	*87*	*100*	*100*	*100*	*110*	*113*
First class	25	30	35	35	35	36	37/6
Index	*71*	*86*	*100*	*100*	*100*	*103*	*107*
Third-service class	–	–	37*	–	–	38/6	42
Index			*100*			*110*	*120*

* Merit class.
Source: Borough of Middlesbrough, Minutes of Watch, Police and Lighting Committee, 6 March 1872, CB/M/C/ 2/101, p. 341. Printed Council Minutes, 2 March 1877, CB/M/.C, 1/29, p. 25, 23 March 1880 CB/M/C, 1/40, pp. 212–13 and 26 March 1889, CB/M/C, 1/49, pp. 234–5. Constables' Conduct Register, CB/M/P, 31 inside front cover.

for sergeants was less than that for constables. The differential between constables and sergeants was not restored until the pay adjustments of 1907 and after. With the reduction in promotion opportunities in the 1880s and 1890s there was no need to increase pay levels for newly promoted sergeants.

Unlike in the mid-nineteenth century, Middlesbrough policemen were better paid than their counterparts in the nearby county forces of Durham, the North Riding and even the West Riding. From the mid-1870s to the mid-1890s the mean weekly wage rate in Middlesbrough (28.5s.) was 2s. (10p) higher. Comparisons with other north-eastern borough forces also reveal that the Middlesbrough force was relatively well paid in the late nineteenth century. In 1880, for example, only Durham City paid a first-class constable more; only South Shields paid a sergeant more; and no one paid an inspector as much. However, given the town's record and reputation, a financial incentive was needed to attract men. The situation deteriorated particularly in the early twentieth century. Comparisons made with other north-eastern forces on the eve of the Great War showed that Middlesbrough men of all ranks were falling behind their counterparts elsewhere. Only

Sunderland paid an experienced constable, that is with 10 years' service, so little. Newcastle paid 2s. (10p) a week more. The differential was even greater for men with 15 and 20 years' experience: they received 4s. (20p) more. The same held for sergeants. A man with 6 year's service at this level earned 39s. (£1.95) a week in Middlesbrough. His counterpart in Sunderland earned 1s. (5p) more and in Newcastle 6s. 6d. (32.5p) more.

A more important comparison was made with wages in other occupations in town. In the early years of the 1870s a constable could expect to be paid 21s. (£1.05) when on probation, rising to 22s. (£1.10) on appointment to the third class. Recruits with previous police experience almost invariably went into the third class or above. This initial pay compared favourably with the pay of local unskilled agricultural labourers who would expect to be paid from 13s. 6d. (67.5p) to 15s. (75p) per week, and labourers in the blast furnaces who were on a weekly rate of 16s (80p). The newly-appointed constable would then receive increments of 1s (5p), assuming no blemish on his disciplinary record, at the end of each of the first two six months of his service and again after a further one year and three years. Thus, five years after his appointment, a first-class constable would receive 26s. (£1.30) a week. This was on a par with wage rates for fitters, turners and pattern-makers in the town's engineering industries, but less than the rate received by boiler-makers for whom the weekly wage rate was 33s. 9d. (£1.70). At the same time, sergeants were paid from 27s. (£1.35) to 30s. (£1.50), the shilling increment being paid at two-yearly intervals. An inspector's pay started at 33s. (1.65) with a maximum weekly wage of 38s. (£1.90), at which point he would be on a better rate than a boiler-maker in the town.[36]

Police remuneration was increased in the mid-1870s in the face of competition from local industry. Constables now earned from between 27s. (£1.35) on appointment to 29s. (£1.45) in the first class and 30s. (£1.50) in the merit class while sergeants received from 31s. (£1.55) to 35s. (£1.75) and 37s. (£1.85) in the merit class. At the same time, engineers and boiler-makers' weekly wage rates were 29s. (£1.45) and £1 11s. 6d. (£1.58) respectively. In the Cleveland blast furnaces wage rates could be as high as 46s. (£2.30) for keepers, 34s. (£1.70) for masons and 30s. (£1.50) for fitters, joiners and metal carriers. Coke fillers, weighmen and keeper's helpers received around 21s. (£1.05), while ordinary labourers would be lucky to get 19s. (95p) a week.

In the 1880s and 1890s the basic wage structure remained unchanged. Probationers were appointed at a weekly wage of 25s. 8d. (£1.28) before moving to the third class at 28s. (£1.40) and then moving up to the first class where they received 30s. (£1.50) a week. Sergeants' weekly pay ranged from 31s. (1.53) to 35s. (£1.75). The constancy of police wage rates compared favourably with conditions in some local industries. Puddlers' wage rates, profoundly influenced by the trade cycle, fell by over 25 per cent by the mid-1880s, and though moving up thereafter did not recover the levels of the early 1870s until the turn of the century. Wage rates for blast furnacemen and steel workers followed a similar pattern in the 1880s and 1890s.[37] Boilermakers, though well paid, saw their weekly wage rates fall for much of the 1880s before returning to their previous levels in the following decade. In contrast wage rates in the local engineering industry rose steadily over these two decades. Fitters and turners, for example, could expect to earn about 29s. 6d. (£1.48) a week in the early 1880s, rising to 33s. (£1.65) in 1890 and 36s. (£1.80) by the end of the 1890s. A similar pattern of change was experienced in the shipbuilding trade. Unskilled labourers also saw some improvement. By the mid-1890s they were paid a rate of about 18s. (90p) a week and between 22s. (£1.10) and 27s. (£1.35) in the early twentieth century.[38]

Finally, the situation in the early twentieth century was as follows. The scale for constables, after promotion, ran from 27s. (£1.35) for the fourth class to 30s. (£1.50) for the first class. Promotion normally took three and a half years. After the same time again a man would be eligible for the first service class and an additional 1s. (5p) a week. Promotion to the second and third service classes followed after another 5 and 10 years' service. In other words, a constable not gaining promotion to sergeant but with an unblemished disciplinary record could earn a weekly wage of 33s. (£1.65) after 17 years. A similar system of promotion and reward for long service applied to sergeants. Their pay range was from 33s. (£1.65) probationer to 36s. (£1.80) as a first-class sergeant. This process would normally take three and a half years. Promotion to the first service class came after another 4 years and to the second service class 5 years later. At this point, 12 years after appointment as a sergeant, a man would earn 38s. 6d. a week.

The significance of these figures can be assessed by putting them in the context of wage rates in local industries in the early twentieth century. Engineers were paid 35s. 9d. (£1.79) a week and boiler-makers 32s. 3d. (£1.61). In the blast furnaces wage rates varied from the top-paid, such as keepers earning £3 a week, metal carriers earning 50s. (£2.50) and chargers and mine-fillers earning 42s. (£2.10), through intermediate occupations, such as slaggers receiving 37s. (£1.75) and coke fillers 31s. 6d. (£1.58), to the lowest paid such as weighmen who received 24s. 6d. (£1.23) and labourers who were lucky to be paid more than 19s. (95p) a week. Middlesbrough policemen, who saw themselves as superior to labourers and comparable with artisans, were well paid in comparison with labourers but, especially for longer-serving men, the comparisons with local industries were not always favourable.

Wage data alone give but a partial picture and must be related to information about the levels of employment and thus actual earnings as well as to the cost of living in the town. Unlike most other occupations, policing did not experience short and medium-term fluctuations in employment, and in addition there was the expectation of progression and promotion. In view of the earlier analysis it is useful to identify three police career categories, that is, two, one and no promotions. Basing the calculations on the actual experience of long-serving policemen we arrive at the figures in Table 7.7.

Three specific points emerge from these figures. First, for successful men, that is those who gained two promotions, the rewards were greater in the latter decades than the former. For those who were promoted once, the situation changes little over time, though rewards were slightly greater for the men of the 1850s and 1860s in this category. Third, for those who did not achieve any promotion, a growing group in both absolute and relative terms, the financial rewards were significantly less for men recruited in the 1890s than for those recruited in the 1870s and even the 1880s.

Finally these figures need to be compared with comparable estimates for local industries, taking into account fluctuations in actual earnings. (See Table 7.8.)

If one compares the figures in Tables 7.7 and 7.8 it can be seen that in terms of real earnings, policing was an attractive alternative for all men

Table 7.7: Growth rates in real earnings (% per annum) for three career categories in the Middlesbrough police force, by decades of recruitment

	Two promotions	One promotion	No promotion
1850s/60s	2.1–2.6	2.1	
1870s	2.4–3.6	1.4–1.8	1.4
1880s	3.5	1.5–1.7	0.6
1890s	2.5–3.5	1.4–1.8	0.3–0.7

Source: Constables' Conduct Register. Earnings have been converted into real earnings by using the cost of living index for Middlesbrough constructed by A. A. Hall, 'Working class living standards in Middlesbrough and Teesside, 1870–1914', unpublished CNAA Ph.D. dissertation, Teesside Polytechnic, 1979.

Table 7.8: Growth rates (% per annum) in real earnings in three Middlesbrough industries by decades

	Blast furnaces	*Puddling*	*Engineering*
1870s		−1.4–0.4	1.0–1.4
1880s	0.9–1.1	0.9–1.4	0.6–1.4
1890s	0.1–0.7	0.3–1.9	0.0–0.2

Source: Calculated from figures in Hall, 'Working class living standards'.

and for almost all of the period, with the important exception of those men who were recruited in the 1890s but failed to gain promotion.

Mention has already been made of the regularity of police-work compared with the cyclical fluctuations that bedevilled the iron and steel trades or the seasonal fluctuations that could disrupt employment in the building trades. In addition, it should be noted that policemen could look forward to a pension at the end of their working life. Prior to 1890 the granting of a pension was at the discretion of the Watch Committee. A superannuation scheme for the police had been introduced in Middlesbrough in 1862. The fund was based on contributions of 6d. a week from inspectors, 5d. from sergeants and 4d. from constables. In addition, fines inflicted on constables for misconduct, the allowance for serving summonses and executing warrants and all of the penalties paid for assaults on the police and half of the fines in drunkenness cases were paid into the fund. In the early years there were few if any calls on the fund. Isaac Wilson told the Select Committee on Police Superannuation Funds that no one except the chief constable was eligible for a pension. Pensions and gratuities were awarded on an *ad hominem* basis. It is clear that the scheme was not popular with the men of the borough force. They wanted a pension as of right, but this was not to be granted by law until 1890. The awards made varied considerably. Unfortunately no evidence has survived of the reasons behind the decisions of the Watch Committee. Sergeant Tomlin served for 10 years before his death in service. His widow was awarded a gratuity of £91 in 1874. Inspector Thomas Temple served for 22 years but was only awarded a gratuity of £60 when he was forced to resign through ill-health at the same time. Wilson was sympathetic to the complaints of the men, and made it clear that he supported the idea of a guaranteed pension after 25 years' service, and saw it as an important element in improving the efficiency of the force by retaining the service of those men who had settled into the force and saw policing as a long-term career. The first pension paid out of the fund was awarded to Inspector John Cooper in 1881 after 20 years' service. Yet in the same year Sergeant Henry Purvis, who had served since 1864, was granted only a gratuity of £20. Only four other men received a pension in the years before the 1890 Act and all had served for more than 20 years – indeed in one case over 30 years had been spent in uniform.

The uncertainty inherent in a discretionary system resulted in men working longer than might otherwise have been the case and at great expense in terms of their health. It is significant that three long-serving men retired on pensions immediately following the implementation of the 1890 Act. The attractiveness of a pension clearly cannot be seen as a contributory factor in the stabilisation of the Middlesbrough police force that that had taken place by the 1880s, but it probably had a more positive effect on the recruits of the 1880s and 1890s and may well have offset some of the dissatisfaction felt among these cohorts at the lack of promotion opportunities. While the precise impact of a police pension cannot be established, its existence undoubtedly added to the relative financial attractiveness of policing. Not only did Middlesbrough policemen enjoy higher and more stable rates of increase in real earnings, they also looked forward to a pension at the end of the working life.

Economic considerations played a crucial role in the transformation of policing in the town, but it would be misleading to suggest that they provide a complete explanation. Changes in the condition of work, the emergence of a sense of belonging and a growing sense of identity about and pride in police-work were also important, if unquantifiable, factors. Policing from the earliest days had always been an arduous occupation. Working the beat in all weathers throughout the year took its toll of men's health. In the mid-nineteenth century policemen were expected to work long shifts (as much as 15 hours in extreme cases) for 7 days a week and 50 weeks a year. In addition, a policeman was expected to maintain the dignity of his post and be prepared to act to uphold the law even when off duty. In addition to the routine demands of the job there were more occasional dangers such as runaway horses, infuriated beasts, dangerous dogs and violent members of the public.

Middlesbrough was no exception to this general pattern, but there is insufficient surviving evidence to build up a complete picture from the introduction of new policing in the town in the 1850s. Nothing is known of the number and length of the early beats, though it is clear that some, most notably the one that covered the docks area, were dangerous. Detailed information does not become available until 1885, but in that year there were 10 beats which varied from the half-hour patrols of the Market Place and Sussex Street to the one-and-a-half hour beat on the Marshes, covering the major industrial district of the town, and the two-hour beat of Cargo Fleet which, again, covered a major industrial area (see appendix Figure A7.1, at the end of this chapter). Patrolling the streets, particularly during winter nights, was physically demanding and sometimes dangerous, but it was often the tedium and loneliness that led constables to slip into a friendly public houses or to find a relatively warm hut in which to snatch a few hours' sleep. As we have seen, many men succumbed to these temptations even in the late nineteenth century.

In a number of important respects the physical demands of the job eased over time. The long shifts of the mid-nineteenth century were reduced. After 1887, for example, following a petition from the lower ranks, the Watch Committee agreed to implement an 8-hour shift system. In other ways conditions were improved locally. The Middlesbrough police were granted 'a privilege which scarcely any other force enjoys' in the form of a half-hour supper break.[39] Holiday allowances were also increased. In 1903, following another petition, this time from 99 officers and men, the Watch Committee granted, in addition to annual leave, one day's holiday every four weeks during the winter months from October to March and extended this to the whole year in December 1907. National legislation also brought benefits. In 1911, for example, police constables were permitted 1 rest day in 8.

Some of the dangers of the job also diminished in the last quarter of the nineteenth century. The large-scale assaults that had taken place in the 1860s and 1870s became much less frequent, though individual assaults on policemen never disappeared.[40] Similarly, the routine dangers continued. Animals were a continuing threat. Runaway horses inflicted damage on several policemen.[41] Percy Freeman was one: he was commended for his action in stopping a runaway horse while on duty in September 1909 but his injuries required the amputation of his little finger. Never fully recovering, he was pensioned off as permanently incapacitated 18 months later. Vincent Brooks, Frank Onions and Arthur Silversides were more fortunate in driving off four mastiffs that had mauled a man to death in 1911.[42] Fires were another common hazard. Robert Hird showed considerable bravery in rescuing an old woman from a burning house in Gauntlett Street in 1909, as did Ernest Hodgson and James Rodger in similar incidents the following year. The most serious fire took place at the Hippodrome in March 1911. Several people were injured and two killed, but the police, notably PC Barnes, distinguished themselves by their bravery. Some incidents were more bizarre. Sergeant George Brett's long career was ended by an incident in which he 'accidentally inhaled a bad smell when assisting to bring a decomposed body from out of a boiler'. Within two months of the incident he left the force on a pension.

None the less, the physical effects of prolonged beat work were painfully clear. Year after year men retired (or were retired) on medical grounds. When Edward Saggerson resigned as chief constable in July 1884 he was described as being 'disabled from infirmity of body from discharging his duty'.[43] In the following year Inspector Mann retired at the age of 46 because he was no longer fit for police-work after 22 years in the force. William Wilkinson was incapable of work after 13 years' service. Inspector John Reed was forced to retire for the same reasons after 31 years' service. But it was not only long-serving men who were physically broken by their job. PC Dennis was pensioned in 1871, having been declared 'totally unfit for further police service' after little more than one year as a policeman. The list of complaints includes predictable cases of varicose veins, sciatica, flat feet and chronic rheumatism as well as illnesses such as pneumonia and ague brought on by the rigours of the job. In exceptional cases, most notably that of Detective Inspector Thorpe, some men died whilst working, quite literally exhausted by their job. Recognition of these problems led to the establishment of a police bed in the North Ormesby Hospital in 1882 and the setting aside of a special bed in the local convalescent home. According to Chief Constable Riches, 'every attention is given to convalescents and the Chief Constable will be pleased to recommend sick leave in all suitable cases for either short or longer periods, as the case merits.'[44] Unfortunately it was not made clear what constituted a suitable case for treatment. The police records do not contain information on the take-up rate for these facilities, but in February 1910 the matron of the convalescent home felt it necessary to suggest that greater use be made of the police facility there.

As policing developed in the second half of the nineteenth century so there developed a greater sense of belonging. In general terms, there was an increased awareness of the importance of policing fostered by the government through the agency of Her Majesty's Inspectors. In similar fashion the emergence of in-house journals, such as the *Police Service Advertiser* which first appeared in 1866 (to become the *Police Guardian* in 1872) or the *Police Review and Parade Gossip*, which dated from 1893, added to a sense of identity as aspirations as well as grievances were shared. More specific changes within the local police force played their part in the development of this *esprit de corps*. The simple fact of shared work experiences in an occupation that set its members clearly apart from the rest of the community fostered a sense of belonging. As the evidence cited above clearly shows, by the 1880s there was a body of men who had joined more or less at the same time and had worked together for 10, 15 even 20 years. This sense of belonging was further strengthened by the practice of men living in or next door to the police station. With the establishment of the police station in Cannon Street, for example, it became common practice to house an inspector, a sergeant and a constable in nearby houses, nos 178–182 Cannon Street.[45] It is also the case that policemen tended to live close to each other in certain parts of the town. Middlesbrough policemen lived in all parts of the town but by the early twentieth century a number of clusters of police residences can be identified. The largest was to be found in the area between Borough Road and Clarendon Road running from Laurel Street to Myrtle Street. Here were some 20 houses inhabited by men of the local police force. A second cluster existed further down Borough Road in the district from Diamond Street to Ruby Street where some 11 houses regularly inhabited by policemen are listed in the local street directories. Finally, there was another cluster of some 7 'police' houses in the Victoria Road/Waterloo Road area. In this area were to be found inspectors and sergeants, which suggests that the police hierarchy was observed outside work. One should not read too much into this patchy distribution but it does suggest that, for whatever reason, some policemen and their families chose to live in close proximity to one another and this can only have enhanced their sense of shared experience and common identity.

Furthermore, there were shared leisure activities that also contributed to the sense of belonging to a team. A police band was established as early as 1866. As well as improving relations with the local community it gave an opportunity for some of the force to come together in the shared pleasure of communal music making. There were organised cricket matches – married versus single men, north of the town versus the south and so on – which involved men of all ranks. Even the Chief Constable, William Ashe, participated. Organised sport extended to football matches in the winter months. By the early twentieth century sporting opportunities were extended with the opening of a recreation room, complete with billiard table and spittoons at the Central Police Station. For the more cerebral there was a general library with newspapers and other reading material opened in

1863. This initiative proved to be short-lived, but in 1906 a new library was opened and there were organised courses for those wishing to improve their educational skills and thus their chances of gaining promotion.

Thus in a variety of ways – at work, at play and at home – there developed among Middlesbrough policemen a sense of belonging. This combined with the changing and improving nature of the job and the relative economic attractiveness of policing helps explain how police-work was transformed from something short-term and stop-gap in the mid-nineteenth century into a long-term career by the late nineteenth and early twentieth centuries.

Appendix

Table A7.1: The growth of Yorkshire borough police forces, 1871 to 1911 (index: 1871 = 100)

	1871	1881	1891	1901	1911
Small					
Dewsbury	12	29	30	37	57
Index	*100*	*242*	*250*	*308*	*475*
Doncaster	18	21	27	36	44
Index	*100*	*117*	*150*	*200*	*244*
Medium					
Halifax	65	75	84	107	126
Index	*100*	*115*	*129*	*165*	*194*
Huddersfield	70	91	112	120	138
Index	*100*	*130*	*160*	*171*	*197*
Middlesbrough	41	52	76	96	134
Index	*100*	*127*	*185*	*234*	*327*
Wakefield	37	37	40	52	69
Index	*100*	*100*	*108*	*141*	*186*
York	44	52	72	80	103
Index	*100*	*118*	*164*	*182*	*234*
Large					
Bradford	159	220	256	390	433
Index	*100*	*138*	*161*	*245*	*272*
Leeds	301	400	423	507	654
Index	*100*	*133*	*141*	*168*	*217*
Sheffield	280	341	385	515	533
Index	*100*	*122*	*138*	*184*	*190*

Source: Annual Reports of Her Majesty's Inspectors of Constabulary.

Table A7.2: Police/population ratios in selected Yorkshire boroughs
(persons per police officer), 1871 to 1911

	1871	*1881*	*1891*	*1901*	*1911*	*% change 1871–1911*
Middlesbrough authorised force	976	1,058	1,000	948	784	–20
Inter-censal % change		+8	–5	–5	–17	
All police*	690	932	938	875	734	+6
Inter-censal % change		+35	+1	–7	–16	
Bradford	918	832	844	718	665	–28
Inter-censal % change		–9	+1	–15	–7	
Halifax	1,015	987	1,071	981	810	–20
Inter-censal % change		–3	+9	–8	–17	
Huddersfield	1,000	901	848	792	783	–22
Inter-censal % change		–10	–6	–7	–1	
Leeds	860	773	870	846	682	–20
Inter-censal % change		–10	+13	–3	–19	
Sheffield	857	836	842	754	854	0
Inter-censal % change		–2	+1	–10	+13	
Wakefield	757	838	825	788	754	0
Inter-censal % change		+11	–2	–4	–4	
York	1,000	962	931	975	796	–20
Inter-censal % change		–4	–3	+5	–18	

* i.e. including privately-paid policemen.
Source: as for Table A7.1. NB: A reduction in the ratio represents an improvement.

Figure A7.1   Police beats, north of the railway, 1885 (beat 5 details have not survived)

Beat 1a – Packet Wharf (1 hour)

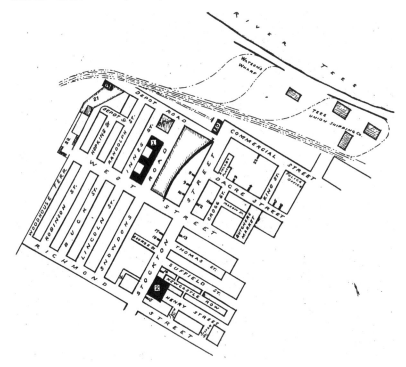

Beat 1b – Durham Street (1 hour)

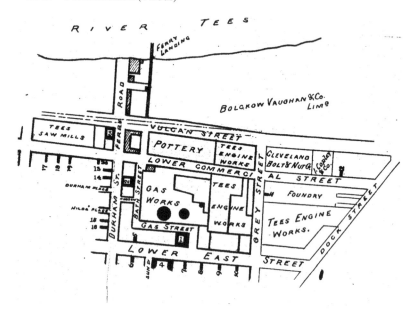

Beat 2 – Cleveland Street (1 hour)

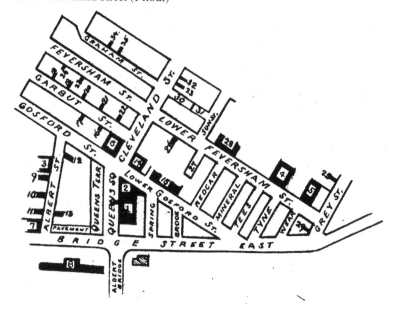

Beat 3 – Market Place (1/2 hour)

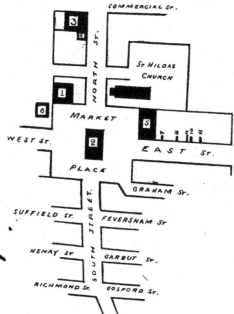

Beat 4 – Sussex Street (1/2 hour)

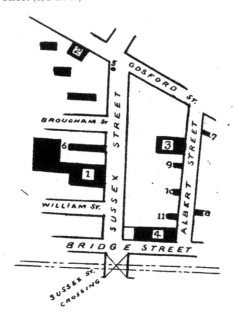

Beat 6 – Stockton Street (1 hour)

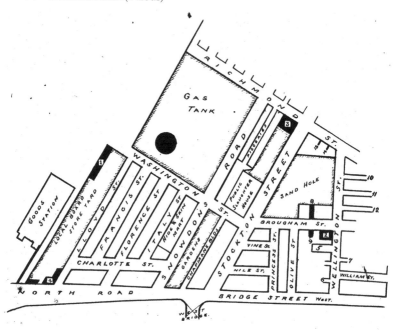

Beat 7 – Marshes (1.5 hours)

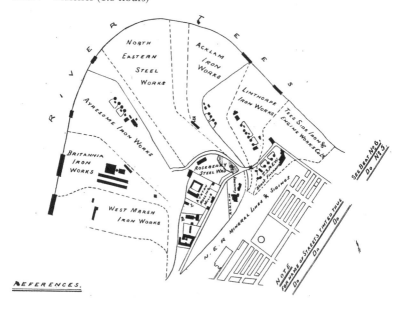

Beat 8 – Cargo Fleet (2 hours)

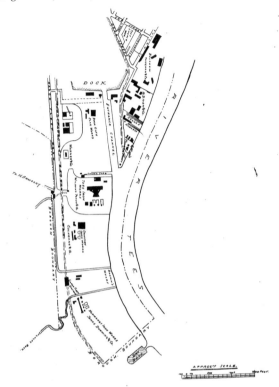

8
The Police and Crime in Middlesbrough after 1870

The last quarter of the nineteenth century saw Britain as a whole become more urbanised, more industrial and commercial, and more prosperous. Notwithstanding the emergence of foreign competitors, the fluctuations of the trade cycle and the re-discovery of poverty amidst plenty, late-Victorian society enjoyed higher standards of living than ever before. Society was more stable and less conflict ridden, though the industrial disturbances and political protests could still shock the sensibilities of late-Victorian commentators. Serious crime against both person and property, at least as recorded in the official statistics, was clearly in decline. Despite a number of significant changes in the legal system, particularly the continuing extension of summary justice in 1879, which make difficult long-term comparisons, it would appear that, contrary to the claims of Howard Taylor, this was a genuine long-term decline for the reasons argued in the introduction to this study.[1] Although there remained an unknown quantity of crime that never formally came to the attention of the authorities, there is good reason to believe that the official statistics reflected a real decrease (at least until the early twentieth century) as working-class living standards improved and as new standards of behaviour were adopted across an ever-widening spectrum of society.[2] However, at the same time, there were growing concerns about immoral and illegal behaviour among the working-class population. Drinking and increasingly gambling were linked with criminality, inefficiency and degeneration.[3]

Middlesbrough continued to grow in a dramatic fashion in the latter part of the nineteenth century. The economic base of the town broadened but its well-being and stability were still threatened by the fluctuating fortunes of the major industries and the persistence of extreme hardship in parts of the town. Notwithstanding these difficulties, overall working-class living standards improved steadily and some workers and their families were able to benefit from changes in retailing, the provision of leisure and the provision of housing. At the same time, not least because of the dominance of the iron and steel industries and the presence of a sizeable port, the town retained its reputation for hard working and hard living. As the country as a whole was becoming more 'respectable' in its behaviour, Middlesbrough still exhibited some rough edges well into the twentieth century, though the incidence of serious crime declined sharply.

The town's early frontier-town reputation was never fully reflected in the official statistics, especially in the 1830s and 1840s. None the less, the contrast with other industrialising areas was clear, though from the 1860s the serious crime rate began to fall. This trend continued in the 1870s. Caution has to be exercised in using the statistics of serious (indictable) offences reported to the police.[4] However, this does not mean that local returns are meaningless as an approximate indicator of actual changes in criminal behaviour. The evidence does not suggest that the police in Middlesbrough consciously sought to manipulate the figures by not pursuing prosecutions, though it may well be the case (though impossible to demonstrate) that ordinary citizens felt more secure in the face of a real decline in serious crime and that this led to an even greater decline in the determination to prosecute. Serious offences reported to the police in Middlesbrough fell in absolute terms even as the population of the town continued to grow dramatically. In the early 1870s the number stood at an annual average of 65 with approximately 50 people actually committed to trial. By the early 1890s the figures were 51 and 19 respectively. The rate of reported indictable offences per 100,000 of population fell dramatically from 163 to 67 (i.e. by some 60 per cent) over the course of 20 years. In part this was a product of the extension of summary justice in 1879, but it was also the product of a genuine decline in criminal behaviour, as can be seen from the figures in Table 8.1. Taking the 1880s as a whole, there was a remarkable change in the overall incidence of serious crime: the number of burglaries (an offence not affected by the 1879 legislation) had fallen by over 50 per cent, while serious crimes against the person fell by over 60 per cent.

To a large extent, the Middlesbrough experience was a more pronounced version of national trends, but one specific point is worthy of note.[5] In general terms, the incidence of burglary remained largely unchanged during the last quarter of the nineteenth century, whereas in Middlesbrough there was a clear decline in absolute, let alone relative, terms.

Table 8.1: Reported indictable crimes, 1870s and 1880s

Offence	1870s Annual average	% total	1880s Annual average	% total
Larcenies	35	54	32	65
Burglary etc.	9	14	4	8
Fraud etc.	8	12	5	10
Receiving	>1		1	2
Subtotal	52	80	42	85
Homicide/attempt	2.5	4	0.5	1
Assaults/wounding	3.5	5	2	4
Sexual assaults	1	2	1	2
Others	4	6	3	6
Subtotal	11	17	6.5	13
Miscellaneous	1	2	1	2
Total	65	100	49.5	100

Source: Chief Constable's Annual Report.

The overall progress in the town was checked in the early twentieth century. The total number of serious offences known to the police increased more or less in line with the growth of population. This again, contrasted with the national pattern of increasing rates in the pre-war years. (See Table 8.2.)

A closer examination of the figures reveals a more worrying trend: offences involving violence increased more rapidly than (the more common) crimes against property without violence, especially in the

Table 8.2: Indictable crimes known to the police, 1903–13 (annual averages)

	1903–4 No.	%	1905–9 No.	%	1910–13 No.	%
All Indictable Offences	466		482		534	
Offences against the person (excluding attempted suicide)	13	3	23	5	56	10
Offence against property with violence	17	4	25	5	31	6
Offences against property without violence	418	90	415	86	427	80
Others (including attempted suicide)	18	4	20	4	22	4

Source: Chief Constable's Annual Reports.

immediate pre-war years. This was particularly true of malicious wounding and sexual assaults (excluding rape) on young girls, though the interpretation of these figures is complicated by a series of legislative changes, from the 1885 Criminal Law Amendment Act, through the 1898 Vagrancy Act, the 1908 Children Act and the Incest Act of the same year to the 1912 Criminal Law Amendment Act, that artificially inflated the recorded crime rate. (See Table 8.3.) Crimes against the person accounted for less than 20 per cent of the total in the 1870s and their share of all crimes fell thereafter. None the less, the fact remains that during the latter part of the nineteenth century the town witnessed, on average, one or two homicides, two to three serious assaults and one rape per year that resulted in prosecution.[6]

Assaults dominated crimes against the person but a change in the nature of such attacks is discernible. The more frightening gang assaults became less common. In 1871 there were two such cases. Three Irish men were sentenced to 12 months' hard labour for violently assaulting and robbing Michael Lockeran, while at the same session a gang of 5 men was charged with wounding with intent to inflict grievous bodily harm on David McCulley in a stabbing incident in Commercial Street. The latter was but one example of the factional fights that still occurred within the Irish community in Middlesbrough. Chief Constable Saggerson, in the summer of 1873, alerted the Watch Committee to the 'numerous cases of assault both on the Police and Private individuals' that had occurred in recent months, while a year later, in discussing a particularly unpleasant 'murderous assault', he ruefully reflected that 'these kinds of assaults have of late been on the increase more especially amongst the lowest of the Irish population'.[7] In fact, Saggerson's

Table 8.3: Offences against the person (known to the police), 1903–13 (annual averages)

	1903–4	1905–09	1910–13
Murder/attempted murder	0.5	1.4	1.75
Manslaughter	0.5	0.8	0.75
Wounding	7	8.2	21
Rape	0.5	0.4	0.75
Indecent assault/defilement	2.5	8	22
Indecency (male)	0.5	1.5	3.25
Others	1.0	2.5	4.5
Total	12.5	22.8	56

Source: Chief Constable's Annual Reports.

concerns proved to be overstated. By the end of the decade there was an easing of the situation, and in his 1878 report, though he lamented the continuing tradition of faction fights, he noted that there had been a slight fall in the number of men committed for trial for serious crimes of violence in the previous year. He pledged continuing firm action against such 'brutal outrages' and, a year later, was able to attribute a 'further decrease' in violent crimes to the firm action of the police and magistrates of the town.[8] The last upsurge of internecine conflict among the working-class Irish occurred in the early 1880s. In July 1882 Saggerson drew the attention of the Watch Committee to 'faction fights ... amongst the lower classes of the Irish population'.[9] This was to be the last reference to gang fights, and the subsequent minutes of the Watch Committee and the annual reports of the Chief Constables contain very few references to the problem of serious violent crime in the last two decades of the nineteenth century.

The nature and causes of these cases varied considerably, but most were mundane. Some of the worst cases involved male violence on family members. In a serious assault that took place in North Ormesby Road, Michael Hird savagely beat his brother. More common were assaults upon wives or partners. John Griffiths and Arthur Blackburn were both tried at York for inflicting grievous bodily harm on their wives in 1898 and 1912 respectively. Patrick Trainor was tried at quarter session for attacking his wife in May 1910 and also assaulting Isabella Dempsey who tried to intervene.[10] Men attempted to murder their wives and on several occasions caused their death.[11] Some were found guilty of manslaughter; some were found guilty of murder. The borderline between the two was fine. Patrick McCarthy was sentenced to 5 years' penal servitude for the manslaughter of his wife in a 'particularly brutal' attack and 'had the witnesses been a little more definite in their statements . . . [he] would have been dealt with for a capital offence.' However, the case had been unusual and attracted considerable publicity. Initially it had appeared to be little more than a rather sordid, but not wholly unexceptional, 'domestic'. Mrs McCarthy was beaten about the head with an iron bar onto which a metal nut had been fastened, and taken to the Workhouse Hospital suffering from serious injuries for which her husband was tried and found guilty at the quarter sessions of inflicting grievous bodily harm. He received a sentence of 12 months' hard labour. However, shortly after this conviction, the unfortunate Mrs McCarthy died and, somewhat unusually, upon application by the secretary of the state for the Home Office, McCarthy was committed to trial at the assizes where he was convicted and sentenced to 5 years' penal servitude.[12] Three

Middlesbrough men were hanged in the early twentieth century. Thomas Mouncer, a 25-year-old butcher in the town, was hanged at Wakefield in 1906 for the murder of Elizabeth Baldwin, with whom he lived. After a night out he returned home and strangled her, and then confessed to the police the following morning. Jealousy led to the execution of Walter Davis in 1909 for the murder of his ex-lover, and William Galbraith was hanged in 1912 for the murder of his wife.[13] Some men were clearly deranged. Thomas Scales, a 64-year-old tailor, indisputably killed his wife, but was not fit to plead because of insanity. Similarly, in 1912, Robert Hessel attacked his wife with an axe and, believing her to be dead, took his own life by jumping from an upstairs window. Other family members were also at risk. John Bell was sentenced to 4 years' penal servitude for the manslaughter of his mother in 1881, and James Fruish was similarly found guilty having administered hydrochloric acid to his mother in 1898.[14]

Not all murders (or attempted murders) were cases of domestic violence. Prostitutes were beaten up by pimps and punters and brawling sailors inflicted serious damage upon one another or other members of the public.[15] Lady Bell was highly critical of the influence of the latter. 'Sailors,' she observed, 'have no responsibility for their words or deeds . . . they seem to bring to the whole world a kinship of lawlessness and disorder.'[16] While the dock area was undoubtedly a continuing trouble spot, there was an element of displacement taking place in her analysis. Sailors were perhaps more visible but they were not the major cause of violence in the town. Finally, and predictably, though infrequently, the police were targets of violence. In 1893 the 'dangerous lunatic' John Henry Gould shot dead PC Henderson, while in 1913 Ernest Younger was sentenced to 3 year's penal servitude at York for attempting to shoot PC Bainbridge. Two men were tried at Northallerton for separate charges of inflicting grievous bodily harm on PC Yelland in 1907.[17]

One category of offences that attracted attention and condemnation involved children. Although the coroner's court dealt with a small but recurring number of cases of newborn children found dead, relatively few cases came to court. Generally speaking such cases were treated sympathetically. Anne Ryder, an 18-year-old, unmarried servant was found not guilty of murdering her infant son. Not all women thus charged were so young. Rebecca Langley was 29 and Elizabeth Smith 42 when found guilty of concealing the birth of a child and secretly disposing of the dead infant. Langley was found not guilty and Smith bound over in the sum of £10. Elizabeth Reece was charged at York with concealing the death of a baby boy. She pleaded guilty to the charge, but being both homeless and friendless and with the promise of assistance from Reverend Rowland of St Peter's, Middlesbrough, she was given a sentence of only 7 days. Other women were deemed to be insane when the offence was committed. Elizabeth Stokes, for instance, was charged with the murder of her young son, David, but though found guilty was detained as a criminal lunatic.[18] In an exceptional case, a mother and daughter, Charlotte and Rebecca Wilds, were tried at York for the wilful murder of a baby girl.[19] Child murder was rare, but in 1884 Mary Cooper, an 8-year-old girl, was murdered in Albert Park. Despite considerable police efforts, including the use of detectives from Scotland Yard, and the offer of a £100 reward, no progress was made. Chief Constable Saggerson was forced to concede that it would be 'hoping too much to expect the murder to be discovered, unless the murderer gives himself up'.[20] Child neglect cases were also infrequent but high-profile. In 1908 John and Mary Ann Suddick were found guilty of the manslaughter of their 11-month-old child who had starved to death.[21]

Serious sexual assaults were less common in late nineteenth-century Middlesbrough, and there was only one gang attack, which took place in 1875. The protection of girls and young women had been a major concern since the 1880s, and the passing of legislation in 1885 led to a sharp increase in the number of recorded sexual assaults in the country at large. However, relatively few cases came from Middlesbrough until after 1900, when over 150 cases were tried at the York assizes, with a particularly sharp increase in the immediate pre-war years that worried the police authorities. Most assailants were in their thirties or forties but the age range ran from 15 to 84. Many cases involved fathers abusing daughters aged 11 or 12, but in some cases the child was as young as 4 or 5.[22] In one particularly scandalous case Anthony Wood was sentenced to 9 months' hard labour for indecently assaulting his daughter and living off the immoral earnings of his wife.[23] Concern was heightened by the existence of a small number of repeat offenders and the young age of certain victims. Both elements came together in 1902 when a 27-year-old chimney- sweep, John Markle, was sentenced to 5 years' penal servitude for 'having carnal knowledge' of a 6-year-old girl. Markle had served 12 months' imprisonment, having been found guilty of a similar offence at Liverpool assizes in 1900. Markle was not alone. George Cross was charged with three different sexual offences involving girls between the age of 13 and 16 in 1912, and Robert Burton was charged with having unlawful sex with a girl aged under 13 at the York assizes in 1911, almost exactly one year after being sentenced to 6 months' imprisonment at Leeds assizes for having unlawful sex with a girl under 16 years old.[24]

Other crimes of violence tended to mundane and drink-related. Sailors regularly fought each other and members of the public. Gambling could give rise to conflict. Thomas Shannon, for example, slashed the throat of John Ditchburn with a razor in a dispute over the number of counters won at cards. William Smith, a violent and short-tempered young man, wounded three people in three separate incidents in 1911. A few involved vicious attacks: Francis Trodden bit some flesh from the face and finger of James Lee. One or two involved women attacking men or other women: Susan Burns was found guilty of wounding Daisy Loughran in 1900. Although only 22 years old, she was a well-known character in the town, with a police record that included convictions for theft, drunkenness and assaults including resisting arrest. Michael Smith was the unfortunate victim of Catherine Scarl and Mary Rowell, two hardened criminals who were sent down in 1903 for 4 and 3 years' penal servitude for robbery with violence. Scarl had 66 convictions for drunkenness, 11 for theft and others for assault and prostitution, while Rowell had been found guilty 8 times of theft and had a further 21 convictions for drunkenness and assault.[25] Such women received little sympathy, but were a significant minority of offenders and not just in Middlesbrough.

Serious property crimes, that is those involving violence, exhibited a similar long-term downward trend in Middlesbrough over the course of the late nineteenth century. As noted above, the annual average incidence of burglary in the 1880s was 50 per cent lower than in the previous decade. As a consequence those cases that came to the public's attention were often seen to be more shocking for being less common. There was something frightening, but almost anachronistic, about the conviction at the 1896 York assize of two Middlesbrough men, John Holting and George Thompson, for robbery with violence on the highway. Likewise, two cases in the following year acted as a reminder that violent robberies were not a thing of the past. In the first, Matthew Conafrey was sentenced to 5 years' penal servitude for robbery with violence, having taken £2, a matchbox, a knife and a penholder from Jacob Smith. Conafrey, with a string of convictions for minor offences such as drunkenness, gambling and petty theft, as well as 7 convictions for serious offences (including one previous case of robbery with violence), was seen as both exceptional and unacceptable. In the second, three men, Robert Cowan, John Nolan and Thomas

Moore, were found guilty of a vicious gang robbery. The downward trend was reversed after 1900, but, though the number of such offences doubled in number, such crimes still accounted for only some 5 per cent of all indictable offences known to the police. Typically these offences involved attacks by two or three men on a solitary victim. The sums involved could vary from a few shillings to several pounds.[26] There were also a number of cases tried at York of housebreaking that involved considerable quantities of goods. Three men broke into the house of Charles Burtt and stole 10 rings, tie-pins, cuff-links and bracelets (all gold), as well as 2 pistols, a watch and several other less valuable items. Others were less spectacular. Robert Kidson stole boots, socks and a shirt from Thomas Nicholson, while James Kay broke into Joseph Barber's shop and stole a brush and two pencils.

The majority of indictable offences committed in Middlesbrough were of a less serious nature. These crimes were tried, not at assize at York or Leeds, but at quarter session at Northallerton and, after summer 1910, at Middlesbrough itself. (See Table 8.4.)

The contrast between the two decades is (unexpectedly) clear, with a very marked decline in the number of offences tried in the second half of the 1880s. In the 1870s the number of Middlesbrough offences peaked in the turbulent years of the first half of the decade – when a third of the cases heard at Northallerton came from the town – but fell slightly in both absolute and relative terms during the second half of the decade. Interestingly, in the 1880s, Middlesbrough's share of crimes tried at Northallerton was significantly lower at about one-fifth of the total. When allowance is made for population growth, an even more striking picture of the incidence of recorded crime in the town emerges. In 1861 some 157 people per 100,000 were committed for trial at the Northallerton quarter sessions. The comparable figure for

Table 8.4: Cases tried at Northallerton quarter sessions in the 1870s and 1880s

	All offences	Middlesbrough offences	Middlesbrough offences as % all	Middlesbrough annual average
1870–4	662	223	33.7	44.6
1875–9	653	193	29.6	38.6
1880–4	435	94	21.6	18.8
1885–9	231	54	23.4	10.8

Source: Northallerton Calender of Prisoners, 1830–99, North Yorkshire County Record Office, Northallerton, MIC 1454.

1871 was 106. By the end of the decade the committal rate had fallen to approximately 58 per 100,000. In other words, the rate declined by some 45 per cent during the 1870s and by some 63 per cent over the two decades of the 1860s and 1870s. A direct comparison with the 1880s cannot be made from these figures because of the extension of summary justice after the legislation of 1879. However, over the course of that decade (i.e. the 1880s) the committal rate fell by almost 60 per cent, from 35 per 100,000 to 15. The significance of these figures is clear. The town's police force was becoming larger and more efficient (and there is no indication that the battle against crime was slackening, nor that the town force was constrained financially) which, *ceteris paribus*, would lead one to expect recorded crime to increase. It did not. To the contrary, it fell sharply suggesting that this was a genuine and major reduction in criminal behaviour in the town.

The offences for which Middlesbrough men and women were sent to Northallerton were overwhelmingly crimes against property without violence. This pattern remained largely constant both before and after the 1879 Summary Jurisdiction Act. (See Table 8.5.)

The stolen items that appear in the indictments of the late nineteenth century bear a predictable similarity to those of the mid-nineteenth and, for that reason, will not be analysed in the same detail as before. None the less, it is important to note a number of significant shifts in the overall pattern. Items of clothing remained the largest single category of stolen goods in the 1870s. Some items were portable,

Table 8.5: Middlesbrough prisoners tried at Northallerton in the 1870s and 1880s

Offence	1870s		1880s	
	No.	%	No.	%
Larceny	243	69	80	66
False pretences	32	9	7	6
Embezzlement	11	3	4	3
Breaking & entering	17	5	7	6
Receiving	6	2	6	5
Counterfeiting	5	1	7	6
All assaults	34	10	10	8
Others	2	>1	1	>1
Total	350		122	

Source: As for Table 8.4.

easily pawned or turned to use: boots, trousers, shirts and skirts remained obvious targets for the needy and opportunistic thief. However, in the late nineteenth century the relative significance of this category declined. Not only were fewer articles of clothing being stolen in absolute terms but also in relative terms. During the 1880s clothing accounted for 30 per cent of all items stolen – a decline of 10 per cent compared with the 1850s and 1860s, and even the 1870s. There was also decline in the relative importance of household goods and food and drink. Even more marked was the decline in industrial thefts, including the theft of tools. This category had accounted for 15 per cent of the total in the mid nineteenth century but had fallen to less than 10 per cent in the 1870s and fell to a mere 3 per cent in the following decade. In contrast, the theft of money and especially of watches and jewellery became relatively more important accounting for just over 50 per cent of the total in the 1880s. New items – notably cigarettes, bicycles and even lawn mowers – make their appearance in the list of stolen items. In their different ways, these trends can be seen to reflect the growing wealth of the town. The overall decline in larceny (and the diminishing emphasis on essential items) is consistent with a gradual improvement in working-class living standards, while the relative increase in the theft of watches and jewellery is equally consistent with rising middle-class standards of consumption, though it remained the case that victims and criminals tended to come from the same social milieu.[27]

The rate of crimes against property without violence continued to fall in Edwardian Middlesbrough. This is somewhat surprising, on the surface, as wage rates rose more slowly, and even stagnated, while the cost of living rose to an extent that checked the late-Victorian growth in real earnings. The total number of offences increased but slightly from an annual average of approximately 420 in the last years of Victoria's reign to almost 430 in the immediate pre-war years. For the victim, such crimes could be traumatic, but for the most part they were mundane and opportunistic rather than spectacular and premeditated. Henry Riches, the new Chief Constable, commenting on an increase in crime in 1909, reassured his audience that they were 'principally petty larcenies from backyards of houses temporarily unoccupied, linen exposed to dry in back streets, and from vehicles left unattended in the streets.'[28] None the less, necessitous crimes were still part of the Middlesbrough crime scene in the early twentieth century. In the winter of 1908/9 it was noted that 'several of the larceny cases were instances where men stole food for their starving families'.[29] These were not isolated cases. The probation officer noted a number of poignant cases including that of a woman who had been driven to theft because of the illness-induced feebleness of her husband. Everything of value in the house, including the pet linnet, had been sold before she stole to survive.[30]

The presence of a flourishing port created problems. The scale of thefts on the river Tees in the 1890s was such that possibility of a separate river police was actively discussed. However, it was not until 1904 that a special river police was established. The figures for recorded crime on the river were surprisingly low, though this may well reflect a greater than usual problem of unrecorded and/or unreported crime. From 1904 to 1913 the number of recorded larcenies never exceeded 20 and in several years was as low as 11 or 12. Furthermore, many of these crimes were fundamentally the same as those committed on land. Clothing, boots and money were the items most commonly stolen. Predictably there were more 'nautical' items taken – oilskins, fishing nets and oars – but also items of cargo and, of course, coal.

Throughout the period indictable offences were a small part of the overall incidence of crime. Whereas some 50 people per year were committed for trial from Middlesbrough in the 1870s, some 2,500 were tried summarily in the town (a ratio of 1 to 50). In the following decade the contrast was even greater with an average of approximately 30 people committed for trial compared with an average of 1,850 tried summarily (a ratio of 1 to 60). Summary justice had been expanded in 1879 but the total number of people proceeded against for petty, that is non-indictable, offences was 25 per cent lower in the 1880s than the 1870s, notwithstanding the continuing growth of the town. When population growth is taken into account, the figures show a 40 per cent drop in petty crime between the early 1870s and the early 1880s.[31]

The distribution of petty offences is detailed in Table 8.6. Despite the increased scope of summary justice the total number of offences in

Table 8.6: Offences dealt with summarily in the 1870s and 1880s

Offence	1870s		1880s	
	No.	*% total*	*No.*	*% total*
Drunkenness	540	22	560	30
All assaults	441	18	233	17
Larcenies	182	7	239	13
Local acts	565	23	225	12
Vagrancy	41	2	52	3
Total	2,498		1,854	

Source: Chief Constable's Annual Reports.

Table 8.7: Cases tried summarily, 1903–13

| | 1903–04 | | 1905–09 | | 1910–13 | |
	No.	%	No.	%	No.	%
INDICTABLE OFFENCES:						
Total	347		311		293	
Of which simple larceny	267	77	244	78	215	73
OTHER OFFENCES:						
Total	2,422		2,806		2,491	
Drunkenness	857	35	1,206	43	1,118	45
Assaults	305	13	269	10	243	10
Prostitution, etc.	74	3	88	3	83	3
Betting & gaming	3	>1	76	3	123	5
Begging	38	2	65	2	38	2
Sleeping out	45	2	40	1	12	>1
By-laws etc.	494	20	435	16	249	10
Education Acts	259	11	169	6	59	2

Source: Chief Constable's Annual Reports.

Middlesbrough changed little between the 1890s and 1900s. Thus, with population still growing, the rate continued to fall and was about 30 per cent lower than a decade earlier.[32] (See Table 8.7.)

Drunkenness, unsurprisingly, was the most common offence, accounting, for about 1 in 5 of all petty crimes in the 1870s, rising to about 1 in 3 in the 1880s; a figure comparable to those of the late 1850s and the 1860s. Once again, these figures have to be related to the town's growth in population. The rate of prosecutions for drunkenness, which had stood at 1,991 per 100,000 around 1861, fell to 1,490 and 1,076 around 1871 and 1881 respectively. The overall decline (46 per cent) was spread evenly over the two decades. The decline continued in the next decade, falling to around 850, but rose thereafter to such an extent that by 1911 the rate was 932 per 100,000. This increase coincides with the appointment of a new Chief Constable, Henry Riches. The evidence of the General Order book suggests that a new determination had been brought to the drink-related problems of the town. Not for the first time complaints were raised about the prevalence of public houses, but greater problems were to be found in the licensed club, in which long hours of drinking could be legally indulged, and in the home, where, as Lady Bell noted, the 'most pernicious drinking . . . goes on constantly'.[33]

Given the vagaries of crime statistics, especially for petty offences, it cannot automatically be assumed that these figures measure a real change in late-Victorian Middlesbrough. However, there is no evidence to suggest that attitudes and practices among public and police altered to such an extent as to explain this marked decline, though Ashe appears to have been less zealous than either his predecessor (Saggerson) or his successor (Riches). On the contrary, there were repeated expressions of concern about the problem of drunkenness among both men and women in Middlesbrough. The Chief Constable, Edward Saggerson, constantly commented on the matter, not least because of his firm conviction that drunkenness was one of the major causes of crime in the town, and he was not satisfied with the extent of the decrease in arrests for drunkenness in the early 1880s.[34] While the trend was downward, there were also important variations from year to year. In the boom years of the early 1870s, for example, the annual figure exceeded 600, whereas in 1874, in a trade recession, the number fell to 322. A similar downturn took place as trade moved into depression in 1877–9. The local police looked to changes in the licensing laws, and variations in their enforcement, as an explanation of short-term variations but, while these factors undoubtedly had some part to play, a more convincing explanation of short-term fluctuations is to be found in the changing economic fortunes of the town. Indeed, Saggerson himself conceded this point in his report for 1880. He noted, sadly, that the incidence of drunkenness had been lower during the trade depression of the previous year, but in 1880 'many persons who during last year suffered so much from want, and were constant recipients of public charity, and who are now in constant work, may be found spending their hard-earned money in intoxicating drinks.'[35]

Somewhat caustically, he concluded by venturing the opinion that 'so soon is trade a little depressed [they] will doubtless be again driven to seek relief from the parish authorities.' He might also have added that prosecutions for drunkenness would also 'doubtless' fall in such circumstances.

Crimes of violence were also an important aspect of summary justice, but, as in the country at large, the long-term trend in the statistics was downward. During the 1870s the number of cases fluctuated between 400 and 500. The overwhelming majority took the form of common assault, usually drunken brawls between men, but a minority comprised aggravated assaults on women and children or assaults on the police. It is not a coincidence that common assaults (and drunkenness) peaked, for example, in the prosperous years of 1872 and 1873 and fell, as trade declined, in 1874. Given the predominant working-class construction of masculinity, with a heavy emphasis on physical strength and the ability to defend oneself, interpersonal violence (of a less serious nature) remained an important part of the town's life and was not fully captured by official statistics. However, it is significant that the number of violent incidents that drew the attention of the police fell, absolutely and relatively, in the last quarter of the nineteenth century. The annual number of assaults for which the police took proceedings fell from over 400 in the early 1870s to less than 300 a decade later. The average annual rate for assaults fell even more dramatically. In 1881 the figure was 515 per 100,000 compared with 1,053 in 1871 and 1,300 in 1861. In the immediate pre-war years the figure had fallen to just over 200. Once again, it is difficult to believe that this was not, in large measure, a genuine decline rather than the product of changes in opinion and police practice. There is no evidence to suggest that there was a greater tolerance of violence in the 1870s or 1880s or any diminution in the determination to prosecute. To the contrary, as Saggerson's repeated comments about and condemnation of faction fights, vicious assaults and 'ruffian wife and women beaters' bear testimony, there was an abhorrence of public violence and a wish to eliminate what were seen as 'brutal outrages.[36]

Larceny cases, as the figures above indicate, were a relatively small part of the overall crime picture, especially in the 1870s. Interestingly, the official figures do not indicate any significant improvement. In absolute terms the number of petty thefts tried summarily increased by some 33 per cent from an annual average of 179 in the early 1870s to 244 in the early 1880s. This rate of increase was almost identical to the town's population growth and as a consequence that rate of petty thefts remained largely constant at around 450 per 100,000. However, the rate was significantly lower in the early twentieth century, averaging around 244.

A substantial part of police time was devoted to the enforcement of, or prosecution under, the local by-laws. More cases fell in this category than any other, excepting drunkenness. On average, in the 1870s some 565 cases a year were brought under this heading and were largely concerned with maintaining order, safety and decency in the streets. It is perhaps a measure of the extent to which the Middlesbrough police were able to bring an acceptable level of order and decorum to the streets that prosecutions under the local by-laws fell to an annual average of 225 in the 1880s.

However, perhaps the most striking feature of summary justice was the sheer range of activities that fell under the purview of the police and the extent to which this involved them in the day-to-day life of the inhabitants of the town at work, at play and even in more intimate aspects of their life. Men were prosecuted – albeit not in large numbers – for deserting or neglecting to support their families, or for disobeying bastardy orders. The spread of elementary education led to a sharp increase in prosecutions for failing to send children to school. The police had considerable powers under various pieces of public health legislation that could bring them into contact (and conflict) with land-lords and shopkeepers. The latter also met the police in their guise as inspectors of weights and measures. Hawkers and pedlars had to be licensed, while other legislation controlled the activities of pawnbro-kers, and so on. Those unwilling to work (or deemed to be so) could also fall foul of the police via the embraces of the vagrancy laws, which caught those with no visible means of subsistence, those begging and those prostituting themselves.

Much police-work was devoted to preserving order in public places. The nature of this work is brought out very clearly in the statistics for street offences that were a regular feature of Riches' annual reports. (See Table 8.8.)

The sheer scale of the powers at the disposal of the police implies an intention (on the part of legislators, at least) to regulate large areas of life – and not just working-class life.[37] However, intention and outcome are not necessarily the same; the former does not guarantee

Table 8.8: Principal street offences, 1903–13

	1903–4		1905–9		1910–13	
	No.	*%*	*No.*	*%*	*No.*	*%*
Total	1,913		2,182		2,194	
Drunkenness	1,042	54	1,296	59	1,273	58
Begging	54	3	68	3	34	2
Prostitution	47	2	48	2	44	2
Gaming	190	10	152	7	119	5
Betting & bookmaking	76	4	49	2	15	1
Damaging property	77	4	56	2	30	1
Brawling	40	2	17	1	2	>1
Fighting	40	2	51	2	32	1
Assaults on PCs	97	5	88	4	87	4
Abusive words	35	2	90	4	109	5
Obstruction	72	4	76	3	57	3
Football	81	4	120	5	104	5

Source: Chief Constable's Annual Reports.

the latter. Complainants to the local press made it clear that the police did too little to clear the streets of such abominations as little boys playing football, adolescents and men gambling and women of varying age following the oldest profession. It is clear that many pieces of legislation were not rigorously enforced. Prosecutions under the vagrancy laws for prostitution, for example, ran at an average of a dozen per year, falling to an all-time low of two in 1872. It is difficult to believe that this gives an accurate indication of the problem in the town. The vagaries of the Edwardian street offences figures strengthen this view. Far fewer people were arrested for gaming, betting and bookmaking at the end, rather than the beginning, of the period. The number of people arrested for brawling dropped dramatically after 1906 but it is highly improbable that brawling itself largely disappeared from the streets. It is also difficult to believe that the increase of over 100 per cent in football-related offences in 1905 could be explained in terms of a sudden upsurge in working-class sporting activity, though Middlesbrough's first-round defeat in the FA cup, and in the same season as Newcastle reached the final, may have been a spur to action. Similarly, the dramatic increase in the number of people prosecuted for using abusive words in 1909 is unlikely to reflect a hitherto suppressed penchant for swearing in public places

An explanation for these fluctuations can be found in the General Order Book that provides an insight into the immediate concerns of the local police. Three characteristics stand out. First, the relatively trivial nature of many of the offences – throwing orange peel on the footpath, obstruction of footpaths by boys playing with tops, the noisy behaviour of both girls and boys at the local ice-cream shop. Second, the underlying continuity of concern, for example with the problem of boys throwing stones or using bad language, throughout the period from the late nineteenth century to the early twentieth century. And third, the sporadic nature of this concern: in 1885 with unruly boys in the free libraries and reading rooms and the practice of bicycling on the footpaths in Albert Park; in 1903 with the practice of chalking and striking of matches on walls; and in 1906 with the playing of football and gambling on recreation grounds on Sunday afternoons. Such changes in emphasis on the part of the police reflected, in part at least, pressure from members of the watch committee and members of the general public who made public their concern with what they saw as undesirable or reprehensible behaviour.[38] The official figures were, therefore, as much a product of changing expectations and police practices as of offending behaviour *per se*.

The relationship between the police, their immediate masters in the form of the watch committee and the general public is complex, variable and difficult to chart with any precision. Undoubtedly, there were times when the police were required to take actions which they considered not to be proper police-work or which were likely to be counter-productive.[39] Differences between watch committees and chief constables were rarely recorded let alone ever becoming public. It is not known to what extent Chief Constables Saggerson, Ashe and Riches (or their men) saw the wanton and public discarding of orange peel as a major problem. However, it is known that they shared a concern about the problem of working-class gambling and sought to stamp out this 'grave national concern'. In this respect the official figures are also a measure of what the police were unable (or in the case of ordinary constables perhaps unwilling) to do.

Working-class gambling had always been a matter of major concern, locally and nationally, being seen as a threat to habits of industry and an encouragement to other crimes.[40] In the 1870s the focus of attention had been working-class drinking, but a generation later this had been replaced by working-class gambling, which had begun to expand in the 1880s. But in no small measure, the growing worry was due to the activities of anti-gambling organisations, such as the National Anti-Gambling League, which took an increasingly high-profile approach especially in the mid-1890s, following a legal decision that street bookmakers could not be prosecuted under the Vagrancy Act. Such was the level of concern that the 1902 House of Lords Select Committee enquiry concluded that the country was in the grip of a gambling fever. The debate on gambling was part of a wider worry about relative economic decline – a point that resonated on Teesside where the local iron and steel industry had found itself faced with increasing competition since the 1870s – and about national deterioration in a broader sense. But there was also a more specific concern: namely, that gambling and the corruption of the police were closely linked. The upshot was the 1906 Street Betting Act, which reflected both public concern and police confidence in their ability to control, or even suppress, street betting. Such confidence was ill-founded. The popularity of gambling and the organisational abilities of bookmakers and their supporters soon revealed the limitations of the police – who, at times, were driven to illegal methods, such as planting betting slips or even using *agents provocateurs*, in an (ultimately unsuccessful) attempt to enforce the law. Caught between two diametrically opposed groups – one wanting the law enforced, the other not – the police developed a form of partial or differential enforcement. Bribes were undoubtedly accepted by some policemen as part of the negotiation of a *modus vivendi* between the police and those for whom the streets were the main site of leisure activity.

In the 1870s and 1880s street betting was endemic in Middlesbrough, but the police rarely acted unless pressured to do so.[41] The volume of complaint and calls to action increased sharply during and after the 1890s in Middlesbrough as in the country at large. There was concern about police collusion and corruption.[42] Sporting clubs, such as the Albert Club, were left untouched and (or so it was alleged) the police protected gamblers, patrolling the betting areas to ensure order.[43] Lady Bell was clearly shocked by the way in which 'among the ironworkers it is indulged in in various forms by men, women and children, with untiring zest'. It was a part of life to which children, from an early age, were accustomed as they played pitch and toss for pennies in the streets or later graduated to becoming runners for adult gamblers.

Street gambling was targetted through local acts and by-laws and the laws relating to vagrancy as well as the 1906 Street Betting Act. Under Ashe, police action was sporadic. There was, for example, a mini-purge in 1896 when 21 people were prosecuted for street-betting in Snowden Road, but there was no concerted action.[44] Riches, unlike his predecessor, was undoubtedly concerned with the problem of working-class betting and expected his men to take action.[45] In one sense success was achieved: the volume of street betting diminished but the problem had been driven underground. Riches confessed to the Watch Committee in 1909 that

> though bookmakers have practically ceased to frequent the streets, there is no doubt that the practice of betting is still carried on to a considerable extent, and many are the devices resorted to for the purpose of escaping detection by the police.[46]

The situation worsened rather than improved. Three years later, Riches ruefully noted in his annual report that there was

> very little street betting . . . but it is doubtful whether betting on horses has decreased to any appreciable extent, and betting by means of coupons on the results of league football matches is, I regret to say, decidedly on the increase.[47]

Attempts at suppressing gambling were not helped by the widespread acceptance of it by many members of the public and the difficulties facing the police. Lady Bell was only too aware of the situation. Gambling had been driven from the streets into the home.

> The policeman may watch as much as he likes, it is difficult to stop every man who calls at a cottage door, or to prove that he is a book-maker if he denies it. Added to which, most of the cottages have back doors and a way out into a back street, and nothing is easier than to go in at one door and out of the other. The bookmaker, therefore, is now playing a game of chance against the police, a new form of gambling added to the rest, in which, if he is successful, the enemy remains outwitted in the street.[48]

It is not altogether clear that the town's police were zealous in their prosecution of bookmakers, though in this respect they were not unique. As one policeman told Lady Bell: 'I feel quite ashamed some-times to think what I spend my time in doing and what I am after. I am neglecting my other duties.'[49] Even if the police achieved a success and brought a man to court the deterrent effect of a fine was under-mined by the practice of holding a 'gathering', 'that is, a collection made among the men at the works'.[50] Police actions were further ham-pered by a belief among many ordinary constables that gambling was not intrinsically wrong. Further, many policemen were involved with those who organised illegal gambling – ostensibly as a means of obtain-ing information on 'serious' crime but often 'to have a flutter'. This had threatened to become a serious problem in Middlesbrough in the 1890s. In 1893 the mayor specifically asked the Watch Committee to ensure that the town's constables were warned 'against Betting and obtaining Refreshment at Public houses while on duty'.[51] A number of dismissals followed and the problem was checked, for the time being at least. A decade later it re-appeared in more serious form. Following a number of complaints the watch committee conducted an enquiry into the relationship between the betting fraternity and certain members of the force and came to the conclusion that certain 'persons who seek to make a livelihood by betting have endeavoured, both directly and indirectly, to corrupt some Members of the Police Force'.[52]

Three constables were given a severe caution for being 'too familiar with Bookmakers and their Touts' while on duty in the Stockton Street Recreation Ground, a place with a reputation as a venue of illegal gam-bling. While such behaviour was probably exceptional – the inquiry unearthed no further miscreants – there was a sympathy for gambling which must have reduced the effectiveness with which Chief Constable Riches' orders were enforced. In inter-war Middlesbrough there was a tacit understanding between police and street gamblers, often involving elaborate façades whereby the police appeared to be attempting to enforce the law while in reality tipping off the supposed targets.[53] Such habits probably had deep roots that went back into the late nineteenth century.

****

The later years of Victoria's reign in England were, in broad terms, a safer time in which to live than the early years.[54] Middlesbrough was no exception to this trend, becoming a less dangerous and insecure town in which to live: and this fact was increasingly recognised by influential figures in the town. Fears, reflecting both class and ethnic prejudices, were always near the surface, particularly in the 1870s. The very fact that the economic progress of the town attracted large numbers of young working men was a continuing source of worry. A belief in a strong link between relatively rootless young men and the incidence of crime was firmly held by people such as Saggerson. In 1871, as the local economy moved into what was to be the greatest boom of the nineteenth century, he warned against 'the daily influx of strangers, having no fixed abode, and many of whom are not of the best character' and promised the 'unceasing vigilance of the police' to contain the threat to order.[55] His fears increased over the next year or so, and in 1873, at the height of the boom, he told the Watch Committee that

> Owing to Trade being good and wages high, Hundreds of men from all parts find their way to this Borough and most of them are of the lowest Class who will not work but commit all kinds of depredations which accounts for the great increase of offences of late.[56]

Such fears were tempered over time by a growing awareness that the labouring classes were not automatically dangerous classes. During the trade depression of the late 1870s Saggerson noted, indeed praised, the 'patience and endurance' of the working classes in times of hardship.[57] This recognition of the presence of ordinary, respectable and law-abiding citizens, coupled with growing confidence in the town's police force, resulted in a more optimistic tone in the annual reports of the 1880s. Indeed, Saggerson had mellowed to such a degree that in 1882 he allowed himself to express publicly his pleasure at the state of affairs in the town. 'On the whole,' he wrote in his annual report, 'the figures are highly satisfactory and there is a total absence of really serious offences against either persons or property.'[58] Two years later he publicly praised those 'respectable and law-abiding inhabitants of the town' who had contributed so much to the prevailing good order.[59] Nor was this simply the complaisant comment of a man who had served over 20 years as chief constable. Such sentiments were echoed by some of the town's opinion formers. The *Daily Exchange* prefaced its coverage of the 1884 annual report with the following observation: 'Middlesbrough may congratulate itself on its comparative immunity from crime.'[60] Though there were still some publicly expressed concerns with the efficiency of the police and their ability to combat crime, a significant shift in attitude had taken place since the late 1850s and 1860s. Middlesbrough was becoming less of a frontier town and more of a regulated and respectable community.

The annual police returns continued to record certain characteristics of the criminal population. A clear majority of criminals were men, though the percentage of male criminals was higher in the 1870s (80 per cent) than the 1880s (75 per cent). As in previous decades, the criminal population was poorly educated, with approximately 90 per cent in the 1870s classified as unable to read or write or able to do so imperfectly, rising to 95 per cent a decade later. As well as being drawn from the less well-educated sections of society, Middlesbrough criminals were also overwhelmingly and increasingly drawn from unskilled and poorly paid employment (or from the unemployed). During the 1870s a quarter of male criminals who gave their occupation said they were unemployed at the time of arrest. In the trade depression of 1878 and 1879 the percentage rose to over 30 percent. During the 1880s the average was nearer 35 per cent, rising to over 50 per cent in the bad years of 1886 and 1887. In addition a further 10 to 15 per cent were employed in the lowest-paid jobs in town.

Contemporary concerns with the criminality of the Irish received apparent confirmation in the official statistics, though to some (immeasurable) extent this was a self-fulfilling prophecy. The situation was not unchanging. The percentage of prisoners identified as Irish had fallen to an average of 35 per cent in the 1870s. In the early 1880s the figure was closer to 20 per cent and fell to about 15 per cent by the end of that decade. While it would be naive to see these figures as an accurate measure of change, the scale of the decline is such that it cannot be entirely dismissed as a vagary of recording. Rather it is more convincing to argue that this reflects a real change. It is more likely that the change was more in policing than in the criminal behaviour of the Irish.

The concern with outsiders and those recently arrived in the town also appeared well-founded. Roughly a third of all criminals were strangers to the town and a further third had arrived within the past five years. Of the latter, half had lived in Middlesbrough for less than a year. However, it was also the case that the majority of people taken into custody were either of good character or unknown to the police. A substantial majority (35 to 40 per cent) were classified, in the somewhat ambiguous terminology of the day, as suspicious characters, but the percentage of known thieves, convicted prostitutes and tramps and vagrants varied between 15 and 20 per cent of the total throughout the period.

The emergence (or recognition) of the habitual criminal was a distinctive feature of the late nineteenth-century discourse on criminality. Part of a wider concern with racial degeneration, itself a product of new scientific theories as well as an awareness of the threats to the industrial and imperial dominance of Britain, the habitual criminal became a convenient scapegoat for wider social and economic problems. However, the 'problem' appeared real enough to contemporaries who could see for themselves (or at least read about) the sad but threatening repeat offenders who appeared in the local courts. Patrick Matthews, for instance, appeared a clear example. Appearing at Northallerton in October 1884, charged with stealing a pint of rum, this 37-year-old labourer had been imprisoned 27 times for drunk and riotous behaviour, wilful damage, theft and assault (including assaulting a policeman) and fined a further 18 times in the past 13 years.[61] Female offenders, who were doubly damned for breaking the law and rejecting the norms of femininity, aroused even greater anxieties. Indeed, late Victorians were increasingly conscious of the fact that recidivism was more often found among women than men. Through the writings of men such as the London police court missionary, Thomas Holmes, women such as Jane Cakebread, Kate Hennessey and Susan Hurley became folk devils.[62] The problem was widespread. In Middlesbrough there were a number of well-known repeat offenders such as Mary Campbell (also known to the courts as Mary Wilkins, Mary Ann Welsh and Catherine Sullivan) who, by the age of 40, had appeared before the sessions or assizes 8 times in 20 years, 11 of which had been spent in gaol. In addition, she had a further 25 convictions for petty offences, ranging from drunkenness, assault and wilful damage to obscene language and prostitution.[63]

The hardened adult criminal (female perhaps more so than male) was the more threatening figure, but the juvenile offender was the more worrying. Sympathy for corrupted youngsters, seen as victims of inadequate parents and harsh circumstances, co-existed with fear that these people represented the next generation of hardened criminals. From the mid-nineteenth century onwards there were demands for separate and specialist treatment for young offenders. And as part of this an industrial school had been established at Linthorpe.[64] Around the turn of the twentieth century there were renewed demands for the establishment of distinct juvenile courts, greater use of probation for young offenders and the introduction of borstals as a means of reforming juvenile delinquents. In addition, it was believed that organisations such as boys' brigade or the scouts could help save young boys from a life of crime.

Middlesbrough's peculiar demographic development meant that it had a particularly young population, but the high population density of the town compounded the situation. Youngsters were very visible on the streets and this added to the sense of concern. Further, late-Victorian society was concerned with the problem of juvenile criminals. Hooligan disturbances in London and 'scuttler' outrages in the north-west of England aroused much comment.[65] Locally such fears rarely surfaced and the number of juvenile offenders brought before the law in Middlesbrough was relatively low, especially in the early 1870s. From an average of approximately 60, the number of juvenile offenders appearing before the magistrates rose sharply to around 100 in the mid-1870s and reached almost 150 in Saggerson's last year as chief constable, 1884. The numbers that appeared in court represented but the tip of the iceberg. Unlike many of his contemporaries, Saggerson took a sympathetic stance towards errant youngsters whom he saw as victims of negligent parents for whom he had little sympathy. In 1872 he commented that

> It is grieving to see the hundreds of children who daily run about the streets, some of them almost in a nude state, and most of these the offspring of parents who are in constant employment and in receipt of good wages and could, if so disposed, keep their children respectable and educate them at their own expense.[66]

Children, allowed 'to run about our streets daily' with no parental guidance, would grow up with habits of 'idleness' which if not checked would result in a growing number of 'pests to society' and a growing burden on the ratepayer.[67] Although some hope of reform lay in the Industrial Schools, Training Ships and Reformatories to which Middlesbrough's juvenile offenders were sent, Saggerson saw education as the most important element in the fight against juvenile crime. The action of the School Board in 'compelling attendance at school of children who were formerly neglected by their parents' was praised on more than one occasion.[68] The problem of parental neglect never disappeared, but by 1880 Saggerson confined his criticisms to 'drunken parents' rather than the generality of working-class parents.[69] The new chief constable, William Ashe, chose not to comment on the question.[70] It is difficult to say whether his lack of interest reflects a more general absence of concern about the problem. The minutes of the Watch Committee contain several references to street disturbances, the playing of football, brawling and the use of bad language, but there is no indication of any preoccupation with the problem of adolescent hooliganism and hooligan gangs.

Growing concerns were expressed in the 1890s for the future of the young. An anonymous contributor to the *North Eastern Daily Gazette* in 1899 highlighted the problem of child neglect. In the town there were children who were

> badly fed, badly clad, morally and religiously almost wholly neglected . . . [C]ertainly the number of neglected boys and girls who are found begging on the streets, and practically living there, seems to be increasing.[71]

Lady Bell wrote in characteristic manner:

> I fear it is incontestable that most of the children who are playing about the streets of Middlesbrough are destined to grow into a generation which will bring down the average of the deserving and efficient. This immense population of workers is growing up among physical and moral influences which are bound to be unfavourable.[72]

Poverty was a major problem. Almost one-third of the families visited by Lady Bell lived in such conditions that they

> never have enough to spend on food to keep themselves sufficiently nourished, enough to spend on clothes to be able to protect their

bodies adequately, enough to spend on their houses, to acquire a moderate degree of comfort.[73]

But in addition, for many juveniles the situation was compounded by the fact that the iron-works offered little in the way of employment for those under 16 years of age. For some there was a succession of dead-end jobs, for others, left to themselves 'for moral training', there was 'nothing to do . . . but to go about the streets, at the mercy of any temptation that may come in their way'.[74]

The Middlesbrough Police Court missionary was briefer and more explicit. These children were 'victims to their surroundings . . . born into and early familiarised with crime'.[75] Idleness, poverty and hunger combined to drive boys and girls to theft. The necessity of child labour had not been removed for all sectors of Middlesbrough's working classes, despite a general improvement in living standards. Youthful street traders were required to be licensed, but not all were. However, older explanations of youth crime remained. In language that would not have been out of place in one of Edward Saggerson's reports of the 1870s, Norman Riches lamented the fact that many parents of juvenile offenders 'had allowed the Children to run about the streets apparently without exercising ordinary supervision'. Such 'lack of discipline and disinclination of parental responsibility' was seen as the cause of the rise in juvenile crime.[76]

Informal methods were adopted to prevent juvenile delinquency. Lady Bell refers unspecifically to boys' clubs in the town that were intended to prevent lads from hanging around in the streets and drifting into petty crime. A Young Man's Temperance Brigade, later the Middlesbrough and Cleveland Boys' Brigade, dated from the early 1890s. Scouting for boys was introduced to Middlesbrough in 1909 and for girls in 1910. The precise number and origins of boys' clubs is not known, but some, such as the Feversham Street Boys' Club, were active from around the turn of the century. In addition, there were a variety of church organisations, both Catholic and Protestant.

Despite the concern with the juvenile and juvenile-adult offender (i.e. aged 16–21), the number of prosecutions remained relatively low. Successive chief constables do not appear to have seen young offenders as a major problem, or, perhaps more accurately, did not see formal action as the best solution to the problem. Likewise many ordinary policemen appear to have turned a blind eye to youthful offences, especially when they involved little more than playing football or roller-skating.

In the early twentieth century the number of juveniles tried for indictable offences averaged 75, of which 85 per cent were larcenies, and a further 60 16- to 21-year-olds also appeared before the town magistrates. This number dropped dramatically to around 25 and 22 respectively following the 1907 Probation Act and 1908 Children Act which led to the establishment of a juvenile court.[77] Many of these offences, especially opportunistic thefts of goods or money from shops, were clearly poverty related.[78] Poverty also explained many of the non-indictable offences for which juveniles were prosecuted. Working in defiance of the Employment of Children Act, theft (especially of food-stuffs including fruit) and begging were the most common offences.

The statistics of the work of the juvenile court in the pre-war years confirm the general picture delineated above: simple larceny accounted for 4 out of every 5 indictable offence. Even the prevalence of youthful gambling is consistent with this interpretation, though for many con-temporaries the latter was more a sign of moral decay. Similarly, lack of discipline was seen to be at the root of certain other offences. On closer examination, many of these offences were little more than youthful pranks such as throwing snowballs or fireworks in the street, acting boisterously outside Pacitto's ice-cream shop, or shouting during the hours of divine service. However, there is also some evidence to suggest that older forms of behaviour had become unacceptable and, perhaps more important, were being dealt with formally. (See Table 8.9.)

In accordance with emerging wisdom that youngsters, or at least first offenders, should be kept out of courts and given an opportunity not

Table 8.9: Juvenile courts, 1910–13

	Annual average	%
Indictable offences: Total	108	
Simple larceny	87	81
Shop-breaking	8	7
Non-indictable offences: total	200	
Obstruction/nuisance	58	29
Vagrancy/begging	15	8
Vagrancy/gaming	33	17
Local acts	45	23

Source: Chief Constable's Annual Reports.

Table 8.10: Probation orders, 1908–13

	1908–9	1910–13
Total (annual average)	100	118
% distribution:		
Male	78	78
Female	22	22
Under 16	60	58
16–21	23	17
Over 21	17	43

Source: Chief Constable's Annual Reports.

to be stigmatised with a criminal record, recourse was made to the use of probation orders. Boys under 16 were the major beneficiaries of this new approach. (See Table 8.10.) Despite the efforts of the juvenile court and the probation service there remained a feeling that juvenile delinquency was an unsolved problem, as the statistics of the immediate pre-war years appeared to show.

More generally, as Middlesbrough approached the turn of the twentieth century, many of its leading inhabitants took pride in the order that had been established in the town. For much of its early history the town had been turbulent, with levels of petty crime in particular startlingly high. Furthermore, despite real efforts by successive chief constables (Hannan and Saggerson) and the support of local politicians (notably Isaac Wilson), the police force was not the most reliable means of protecting property and persons. However, in the last quarter of the century significant changes had, gradually and almost imperceptibly, taken place. Crime rates had dropped significantly; the police force was more mature and efficient and the town itself had achieved a greater degree of stability and prosperity. This confidence was somewhat shaken in the early twentieth century, not least because of the growing preoccupation with the unresolved (or at best, partly resolved) problems of the young. None the less, there were considerably fewer worries than had been expressed in the mid-Victorian years. Middlesbrough was indisputably a policed town and levels of crime had diminished markedly. English society as a whole had become more civilised and more secure, but nowhere more so was this the case than in Middlesbrough.

Appendix

Table A8.1: Other police activities, 1903–13

	1903–4	1905–9	1910–13
A. Quasi-criminal Matters: orders made			
Total	197	178	210
Maintenance	106	97	110
Children	36	33	25
B. Certificates granted			
Total	132	174	196
Pedlars	90	108	121
Marine stores	10	25	36
Ticket porters	31	39	37
Chimney-sweeps & shoe blacks	1	1	2
C. Habitual criminals & persons under police surveillance			
Habituals	32	22	25
Surveillance	11	18	16

D. Premises registered under Explosives Act & licences issued Petroleum Act

		(1907–9)	(1910–13)
Explosives:	Premises	86	77
	Inspections	241	294
	Prosecutions	1	1
Petroleum:	Licences	22	39
	Inspections	67	108
	Prosecutions	0	1

E. Accidents and illness in the streets, 1909–13 (annual average)

	(1909–13)
All Accidents	198
All Illness	83
Illness leading to death	4
Accidents leading to death	4
Accidents leading to personal injury	141
Accidents with no injuries	53

9
The Police and the Public from the 1870s to 1914

Late-Victorian and Edwardian England was a policed society in a way that set it apart from Regency and early-Victorian England and that had more in common with the twentieth-century experience, at least until the 1970s. This did not mean that the police were universally liked. *The Times* painted an over-rosy picture of working-class attitudes with its reference to the 'handyman of the streets' but the very fact of a policed society was evidence of the ability of the police to win support and defuse or disperse opposition to such an extent that much of their work was unquestioned and many of their men went about that work unchallenged.[1] Despite the importance of this development, policing late-Victorian and Edwardian England has not attracted the same degree of detailed attention from historians. The broad outlines have been established and offer a relatively comforting image of society that contrasts with the experience of the late twentieth century.[2] However, there is a danger not only of losing the subtlety that comes from an appreciation of the variety of local experience, but also of underestimating the problems that still faced the police in the second and third generations, and thus of overstating the stability of that policed society so praised by *The Times* in the early twentieth century.

Middlesbrough's peculiarly rapid growth had created a range of social troubles and social tensions that, in part, manifested themselves in conflicts between the town's still inexperienced police and certain sections of its working-class population, especially in the 1860s. The last quarter of the nineteenth century saw an easing of tensions as the town, its inhabitants and institutions, moved from the turbulence of its 'frontier' days to greater stability and maturity. At the same time as the town's police force became more professional, the recorded crime rate in Middlesbrough fell dramatically. The creation of a policed society was a considerable achievement and not easily or simply achieved. None the less, a profound change had taken place and with it a significant shift in the relationship between the police and the policed. Behaviour among both the police and the policed changed and, almost symbiotically, the police benefited from wider societal changes while local society (for the most part) benefited from improvements in local policing. The police were never universally popular, especially in certain quarters, but there were clear signs that overt hostility declined over the course of the second half of the nineteenth century. The number of recorded assaults on police officers in the town fell steadily notwithstanding the growth in the size of the town and of its police force.[3]

During the 1860s there was an average of almost 60 assaults per year with over 100 cases recorded in the worst year. In the following decade the average fell to just over 40 with an annual peak of 53. In the following decade the average number of incidents fell below 50 while in the 1880s it had fallen to 26 with a maximum of 40 cases in one year. This decline of over 50 per cent took place at a time when the population of the town had almost trebled and its police force had grown in overall size by nearly 50 per cent. The position deteriorated somewhat thereafter and in 1893 the only murder of a serving policeman took place when the 'dangerous lunatic' John Henry Gould shot PC Henderson. By the first decade of the twentieth century the annual average figure had risen to approximately 90 (more than a three-fold increase) but the population of the town had more than doubled, as had the borough's police force during this period. Put simply, the 1870s and 1880s saw a dramatic reduction in the level of assaults on the police in relative terms. Furthermore this trend continued, albeit much more modestly, in the following decades.[4] The figures have to be interpreted with care. Society was becoming less violent generally and the police in Middlesbrough – and indeed elsewhere – may have been no more than beneficiaries of this trend. Legislative change that increased the penalty for assaulting the police will also have influenced the figures, and it is also possible that the police were more prepared to turn a blind eye to, or at least deal informally with, incidents which previously would have led to a court appearance. Nevertheless, it is difficult to escape the conclusion that a real change was taking place in this period.

It is also the case that there was a decline in the incidence and scale of mass anti-police incidents. The majority of such incidents that did take place occurred in the 1870s. Holiday periods, involving long drinking sessions, could lead to violence, as in 1869/70 when the Christmas and New Year period saw a number of violent assaults upon the police, but it was not only at these times that trouble broke out.[5] Hostility flared up in May 1870 when Sergeant Bellamy received serious head injuries when thrown to the ground and kicked by members of 'a chiefly Irish crowd' of between 50 and 60 people.[6] James Bull found himself in conflict with PC Hart in March 1872 but was rescued twice by the crowd that had gathered to witness the skirmish.[7] The rising number of assaults on the police (and members of the public) aroused concern in the summer of 1873, and, though the problem died down somewhat thereafter, as the local justices sent most offenders to prison rather than give them the option of a fine, troubles continued in the following years.[8] The problem soon reappeared. In 1875 Sergeant Raisbeck was attacked and 'violently assaulted by a gang of low Irishman' of whom 6 were arrested and sentenced to 6 months' hard labour. Raisbeck, for his pains, was unfit for work for several weeks.[9] The situation was compounded by the refusal of many in the town's Irish community to collaborate with the police even when they themselves had been victims of a crime. In his report for 1876 Saggerson lamented that it was 'a most difficult matter' to obtain evidence both from those directly involved and those who witnessed the events. Intimidation of shopkeepers and the like particularly aroused Saggerson's ire.[10] However, in the event, this was to be the last time that such a complaint was made by the police.

The old practice of mob rescues did not disappear entirely but the number of incidents dropped markedly. Patrick MacEwan was sentenced to 3 months' hard labour in 1883 for orchestrating an attack by 'a number of roughs' who 'violently assaulted [PC Gatenby] in Gladstone Street'.[11] A similar fate befell PC Neesam, who had been sent to arrest a number of people suspected of theft in March 1887. Eventually two men and a woman were arrested, but in the skirmish that took place Neesam suffered a broken rib.[12] The most serious incidents of the decade took place late in 1889. In the first, PCs Redding and Sledge, having been sent to arrest a soldier named Thomas Rooney, were set upon by 'a disorderly mob' and were fortunate to escape with minor injuries, though Redding was knocked unconscious from a blow on the head with a bottle when the prisoner was rescued by his riotous friends. In the second, PC Sutherland was less fortunate and suffered severe injuries when he arrested John Scully for being drunk and disorderly, only to have his prisoner snatched back by the crowd that had gathered. Later Scully and three others were arrested, tried and sentenced to terms of imprisonment of 4 to 6 months.[13] Few major incidents were reported after this. In October 1902 three men were prosecuted for leading an assault on PC Fuller who was attempting to arrest a drunk and disorderly individual. PC Barker was less fortunate. He was thrown to the ground, dislocated his shoulder and then received a severe kicking from a group of labourers.[14] However, such incidents were but a pale shadow of the events of the 1860s.

Most of the cases of assaults on the police were predictably mundane and the majority was dealt with summarily. As in previous decades alcohol played a part in precipitating the incident, but domestic events (celebrations as well as conflicts) could also lead to trouble with the police.[15] Policing morals could be hazardous. Prostitutes and their customers, for example, did not take lightly to police intervention. Alice Kilvington and her client Thomas Lynch were both sentenced to 6 months' hard labour for attacking PC Burney.[16] In an unintentionally humorous incident (but one which casts indirect light on shadier police practices) PC Raisbeck found himself under attack following an awkward scene behind St John's School, where he had gone to discover the source of some mysterious voices one November night in 1893. Having found 'a man and a woman laid down having connections', he asked, somewhat naively in the circumstances, what they were doing. To which 'the man said; what the H- - - is that to do with you, you B- - - - - -; it's money you want', and proceeded to attack Raisbeck with his fists. Raisbeck used his staff in self-defence and the man ran off. However, he was sufficiently incensed by police behaviour to make a counter-charge of violence against Raisbeck. The accusation was dismissed, but no action appears to have been taken against the unnamed man and his companion![17] Likewise, drunks – male and female – attacked officers sent to arrest them. PC Henderson had his nose broken as he arrested Cornelius Hargreaves; PC Cox was attacked in Commercial Street by the MacArdle brothers, Patrick and Charles, who sought to avoid arrest; while in a repeat incident, another pair of drunken brothers, Peter and William Burgess, attacked PC Stainthorpe a month later.[18] Such incidents were a product of the inevitable tension that grew out of the policing of working-class leisure, but cannot be seen as a fundamental rejection of policing as such. However, there is some evidence to suggest that certain individuals were involved in ongoing conflict with the police. Richard Naven, a small-time thief, and Robert Cairn were found guilty of assaulting the police on a number of occasions.[19] Other well-known 'characters' such as the habitual drunkard Annie Lee and Arthur Chaplin, the latter 'a well-known Cannon Street hooligan', vented their spleen at various times and on various officers.[20] Such incidents indicate the continuing opposition to the police, albeit on a considerable smaller scale than a generation before, in certain parts of the community.

As the number of people participating in anti-police disturbances decreased, so reports of people coming to the aid of the police increased, especially after 1900. Although one must be careful not to exaggerate the extent of change, there was a shift from intervention to increase the difficulties faced by the police in the 1860s and early 1870s to intervention to reduce them. PC Robinson, for example, found himself under attack as he attempted to address two drunks, but was helped by two members of the Territorial Army.[21] In September 1912 an attempted crowd rescue failed when two men and a woman came to the assistance of PC Lawrence.[22] Potentially more serious was an incident in the spring of 1914 that saw a brawl among seamen develop into a concerted assault on three policemen. Again indicative of changing attitudes, four members of the public came to the assistance of the police and three men were arrested and brought to trial.[23] Policing late-Victorian Middlesbrough was less hazardous than it had been in the 1850s and 1860s. The town itself was better lit, the local community was becoming more settled and less violent, but, more importantly, there was a more positive attitude towards the police that manifested itself more commonly in commendation of their action and also, if less often, in active intervention on their behalf. None the less, the danger of physical assault remained. Cuts and bruises, sore ribs and broken noses were recurring features.[24] PC Gatenby, the victim of at least three assaults in the 1860s, was further attacked in 1873 and again in 1883. A generation later, PC Bate found himself involved in three attacks in 3 years.[25] Most assaults involved fists and boots but some policemen were knifed. PC Hatfield was stabbed when seeking to prevent a man from pestering two women in the street, while Sergeant Booth was stabbed in the police station.[26] Officers could also be attacked when off duty. In one incident Detective Constable Morton was so severely injured that he was off work for 5 months.[27] As noted earlier, it is not easy to interpret these figures in the absence of more detailed contextual information. Some parts of town were more dangerous than others and some styles of policing – the overzealous or the officious – were more likely to provoke a violent response but conflict could also be more the product of accident.

The number of incidents of assault gives but a crude indication of the seriousness of the problem. A more accurate indicator is given by the numbers of days lost due to injury. Unfortunately, the police returns for Middlesbrough do not allow for a long-term comparison.

However, partial statistics for the 1900s provide a snapshot. In the worst year 432 days were lost due to injury or an average of between 6 and 7 days per reported incident. Earlier in the decade the average number of days lost to injury was approximately 2, and in the two immediate pre-war years less than 1. Considerably more police time was lost because of sickness. For every 1 day lost to injury 4 were lost to sickness in these years.[28]

The decline in outright hostility towards the police is an indication of a new and more positive relationship between the police and most parts of the local community. Explaining that new relationship is less easy in the absence of direct evidence. A considerable amount of police time was spent dealing with petty crimes. The beneficiaries of such actions were, more often than not, working-class men and women. The image of the ever-watchful policeman, protecting the innocent while they slept, was captured in the statistics of insecure windows and unlocked doors checked by the patrolling bobby. Further, in so far as the police were involved in maintaining local order against a commonly-seen threat posed by itinerants and outsiders, public support was enhanced. In certain cases the bravery and determination of the police brought commendation not simply from the Watch Committee but also from individual members of the public. Such incidents when reported in the local press helped to build up a positive image of the vigilant policeman, defending the public even at the cost of personal injury.[29]

In addition to their crime-fighting role, the police carried out a variety of welfare functions that again, in all probability, reduced hostility towards them and may well have engendered more positive feelings. For many years the police doubled as the local fire brigade and even when this practice ceased individual policemen distinguished themselves on a number of occasions at fires in the town. The vast majority of these incidents were relatively minor but this did not diminish the importance of rescuing individuals, particularly if they were in some way vulnerable. Inspector Hird's bravery and gallantry in rescuing 68-year-old Elizabeth Thomas from a fire in Gauntlett Street in 1909 is a case in point. Likewise, the meritorious actions of PC Bate at another fire, which brought him both a commendation and promotion, or the coroner's comments about PC Rodger's brave, if unavailing, attempts at rescue, showed the police in a very positive light.[30] Occasionally, the incident was more dramatic, most notably in 1911 when there was a serious fire at the Hippodrome. Two people were killed and several injured, but the 'heroic conduct' of PC Barnes brought him high praise.[31] The police presence in street accidents also brought praise. Runaway horses were a particular danger and a number of constables were praised, paid and promoted for their courage in dealing with them.[32] Police training in 'ambulance work' enabled them to give first-aid on the street before conveying, when necessary, people to their homes or the local hospitals. More generally, busier streets and the advent of motorized transport required greater police vigilance. Ever concerned with the safety of children, Riches made a particular point of commenting on the increased police presence on the streets to ensure that children arrived safely at school. The police also contributed to general welfare in a variety of informal ways. The police band provided entertainment in a number of places, including Albert Park. They organized the distribution of boots and clothes to poverty-stricken children, returned lost children to parents as well as lost property to careless or unfortunate owners, and also rounded up stray dogs. It is impossible to assess the impact of these actions, but it is not implausible to argue that they helped build up the image of the policeman as an essential element in a safe and smoothly functioning urban environment.

Policing by consent and the use of minimal force have been rightly seen as key elements in the creation of police legitimacy.[33] Policing necessarily involved the use of force at times. Furthermore, policing involved each and every constable using his discretion in determining how to handle a situation. The potential for the use of force that was excessive (or seen to be excessive) was considerable, especially with inexperienced constables. Police violence could undermine police legitimacy but, equally, firm action by the Watch Committee could help in part to create a positive image. Isaac Wilson, the long time chair of the Watch Committee during the critical transitional years in the 1860s and 1870s was determined to take firm action against men found guilty of using unwarranted violence against the public. However, it is difficult to establish the scale and precise nature of the problem from the official record, especially from enigmatic references to 'exceeding his duty' or 'unsatisfactory conduct'. Dismissals and prosecutions were the tip of an unmeasurable iceberg.

A number of serious cases of assault occurred in the early 1870s. In September 1872 PC Darley was fined the considerable sum of £4 and dismissed from the force for assaulting John Dickinson, and two years later PC Caraher was also dismissed, having been sentenced at the Northallerton quarter sessions to 6 months' imprisonment for assaulting James Long in the street. However, these were exceptional incidents. The next prosecution for assault came almost twenty years later and the outcome was quite different. PC Atkinson was fined £2 on 23 July 1893 for an unprovoked attack on a boy but was allowed to continue in the force, as was PC Bainbridge, another ex-soldier, who was fined £2 and given a warning for a similar attack on a youth. PC Beamire, who was found guilty of assaulting Frederick Skillen and bound over and ordered to pay 35s. (£1.75) for a new set of false teeth, also remained in post.[34] More surprisingly, so did Sergeant Blakeborough and PC Sparks, who were fined £15 in damages for personal injuries sustained by Ernest Evans in a case at the county court.[35]

It was more common for the Watch Committee to take action. In less serious incidents this took the form of either reprimanding men, as in the case of Francis Hudson, or fining them, as in the case of William Blakeborough, who was fined £1 and ordered to pay £2 compensation. In more serious cases, roughly one-third of the total, men were either dismissed outright, as in the cases of Francis Carter, an ex-Grenadier Guard whose unprovoked but drunken attack on a member of the public was his undoing, or ordered to resign, as in the case of PC Brown who committed a drunken assault on a woman, Fanny Farrell.[36] Similarly, a relatively small number of policemen were either reprimanded or dismissed for mistreating prisoners on the streets or in custody, though the Watch Committee minutes and police conduct registers are less than illuminating.

In all, for the period from 1870 to 1914, the police conduct registers contain information relating to little more than 20 cases of action being taken because of a police assault.[37] On average, there was one case every two years. The incidents, however, were very unevenly distributed. Only two incidents were recorded for the whole of the 1880s, while almost a half took place in the last third of the period, and, not entirely coincidentally, after a new chief constable had been appointed. None the less, even in the early twentieth century there was less than one such incident a year. The figures are open to a number of different interpretations. They might reflect the fact that the more mature force of the late nineteenth century was also a more disciplined force. There is undoubtedly an element of truth in this. The General Orders reminding constables how to conduct themselves on the streets – especially where respectable ladies and tradesmen were concerned – appear to have been observed. But it is also highly likely that such incidents are but a small part of a larger number of unrecorded incidents (or incidents that were not acted on) which stemmed from the policing of the working-class districts of the town in general, and the Irish areas in particular. In so far as incidents happened in these districts they were either unnoticed by the town's respectable population, who no longer lived in such close proximity to the old working-class district 'over the border', or were considered 'appropriate' in view of the problem presented by the 'less civilized' inhabitants of the town. Such behaviour directed at more respectable people was a different matter. When in 1877 Mr Eales complained to the Watch Committee about his treatment at the hands of Inspector Sample and PC Hopper, he received a profuse apology, expressing 'great regret at the annoyance which has been caused' and stressing that the officers had behaved 'without any malice' but had 'committed an error of judgement'.[38] PC Proudlock was reprimanded for the way in which he had ejected the respectable Mr Piercy from the police station; PC Jordison was in trouble for 'interfering with tradesmen in the conduct of their business', while PC Mardon was dismissed for his treatment of two engineers.[39]

Indeed, the general impression gained from these Watch Committee minutes is that most cases of police assault were treated leniently. As noted above, two men convicted of assault were not dismissed.[40] PC Collinson was merely cautioned for 'unsatisfactory conduct' in arresting Ernest Hill, and no action was taken even though there had been complaints from several people that he had assaulted another member of the public. Another who continued in uniform was PC Weaver, despite having been found to have assaulted two members of the public in separate incidents in August and September 1897. For the first incident he was reduced from the fourth to the fifth class, with a consequent reduction in pay, but for the second he was merely reprimanded.[41]

The extent to which low-level violence was part of routine policing cannot be established precisely. Anecdotal evidence (and not just from Middlesbrough) suggests that it was common for young lads to be cuffed about the ears as an informal punishment and for 'awkward' characters to suffer a back-street beating, but this rarely, if ever, reached the official record.[42] However, the absence of formal complaint and official concern is significant in itself. The concerns with 'police brutality', expressed in the 1860s become less common in the 1870s and all but disappear by the end of the century.

Public attitudes towards the police became more positive over time. In the 1870s there were relatively few editorials or letters praising the police.[43] An editorial in the *Middlesbrough Exchange* in 1872 conceded that 'as a rule there is not much to complain of in the conduct of the Middlesbrough police'.[44] The Watch Committee also on occasions expressed its approval of the town's police and of 'the great success of their efforts'.[45] More attention was paid to their shortcomings. Drunken policemen were ridiculed. In March 1872 the *Middlesbrough Exchange* noted an incident during the previous weekend when 'Two policemen, in uniform and also in an advanced state of inebriation, staggered towards a place not altogether unfamiliar to them in times past, to seek the repose which their condition so urgently required . . . But the fates were against them. They were ignominiously thrust from the coveted shelter, and exposed to the derision of an amused group of onlookers.'[46]

The same paper returned to the issue of police ill-discipline later in the same year. Conceding that the police needed protection from 'rascaldom', its editorial stressed the need for magistrates to protect the public from the police. 'In too many cases the blow or the rough shake follows the word', it complained. Indications of dissatisfaction are also seen in the letters of complaint recorded in the minutes of the Watch Committee and the General Order Book. Some drew attention to the police using excessive force used in taking prisoners to or ejecting them from the police station.[47] More were concerned with the failure of the police to deal with a variety of nuisances. Following complaints, William Ashe was forced to remind his constables on a number of occasions in 1885 not to gossip and go with civilians but to ensure that footpaths were kept clear, stray cattle impounded and disturbances quelled. The vicar of St Hilda's church in the old town was upset by the failure of the police to stop 'riotous young men' from playing football, breaking windows, gambling and swearing.[48] Failure to keep the streets clear and quiet was a common cause of complaint. Young boys 'shouting and bawling' in the streets as they sold their newspapers on Sunday mornings were unpopular particularly with churchgoers. Young males were not the only cause of concern. Complaints were made about early carol singers and even the Salvation Army for obstructing the footpath and creating unacceptable noise on a Saturday night.[49] Other complainants were worried about the extent of immorality in the town. The police were asked to send out patrols at night to prevent 'couples committing immoral acts' in Ayresome Green Lane and to stop gambling in the Marsh Road and Stockton Street Recreation Grounds.[50] Occasionally, there are signs that the police were over-zealous. In November 1902 Ashe instructed his inspectors and sergeants to

> impress upon the constables under their charge the necessity of using discretion in dealing with persons standing on or obstructing the pathway. For instance two ladies or more examining goods in shop windows are not to be interfered with . . . All persons are to be treated with civility, forbearance and good temper by the Police.[51]

Despite recurring complaints, during the 1890s and 1900s there is evidence of a shift in the balance of opinion. For example, the number of instances of policemen being rewarded by grateful members of the public increased.[52] As noted earlier, the bravery of the police in dealing with fires, runaway horses and dangerous dogs brought praise from individuals and in the pages of the local press while the murder of PC Henderson, an exceptional event it is true, further revealed generosity towards the police when some £540 was collected in little over a month.[53] Early twentieth-century annual yearbooks, unsurprisingly, took a very positive stance. In 1901, which proved to be the last year of service of Chief Constable William Ashe, there was an eloquent comment not only on his career (and in particular his antipodean exploits) but also on the wider success of the force under his command.

> Few towns the size and character of Middlesbrough can boast of so little serious crime. Serious crimes of violence are practically unknown, while cases of housebreaking are very few and far between. The state of affairs is largely due to the increasing vigilance and the admirable organization of the Police Force.[54]

But if Ashe's achievements were seen as considerable those of the grammar school-educated Henry Riches were 'superhuman' as he 'thoroughly modernised the force and the police system generally'.[55] Similar sentiments were also to be found in the pages of the local press. The *North Eastern Daily Gazette*, for example, described Ashe as a 'benign' figure, exercising his considerable authority to ensure the 'protection and welfare of the people'. Although concerned with the level of drunkenness, the paper was encouraged by the decline in serious offences and the absence of a criminal class that, in turn, reflected positively on the work of the town police.[56]

As ever the evidence most readily available throws light on middle-class attitudes towards the police. The testimony of those most directly affected is rarely found in the official record. Occasionally there are tantalising hints. The accusation that PC Raisbeck was after money, when he caught a couple having sex, raises the question of police malpractice regarding prostitutes and their punters. Allegations of demands for protection money (or favours) being asked by the police were regularly made but little action taken. The Watch Committee was concerned that certain officers were too familiar with prostitutes and their pimps but only occasionally were there dismissals. Similarly, police tolerance of (and even collusion in) street betting was not done simply for a quiet life. Unfortunately, the scale of such activities are unknown. Hostility to the police was still to be found in certain districts. 'Over the border' in the old town was still the major location for criminal behaviour but Cannon Street had also acquired a reputation for violence against the police. Particularly in these districts there were 'well-known characters' and 'hooligans' who waged an intermittent war on the police. However, making long-term comparisons over the reign of Victoria (and particularly between the mid- and late-Victorian years) one is forcibly struck by the scale of change. Despite its continuing growth and despite the persistence of areas of considerable poverty and squalor, the town was a safer place to live in as the rate of crimes against property and the person declined. Middlesbrough could still be a violent and unsafe town but with a more disciplined and more experienced police force it was a securely policed town in a way that it had not been as late as the 1860s. The 'frontier town' had been conquered and disciplined. Credit for this is not easily apportioned. Change was in part generated from below and from within the predominantly working-class community. That community (or more accurately communities) became more stable over time as families grew up in Middlesbrough.[57] Modest, if irregular, increases in living standards, a wider range of leisure activities and new standards of behaviour contributed to a more disciplined and law-abiding society. Institutions (both religious and secular) played their part but so too did the Middlesbrough police force. A double transformation was achieved especially in the last quarter of the nineteenth century. Internally, it became a disciplined and mature force; externally, it neutralised much opposition and even won over some popular support. Neither transformation was total. Some early twentieth century policemen were inefficient, even corrupt – but not on the scale experienced 50 years before. Some Middlesbrough men and women in the early twentieth century loathed the police, more were suspicious – but not on the scale experienced 50 years before. As a consequence of these changes, as a consequence of the growing convergence of interests between a majority of the community and the police, Middlesbrough was transformed. The British Ballarat was no more.

Middlesbrough was not a typical Victorian town. Its peculiar economic and demographic characteristics set it apart but, despite its singularities, the town experienced, albeit in more acute form than most, more common problems of establishing the rule of law and of imposing order and decorum at a time of rapid urbanisation. The changes that took place in that somewhat grim part of the north-east of Yorkshire throw important light on the complex interplay of factors, involving local politicians and opinion-formers, the police and the policed communities, that ultimately led to the creation of a stable, policed society. Superficially, it is tempting to see Middlesbrough as something exceptional, a classic example of planning that went wrong, or at least was overwhelmed by unforeseen changes. To some extent this is true, particularly regarding the physical development of the town, but such a perspective can also be misleading. The intentions of the founding fathers to create a morally, as well as physically, ordered society were never abandoned. The continuing commitment of local political leaders, drawn initially from the iron masters but later from the local 'shopocracy', ensured that actions were taken to improve the security and decorum of the town. It is also the case that, over time, the community – and particularly its working-class components – adopted codes of behaviour that resulted in a less tumultuous and more law-abiding town. The passage of time in itself was a key element as the difficult-to-adapt-to novelties of industrial development, urban life and policing in the 1840s and 1850s turned into the routine and commonplace events of the 1890s and 1900s. But also, change was driven by the various men who comprised the town's police force. Whether almost-anonymous constables or well-known senior officers of standing in the town, these men – for all their imperfections – played a central role in the process of change. It is somewhat paradoxical that a group of men, who in the early years were seen as part of the problem, made (and had to make) a major contribution to its solution. The often flawed and poorly-trained beat constables of the nineteenth and early twentieth century, learning the skills of their trade by sheer hard experience and developing a *modus vivendi* with the communities they policed, were the men at the interface between the police and the public. The long-term success of policing rested in no small measure on their ability to develop tactics and a style of policing that enabled a heavily outnumbered body of men to enforce laws, and through them codes of behaviour, that emanated from the ruling elites and, furthermore, which were often viewed as irksome, if not alien, by those members of the working-classes who felt the 'force of the law' most directly. There was never total success. Some laws were too unpopular, some policemen too crass and clumsy (and worse) and some sections of society ignored or rejected the police and what they stood for. None the less, there were real successes. At the death of Victoria there was in Middlesbrough (and the country at large) a policed society in a way that simply did not exist in the early years of her reign. The police were an accepted, though not always respected, part of everyday life and they had played their part in establishing their position in society. To that extent, they played a more important role than their more-commonly praised seniors in the realisation of those aspirations to respectability and order that were to be found increasingly among working-class, as well as middle-class, society; to that extent the humble constable was the unsung hero in the complex process of creating a viable policed society not just in the British Ballarat but in the country at large.

Notes

Chapter 1: Introduction

1 C. Emsley, *The English Police: a political and social history*, Hemel Hempstead, 2nd edn, 1996, C. Steedman, *Policing the Victorian Community: the formation of the English provincial police forces from 1856 to 1880*, London, 1984, and R. Swift, 'Urban policing in early-Victorian England: a re-appraisal', *History*, 73, 1987. In addition, there are a large number of histories that provide useful detail of specific borough and county forces. For example, A. A. Clarke, *The Policemen of Hull*, Beverley, 1992, and *Country Coppers: the story of the East Riding Police*, Bridlington, 1993, B. J. Davey, *Lawless and Immoral: policing a county town, 1838–1857*, Leicester, 1983, and J. Woodgate, *The Essex Police*, Lavenham, 1983. See also D. Taylor, *The New Police in Nineteenth Century England: crime, conflict and control*, Manchester, 1997. In addition, there are a number of very valuable studies of the evolution of specific pieces of legislation, including E. A. Reynolds, *Before the Bobbies: the night watch and police reform in Metropolitan London, 1720–1830*, Basingstoke, 1998 and D. Philips and R. D. Storch, *Policing Provincial England, 1829–1856: the politics of reform*, Leicester, 1999.

2 V. A. C. Gatrell and T. B. Hadden, 'Criminal statistics and their interpretation', in E. A. Wrigley, ed., *Nineteenth-century Society: essays in the use of quantitative methods for the study of social data*, Cambridge, 1992. and V. A. C. Gatrell, 'The decline of theft and violence in Victorian and Edwardian England', in Gatrell, B. Lenman and G. Parker, eds., *Crime and the Law: a social history of crime in Western Europe since 1500*, London, 1980. See also the two books by G. Rude, *Protest and Punishment*, Oxford, 1978, and *Criminal and Victim: crime and society in early nineteenth-century England*, Oxford, 1985. For the broader context see Gatrell, 'Crime, authority and the policeman-state', in F. M. L. Thompson, ed., *The Cambridge Social History of Britain*, vol. 3, Cambridge, 1990, and F. M. L. Thompson, *The Rise of Respectable Society*, London, 1988.

3 D. Philips, *Crime and Authority in Victorian England*, London, 1977, which provides a powerful counterweight to the popular but misleading interpretation in J. J. Tobias, *Crime and Industrial Society in the Nineteenth Century*, London, 1972.

4 D. J. V. Jones, *Crime, Protest, Community and Police in Nineteenth-Century Britain*, London, 1982. See also his *Crime in Nineteenth-century Wales*, Cardiff, 1992.

5 A. Briggs, *Victorian Cities*, London, 1963, explicitly compared the growth of Middlesbrough with the notorious Australian frontier town of Ballarat. The dramatic industrialisation of this part of the north-east of England in the mid-nineteenth century transformed declining agricultural villages, such as Eston, and led to the creation of totally new industrial villages such as Tow Law. However, dramatic demographic growth was not simply caused by

industrialisation, as the development of Blackpool in the second half of the nineteenth century amply illustrates.

6 Briggs' *Victorian Cities* was one of the pioneering studies of urban development, and since its appearance a wealth of literature has followed, encompassing analysis of the creation of the built environment and of the social and political structures that emerged. For a thoughtful and succinct introduction see the editors' introduction to R. J. Morris and Richard Rodger, *The Victorian City: a reader in British urban history*, Harlow, 1993

7 The literature on industrialisation is overwhelming, but R. Floud and D. N. McCloskey, *The Economic History of Britain since 1700*, Cambridge, 1994, 2nd edn, provides an excellent introduction. See also N. F. R. Crafts, *British Economic Growth during the Industrial Revolution*, Oxford, 1985, E. A. Wrigley, *Continuity and Change: the character of the industrial revolution in England*, Cambridge, 1988, P. Hudson, *The Industrial Revolution*, London, Arnold, 1992, W. H. Fraser, *The Coming of the Mass Market*, Basingstoke, 1981, J. Benson, *The Rise of Consumer Society in Britain, 1880–1980*, London, 1994, and P. J. Cain and A. G. Hopkins, *British Imperialism: Innovation and Expansion, 1688–1914*, London, 1993.

8 An early study of Preston revealed that over half the population of the town in 1851 had been born outside the town. However, and notwithstanding a sizeable Irish population, almost three-quarters of the migrants had been born within some 30 miles of the town. M. Anderson, *Family Structure in Nineteenth Century Lancashire*, Cambridge, 1971.

9 D. Cannadine, *Class in Britain*, London, 2000, provides an excellent introduction to the extensive and complex literature on the subject. Cannadine, as well as arguing that the importance of class has been underplayed by recent historians preoccupied with 'the literary turn', claims (pp. 19–20) that there have been three 'basic and enduring models: the hierarchical view of society as a seamless web; the triadic version with upper, middle and lower collective groups; and the dichotomous, adversarial picture, where society is structured between "us" and "them".'

10 This is not to suggest that riots did not carry a potentially serious threat to order nor that everyone subscribed to the notion of the freeborn Englishman and his rights in every riot. However, there was a greater acceptance in the eighteenth century that some rioters had a claim to legitimacy as their actions could be seen as a defence of traditional rights. With the passage of time such recognition diminished and greater emphasis was placed on the threat to order posed by any rioters, irrespective of their cause.

11 The problems faced by London costermongers are well known to readers of Mayhew. The problem did not disappear in the mid-nineteenth century. The continuing appearance of ice-cream vendors before magistrates in various parts of the country provides a somewhat amusing index of the determination of local authorities to stamp out activities that disrupted the order and decorum of the streets. Similarly, the town police clauses, which were incorporated into many local improvement acts, contain a vision (never fully realised) of urban order. See also M. Ogborn, 'Ordering the city: surveillance, public space and the reform of urban policing in England, 1835–56', *Political Geography*, 12, 1993, and A. Croll, 'Street disorder,

surveillance and shame: regulating behaviour in the public spaces of the late-Victorian British town', *Social History*, 24, 1999.

12 R. B. Shoemaker, *Gender in English Society 1650–1850*, London, 1999, provides a good overview. See also J. Tosh, *A Man's Place: masculinity and the middle-class home in Victorian England*, London, 1999. More specifically see M. J. Wiener, 'Judges v jurors: courtroom tensions in murder trials and the law of criminal responsibility in nineteenth-century England', *Law and History Review*, 17, 1999, and 'The sad story of George Hall: adultery, murder and the politics of mercy in mid-Victorian England', *Social History*, 14, 1999.

13 The concern with drunk and disorderly behaviour is an obvious example, but note also the growing concern with 'indecent' behaviour in the increasingly well-lit streets. See M. J. D. Roberts, 'Public and private in early nineteenth century London: the vagrant act of 1822 and its enforcement', *Social History*, 13, 1988.

14 See e.g. the writings of the Reverend John Clay, chaplain to the Preston house of correction, Mary Carpenter, the Reverend Andrew Mearns, William Booth and the Reverend Osborn Jay.

15 Gatrell, 'Crime, authority and the policeman-state'.

16 Reynolds, *Before the Bobbies*.

17 Philips and Storch, *Policing Provincial England*. Steedman, *Policing the Victorian Community*.

18 The demographic, social and economic growth of the town is discussed more fully in Chapters 2 and 6 below.

19 4 & 5 Victoria, cap. LXVIII, 1841.

20 Ibid.

21 See fnn. 2 to 4 above and C. A. Williams, 'Counting crimes or counting people: some implications of mid-nineteenth century British police returns', *Crime, History & Societies*, 4, 2000.

22 H. Taylor, 'Rationing crime: the political economy of criminal statistics since the 1850s', *Economic History Review*, 51, 1998, p. 571. See also J. J. Tobias, *Crime and Industrial Society in the Nineteenth Century*, London, 1972, and R. Sindall, *Street Violence in the Nineteenth Century: Media Panic or Real Danger?*, Leicester, 1990, for earlier statements of a highly sceptical view of the value of recorded crime figures.

23 This point has recently been made by Williams, 'Counting crimes', but see also D. Taylor, 'Crime and policing in early-Victorian Middlesbrough, 1835–55', *Journal of Regional and Local Studies*, 11, 1991.

24 The absence of annual reports is less surprising given the observation in 1903 of the newly-appointed Chief Constable, Henry Riches, that he did not have 'a single Officer or Constable serving in the force who can prepare the Criminal Statistics as required by the Home Office': Printed Council Minutes, CB/M/C, 1/63, 29 Jan. 1903. Two years later he requested permission of the Watch Committee 'to destroy a number of old duty books etc. that are useless to the requirement of the service': CB/M/C, 1/65, 30 March 1905.

25 This view, popularised notably by Charles Reith in, for example, *A Short History of the British Police*, Oxford, 1948, was severely criticised by 'revisionist' historians who saw police reform more in terms of bourgeois attempts to regulate working-class life. However, few historians would now subscribe wholeheartedly to such an interpretation. Recent local studies suggest that

the concern with the threat of ordinary crime was of considerable impor-
tance in the growing demand for police reform from the 1830s onwards.
See Taylor, *The New Police* and especially Philips and Storch, *Policing
Provincial England.*

Chapter 2: The Birth of the 'Infant Hercules'

1 Parts of this chapter appeared in D.Taylor, 'The infant Hercules and the
   Augean Stables: a century of economic and social development in
   Middlesbrough, *c.* 1840–1939', in A. J. Pollard, ed., *Middlesbrough: town and
   community: 1830–1950*, Stroud, 1996. The classic short history of
   Middlesbrough is A. Briggs, 'Middlesbrough: the growth of a new community', reprinted in Pollard, *Middlesbrough*, but first published in 1963.
2 This was expanded to 11 acres in 1872.
3 There were also important developments in terms of the scale of operation
   and the technology used in the local industry. See Taylor, 'Infant Hercules',
   for a summary. More detailed technical information is contained in
   C. Hempstead, ed., *Cleveland Iron and Steel*, Teesside, 1979.
4 C. Postgate, *Middlesbrough, Its History, Environs and Trade*, Middlesbrough,
   1898, p. 23.
5 The following section draws heavily on J. W. Leonard, 'Urban and
   demographic change in Middlesbrough, 1841–1871', unpublished D.Phil.,
   University of York, 1974, and L. Polley, 'Housing the community,
   1830–1914', in Pollard, *Middlesbrough*.
6 Jones, *Crime in Nineteenth-Century Wales*, p. 93.
7 Cannon Street was not exclusively populated by the Irish and its experience
   is thus somewhat different to that found, for example, in Stafford Street,
   Wolverhampton. R. Swift, 'Another Stafford Street row', *Immigrants and
   Minorities*, 3, 1984.
8 L. Polley, *The Other Middlesbrough: a study of three nineteenth-century suburbs*,
   University of Teesside, 1993.
9 There is an anomaly in 1851 when the percentage of local-born heads of
   household increases, but this is explained by the slower population growth
   of the 1840s.
10 This issue is discussed in detail in R. Swift, 'Heroes or villains? The Irish,
   crime and disorder in Victorian England', *Albion*, 29, 1997.
11 Middlesbrough was not unique in this respect. St Helens, West Bromwich and
   West Ham were also more attractive to male than female immigrants during
   the nineteenth century. The prominence of young males is doubly significant.
   First, this was a group with a higher than average propensity to fall foul of the
   law, but it was also a group whose criminal inclinations were greatly exaggerated in the popular imagination. Further, the demographic development of
   the town was such that there was an above average percentage of young children and adolescents who also gave rise to concern. There were a number of
   general moral panics, notably in the 1840s and 1850s and again around the
   turn of the twentieth century. The latter panic is particularly interesting in
   that recorded juvenile crime was falling at the time. See Taylor, *Crime, Policing
   and Punishment*, pp. 62–4, for a brief discussion and further references.

12 W. Ranger, *Report to the General Board of Health on a preliminary enquiry into the sewerage, drainage, and supply of water, and the sanitary conditions of the inhabitants of the Borough of Middlesbrough in the North riding of the County of York*, 1854.
13 Briggs in Pollard, *Middlesbrough*, p. 6.
14 *Middlesbrough Weekly News*, 8 July 1864.

Chapter 3: The New Police in Middlesbrough

1 Some of the material in this chapter first appeared in D. Taylor, 'Crime and policing in early-Victorian Middlesbrough, 1835–55', *Journal of Regional and Local Studies*, 11, 1991.
2 D. Philips and R. D. Storch, 'Whigs and Coppers: the Grey ministry's national police scheme, 1832', *Historical Research*, 67, 1994.
3 Philips and Storch, *Policing Provincial England*, argue for the importance of the Rural Constabulary Act but, as they amply demonstrate, the debate about rural policing was complex. Even in counties such as Kent, where the need for reform was accepted, there was a powerful desire to develop existing forms of policing rather than move to a new system.
4 Cited in Anon., *1856–1956: the first hundred years of the North Riding of Yorkshire Constabulary*, Guisborough, Stokeld & Sons, n.d. (probably 1965), pp. 7–8.
5 Ibid., p. 8. In Durham almost three-quarters of the townships in the county petitioned – though unsuccessfully – for the disbanding of the police set up under the Rural Constabulary Act. Similar sentiments were expressed in other counties such as Bedfordshire. Emsley, *The English Police*, pp. 45–6.
6 Petition to the Worshipful Magistrates acting for the North Riding of Yorkshire in Quarter Session assembled, ibid., p. 9. Original in North Yorkshire County Record Office, Northallerton (NYCRO). Philips and Storch, *Policing Provincial England*, details the debate across the country.
7 *Middlesbrough Weekly News* (hereafter *MWN*), 31 March 1864.
8 Quarter Session Minute Books, 1837–57, Midsummer 1839 and Easter 1840. Microfilm reel 117, NYCRO.
9 Quarter Session Special Order Book, 1833–45, Easter Session 1839, Microfilm reel 119, NYCRO.
10 Cleveland Association for the Protection of Persons and Property and for the Prevention of Poaching and Vagrancy, Minute Book 1839–42, 19 Dec. 1839. Microfilm reel 1430, NYCRO.
11 The role of private prosecution associations is explored in P. King, 'Prosecution Associations and their impact in eighteenth-century Essex', and D. Philips, 'Good men to associate and bad men to conspire: associations for the prosecution of felons in England, 1760–1860', both in D. Hay and F. Synder, eds., *Policing and Prosecution in Britain, 1750–1850*, Oxford, 1989.
12 Improvement Act, 1841, 4 & 5 Victoria, cap. lxviii, para. ccxxiii, p. 1481. Cleveland County Archive, Middlesbrough, CB/M/P, 58.
13 Preamble to 4 & 5 Victoria, cap. LXVIII, 1841.

14 In addition to the provisions of the Improvement Act there were a further 22 specific by-laws that, in addition to the issues mentioned in the text, covered such things as hoisting goods to and from warehouses, washing or burning rags, bones and animal matter, exposing unsound meat for sale, the fraudulent sale of coal, permitting drains to become blocked, supplying alcoholic drink to children and bribing police officers.

15 Borough of Middlesbrough, Bye-Laws 1854 and 1868, CB/M/C 7/1.

16 Middlesbrough Improvement Commission Minute Book, 1846–53, 2 June 1848 and 6 Oct. 1848, CRO, CB/M/C, 1/2, pp. 95 and 107.

17 M. Stallion and D. S. Wall, *The British Police: Police Forces and Chief Officers, 1829–2000*, Gateshead, 1999.

18 *The Police and Constabulary List*, 1844, Police History Society, 1990. The ratio of police to population among the small boroughs and towns ranged from 1:2,000 or above in Bridnorth, Tavistock and Walsall to 1:700 or less in Evesham, Lyme Regis and Stamford. Middlesbrough's ratio was approximately 1:3,000.

19 'Recollections of Old Middlesbrough', *Weekly Gazette*, 2 Feb. 1889. Miscellaneous Newspaper Cuttings, CRO, CB/M/C, 12/1.

20 Middlesbrough Improvement Commission, Minutes, 1841–53, CB/M/C, 1/1, p. 144.

21 Ibid., p. 191.

22 Ibid., p. 193. Middlesbrough Improvement Commission Minute Book, 1846–53, CRO, CB/M/C, 1/2, p. 41.

23 Ord was not the first man employed by Bolckow & Vaughan to be sworn in as a constable. The first recorded instance, that of Thomas Kelly, dates from June 1847 (ibid., p. 11). Similarly, John Robinson, one of the police officers of the Stockton & Darlington Railway Co., was sworn in as a constable under the Improvement Act in February 1846.

24 Ibid., pp. 211 and 215.

25 Ibid., pp. 215 and 219.

26 Ibid., pp. 291, 318 and 321. Middlesbrough Commission, Light, Watching and Police Committee Minute Book, 1848–53, CB/M/C, 1/5, p. 37.

27 The situation was less clear than this suggests. In January 1844 the Improvement Commissioners' Minutes record the appointment as constable of Christopher Smith, William Peacock and Joseph Sedgwick. No conditions of service or salaries are specified and there is no further record of these men.

28 Middlesbrough Improvement Commission Minute Book, 1846–53, CB/M/C, 1/2, p. 72.

29 Ibid., pp. 11, 78, 79 and 89.

30 Ibid., pp. 142 and 143.

31 Ibid., p. 173.

32 Ibid., pp. 178–9 and 182–3.

33 William Buckton, for example, served for only two months in the winter of 1850/1, while Joseph Stainsby, one of the few men known to have previous police experience (with the Durham County Constabulary in this case), served for 12 months in 1851/2.

34 Davey, *Lawless and Immoral*.

35 *Report from the Select Committee on Police Superannuation Funds*, 1875 (352), vol. XV, Minutes of Evidence, Q.3249. The decision to increase wages in 1857, for example, is detailed in CB/M/C 2/100 24 May 1857.

36 This is discussed in detail in D. R. Welsh, 'The reform of urban policing in Victorian England: a study of Kingston upon Hull from 1836 to 1866', unpublished Ph.D. dissertation, University of Hull, 1997.

37 This does not imply equality. Watch Committees, especially in northern industrial towns, regarded policemen in general as workers and chief constables as trusted but inferior men. Steedman, *Policing the Victorian Community*, pp.44–6. D. S. Wall, *The Chief Constables of England and Wales: the socio-legal history of a criminal justice elite*, Aldershot, Dartmouth, 1998, p. 94.

38 Welsh, 'The reform of urban policing'.

39 Borough of Middlesbrough, Minutes of the Watch, Police and Lighting Committee, 1853–9 [hereafter Middlesbrough Watch Committee], CB/M/C, 2/100, pp. 2 and 3, 19 April 1853 and 6 July 1853.

40 Unfortunately the minutes of the Improvement Commission and the Borough Watch Committee make but tantalisingly oblique references to Hannan's previous career.

41 Middlesbrough Watch Committee, CB/M/C, 2/100, p. 3, 19 May 1853.

42 Ibid., p. 8, 24 Aug. 1853.

43 Ibid., p. 24, 6 June 1854.

44 Ibid., p. 36, 19 Oct. 1854.

45 Ibid., p. 49, 20 Feb. 1855.

46 Ibid., p. 53, 20 March 1855.

47 A similar practice was to be found in Merthyr Tydfil. Jones, 'The conquering of "China": crime in an industrial community, 1842–64', in *Crime, Protest, Community*, p. 92.

48 Middlesbrough Watch Committee, CB/M/C, 2/100, p. 53, 20 March 1855.

49 Vaughan to Middlesbrough Town Council, 14 Dec. 1858, reported in *Stockton and Hartlepool Mercury*, 18 Dec. 1858. He also pointed out that it was deliberate policy to keep changing the individual constable so that 'there would not be much chance of his becoming known'.

50 Ibid., p. 83, 21 August 1856

51 Middlesbrough Watch Committee, 25 June 1861 and 9 October 1863

52 The first detective officer had been appointed in 1859 but there was no expansion in numbers for this aspect of police work until much later in the century.

53 *Middlesbrough Exchange* [hereafter *ME*], 25 June 1869.

54 Middlesbrough Watch Committee, CB/M/C, 2/100, 6 Aug. 1857.

55 Middlesbrough Watch Committee, 19 April 1860, CB/M/C, 2/101, p. 17. *Select Committee on Police Superannuation Funds*, Q.3228. Isaac Wilson was convinced that a proper superannuation scheme would improve the efficiency of the force as well as offering proper rewards for long-serving men. See QQ.3246–8.

56 Middlesbrough Watch Committee, 8 Feb. 1864, CB/MC/C, 2,101.

57 Ibid., 20 Nov. 1865.

58 *MWN*, 14 April 1865. Complaints from below continued. See for example the demand for a merit class for both constables and sergeants. Middlesbrough Watch Committee, 15 Nov. 1872.

59 *Select Committee on Police Superannuation Funds*, Q.3234.

60 Ibid.

61 Despite talk of 'new' police, officers such as Bowes still carried out old township functions.

62 This excludes Edward J. Saggerson, who was appointed Superintendent of Police in 1861, having previously risen to the rank of inspector in the Oldham force, and who served for 23 years in Middlesbrough.

63 *MWN*, 5 Feb. 1876.

64 *Middlesbrough Daily Gazette*, 15 Dec. 1875.

65 *MWN*, 12 Feb. 1876.

66 *MWN*, 22 April 1876.

67 *The Dominie*, 22 April 1876.

68 *MWN*, 12 Aug. 1876.

69 Report of Her Majesty's Inspector of Constabulary, 1859, pp. 68, 70 and 71.

70 Ibid., 1868. Isaac Wilson was proud of the Watch Committee's reputation for being 'very strict with our men' and the fact that 'we have always been well reported upon by the Government inspector'. *Select Committee on Police Superannuation Funds*, Q.3249.

Chapter 4: The British Ballarat?

1 See for example V. A. C. Gatrell, *The Hanging Tree: execution and the English people, 1770–1868*, Oxford, 1994, and Philips, *Crime and Authority in Victorian England*, London, 1977, esp. ch. 2.

2 Philips, *Crime and Authority*, pp. 5,14, 179 and 266.

3 Rude, *Criminal and Victim*, Oxford, 1985. Though stressing the 'somewhat modest role of crimes of violence in the record of metropolitan crime', he does concede that victims could find the experience of violent robbery terrifying (p. 29).

4 Jones, 'Conquering "China"', p. 111.

5 H. Taylor, 'Rationing crime', esp. p. 578. See also Introduction pp. 10–11.

6 Gatrell and Hadden, 'Criminal statistic'; Philips, *Crime and Authority*, esp. chs 6–8.

7 There were also an above-average number of women brought to trial in the iron towns of south Wales. Jones, *Crime, Protest, Community*, p. 7.

8 J. W. Leonard, 'Urban and demographic change in Middlesbrough, 1841–1871', unpublished D.Phil. dissertation, University of York, 1975.

9 R. Swift, 'Heroes or Villains?', p. 401.

10 Philips, *Crime and Authority*, p. 260.

11 This is not to suggest that these figures give an accurate representation of the incidence of the various crimes listed in the table. Crimes of violence against women (sexual and non-sexual) were notoriously under-recorded.

12 Middlesbrough Watch Committee, 9 June 1870, pp. 282–4.

13 The following examples are all drawn from the Northallerton Calendar of Prisoners, 1830–99, North Yorkshire County Record Office, Northallerton, MIC 1454.

14 Thomas Kneeshaw, likewise, appeared on a number of occasions at Northallerton. James Wilson was prosecuted for the theft of a jacket and William Crosby for the theft of a pair of trousers in 1843. Thirteen years later Mary Atkins, a 50-year-old married woman, was charged with the theft of a cloth cap and a pair of flannel drawers from his shop.

15 *MWN*, 11 Dec. 1864.

16 Taylor, *Crime, Policing and Punishment*, pp. 41–3, for a brief discussion and further references.
17 See for example the cases of John Carroll (1841), James Leach (1840) and James Morris (1854), all labourers accused of stealing shovels.
18 Among the women prosecuted for the theft of coal by the Stockton & Darlington Railway Company, Mary Spenceley was charged with stealing 19 pounds in 1850. Ellen Patton 76 pounds in 1848 and Mary Short 86 pounds in 1848. Andrew Joseph was prosecuted for stealing the relatively small quantity of 5 pounds of coal but Robert Cowley was more ambitious, stealing 18 stone of coal in 1851.
19 S. Chapman, *The Early Factory Masters: the transition to the factory system in the midlands textile industry*, Newton Abbott, 1967; D. Hay, 'Manufacturers and the criminal law in the later eighteenth century: crime and "police" in South Staffordshire', *Past and Present Colloquialism on Police and Policing*, 1983; D. Philips, 'The Black Country magistracy, 1835–60: a changing elite and the exercise of its power', *Midland History*, 3, 1976, and *Crime and Authority*, esp. ch. 6; and R. H. Trainor, *Black Country Elites, the exercise of authority in an industrialized area, 1850–1900*, Oxford, 1993.
20 B. Godfrey, 'Law, factory discipline and "theft": the impact of the factory on workplace appropriation in mid to late nineteenth-century Yorkshire', *British Journal of Criminology*, 39, 1999, and 'Judicial impartiality and the use of criminal law against labour: the sentencing of workplace appropriators in Northern England, 1840–1880', *Crime, History & Societies*, 3, 1999.
21 The situation in Middlesbrough has more in common with Merthyr. Here the Dowlais Iron Company was the major force in bringing prosecutions for industrial theft.
22 *Middlesbrough Weekly News (MWN)*, 4 Aug. 1865.
23 *Stockton, Guardian, & Middlesbrough Times* [hereafter *SGMT*], 21 March 1862.
24 Ibid. 26 Dec. 1862. In the first case the youngest of the accused was sentenced to one year's hard labour and five years in the reformatory at Castle Howard. In March of the same year another rape case involving three men in their twenties was also tried at York, but all three were found not guilty.
25 C. Conley, *The Unwritten Law: criminal justice in Victorian Kent*, Oxford, 1991, p. 67.
26 *MWN*, 6 Oct. 1865.
27 This is discussed further in Chapter 5.
28 Suicide is a topic worthy of extended research, but one that falls outside the scope of the present study. The best general introduction is O. Anderson, *Suicide in Victorian and Edwardian England*, Oxford, 1987. For an impressive detailed study of suicides in one city (Hull) see V. Bailey, *This Rash Act: suicide across the life cycle in the Victorian city*, Stanford, 1998. As the title indicates, Bailey is particularly concerned with the vulnerabilities associated with certain stages of the life-cycle, such as early old age for men. However, he also stresses, contrary to Anderson, the importance of social isolation as a cause of suicide. Anderson makes one reference to Middlesbrough in the context of a general reference to suicide rates being lowest in fastest growing towns. *Suicide*, p. 93. It is not entirely clear that this optimistic statement holds true. See Chapter 8.
29 *MWN*, 18 Nov. 1864 and 6 July 1866.

30 A. C. Postgate, *Middlesbrough: its history, environs and trade*, Middlesbrough, 1898, p. 39.

31 See e.g. the editorial comment on the annual report of the chief constable in the *MWN*, 21 Oct. 1864.

32 *MWN*, 14 Jan. 1860.

33 *MWN*, 8 Jan. 1859.

34 *MWN*, 8 July 1864.

35 *MWN*, 14 June 1867.

36 *ME*, 26 Feb. 1869.

37 *MWN*, 12 April 1867.

38 *SGMT*, 11 April 1862.

39 *MWN*, 21 Oct. 1864. Fall was sentenced to a month's hard labour for his 'cowardly and inhuman' conduct.

40 *MWN*, 29 April 1864.

41 See e.g. the cases reported in 1859: *MWN*, 8 and 15 Jan., 5 Feb., 26 April., 7 and 14 May, 16 July, 13 and 20 Aug., 10, 17 and 24 Sept., 1, 8, 15 and 22 Oct., 5, 19 and 26 Nov., 3, 17 and 31 Dec. Similar examples can be found from other years.

42 N. Tomes, 'A "torrent of abuse": crimes of violence between working-class men and women in London, 1840–1875', *Journal of* Social History, 11, 1978. See also E. Ross, '"Fierce questions and taunts": married life in working-class London, 1870–1914', *Feminist Studies*, 8, 1983, and *Love and Toil*, Oxford, 1993; C. Bauer and L. Ritt, '"A husband is a beating animal" – Frances Power Cobbe confronts the wife-abuse problem in Victorian England', *International Journal of Women's Studies*, 6, 1983, and 'Wife-abuse, late-Victorian English feminists and the legacy of Frances Power Cobbe', ibid., and A. J. Hammerton, *Cruelty and Companionship: conflict in nineteenth-century married life*, London, 1992. See also Conley, *Unwritten Law*, on the ambivalence of the police.

43 In this respect the distinction that Conley observes in Kent between acceptable and unacceptable violence holds. See also the collection of essays edited by S. D'Cruze, *Everyday Violence in Britain, 1850–1900*, London, 2000.

44 For instance, William McCormick and Hugh Garon were both fined 10s. (50p) for taking part in an arranged prize fight in Stockton Street: *MWN*, 21 May 1859.

45 *MWN*, 5 Nov. 1859 and 9 Sept. 1864.

46 In the most serious outbreak of fighting between men of Connaught and men of Cork two men were stabbed to death and three subsequently tried at the York assize. *MWN*, 9 June and 4 Aug. 1865. For assaults on the police see Chapter 5.

47 *MWN*, 22 Oct. 1859 and 2 June 1860. In another case tried summarily Robert Messiter was charged with an assault on Jessy Bone which resulted in the latter losing three teeth and suffering severe wounds to the head and body. *SGMT*, 15 Sept. 1860.

48 *MWN*, 8 July 1864 and 21 April 1865.

49 Conley, *Unwritten Law*, p. 79.

50 *MWN*, 5 Feb. 1859.

51 *MWN*, 10 Sept. 1859.

52 *MWN*, 12 March 1859.

53 *MWN*, 13 Aug. 1859.
54 *MWN*, 6 Oct. 1865. The paper was particularly concerned that the court-room incident arose out of 'another serious case of stabbing, or cutting and wounding, arising out of those beer-houses frays so common in the town.'
55 *MWN*, 13 Aug. 1859.
56 *MWN*, 29 April 1864.
57 *MWN*, 14 May 1859, 23 March 1861, 11 May 1861 and 8 March 1867.
58 *MWN*, 15 and 22 Jan. 1859. See also, in the same period, 5 Feb., 12 March, 16 July, 13 Aug., 17 Sept., 8 Oct., 19 Nov., 3 Dec. 1859; 4 Feb., 2 and 9 June, 21 July, 8 Sept., 17 Nov. 1860. Men were also given the option. See e.g. George Thomas, 5 Feb. 1859, or Patrick Kelly, 3 March 1860. Michael Mulvey declined such an offer and was fined 7s. (35p), 3 March 1860.
59 *MWN*, 28 May and 30 July 1859.
60 *MWN*, 14 May 1859.
61 For a discussion of police attitudes to prostitution in London see S. Petrow, *Policing Morals: the Metropolitan Police and the Home Office, 1870–1914*, Oxford, 1994, part 3.
62 *MWN*, 24 Aug. 1864.
63 George Chapman, the unfortunate sailor, was fined 10s. (50p) for this escapade. *MWN*, 3 Sept. 1859. More generally, complaints about soliciting were commonplace in the press. See e.g. *MWN*, 28 Sept. 1861. The Brownless/Brierly case was reported in the *SGMT*, 12 Feb. 1864. For similar incidents see *MWN*, 11 Dec. 1868 for misconduct in Albert Park.
64 *MWN*, 28 July 1860.
65 *MWN*, 6 April 1871.
66 *MWN*, 22 Jan. 1859.
67 For examples see *MWN*, 7 Feb. 1861 or 21 Feb. 1862.
68 *MWN*, 2 April 1869.
69 *MWN*, 21 Sept. 1861. See also Middlesbrough Watch Committee, 1 May 1861, p. 229.
70 For examples see *MWN*, 15 Jan. 1859 and 18 Feb. 1860.
71 *SGMT*, 10 Jan. 1862, 16 Jan. 1863 for examples.
72 *MWN*, 8 Jan. 1859. James Hester stole a piece of beef from an eating-house window at 5 a.m. on New Year's Day. For thefts of turnips see 28 Sept. 1861 and 15 Nov. 1867.
73 *MWN*, 2 Feb. 1861.
74 *MWN*, 4 Aug. 1860.
75 *MWN*, 22 Jan. 1859.
76 *SGMT*, 21 Feb. 1861.
77 Middlesbrough Watch Committee, 10 May 1856.
78 Middlesbrough Watch Committee, 11 Oct. 1858, p. 136.
79 See e.g. Middlesbrough Watch Committee, 29 Sept. 1864, 18 April 1868, 8 April 1869 and 14 Nov. 1867. Similar confident reports were given on a further five occasions in both 1868 and 1869.
80 Of over 900 incidents reported in the local press in the 1860s, only 77 (8 per cent) were located south of the old town. A further 24 took place in two streets just to the south of the railway. Of the 53 incidents that took place in Linthorpe Road it is impossible to say how many took place at the northern end. Over 70 per cent took place on Saturday and Sunday.

Chapter 5: The Police and the Public

1   Davey, *Lawless and Immoral*, Steedman, *Policing the Victorian Community*, Swift, 'Urban policing', Storch, 'The plague of blue locusts'. Although Storch quotes incidents of popular resistance to Superintendent Heaton's 'Crusade' in Huddersfield, a more detailed examination of the local press reveals relatively few anti-police incidents. Indeed, there is evidence of support for Heaton's determination to clean up the Castlegate district of the town.

2   W. L. Melville Lee, *A History of Police in England*, London, 1901; C. Reith, *The Police Idea*, Oxford, 1938, *The British Police and the Democratic Ideal*, Oxford, 1943, *A Short History of the British Police*, Oxford, 1948, *A New Study of Police History*, London, 1956; L. Radzinowicz, *A History of Criminal Law*, 4 vols, London, 1948, 1956 & 1968. T. A. Critchley, *A History of Police in England and Wales*, London, 1967; Emsley, *The English Police: a political and social history* and R. Reiner, *The Politics of the Police*, Hemel Hempstead, 1992. On social control see A. P. Donajgrodzki, ed., *Social Control in Nineteenth-Century Britain*, London, 1977, and R. D. Storch, ed., *Popular Culture in Nineteenth-Century Britain*, London, 1982.

3   *MWN*, 6 May 1864.

4   There is no direct evidence to support this last claim, but interviews with ex-policemen who served in the early twentieth century suggests that they (and their predecessors about whom they reminisced) thought in this way. A similar point has been made about twentieth-century policemen by Barbara Weinberger, *The Best Police in the World: an oral history of English policing*, Cambridge, 1995, p. 157.

5   Storch, 'Plague of blue locusts'.

6   North Riding of Yorkshire, General Quarter Session, 16 Oct. 1855.

7   Middlesbrough Watch Committee, 6 June 1854, 19 Oct. 1854 and 8 Dec. 1857.

8   Middlesbrough Watch Committee, 29 Jan. 1856.

9   Ibid., 8 Oct. 1868.

10   Swift, 'Another Stafford Street row', and 'Crime and the Irish in nineteenth-century Britain', in R. Swift and S. Gilley, eds, *The Irish in Britain, 1815–1939*, London, 1989. See also G. Davis, *The Irish in Britain, 1815–1914*, Dublin, 1991, and F. Finnegan, *Poverty and Prejudice: a study of Irish immigrants in York, 1840–1875*, Cork, 1982.

11   J. Davis, 'From "rookeries" to "community": race, poverty and policing in London, 1850–1985', *History Workshop Journal*, 27, 1989.

12   C. Emsley and M. Clapson, 'Recruiting the English Policeman', *Policing and Society*, 3, 1991.

13   *MWN*, 6 May 1864.

14   Ibid., 6 Oct. 1864.

15   Middlesbrough Watch Committee, 8 Oct. 1868, pp. 225–6.

16   *MWN*, 6 Jan. 1865.

17   *Idem.* See also the incident in 1860 in which PC Hughes was 'knocked down by some person in the crowd' to facilitate the rescue of a drunk who had been arrested, *MWN*, 19 July 1860; or the arrest and trial of the Keogan brothers for drunk and riotous behaviour. It was alleged that John Keogan

had 'excited a mob and attempted a rescue', clearly without success. *MWN*, 6 May 1864. PC Stainsby, not for the last time, was less fortunate. A crowd 'fell on him and struck him on different parts of his body [while] one of his assailants cried out "Knife the b****r"'. *MWN*, 2 Aug. 1864.

18 *MWN,* 8 Jan. 1858.
19 The evidence for Middlesbrough is less than clear-cut. The lack of evidence might betoken a high degree of organisation. One local Catholic priest, Father Burns, was convinced that Fenianism was rife in the town. Burns' attitude (which contrasted with the support for the Land League and Home Rule by his rival, Father Lacey) may well have driven some of his parishioners into the ranks of the fenians.
20 *MWN*, 4 Oct. 1867.
21 *MWN*, 11 Oct. 1867. Middlesbrough Watch Committee, 3 Oct. 1867.
22 *MWN*, 22 Dec. 1865. See also 5 May 1870 for a 'cowardly assault on a policeman' which resulted in scalp wounds for PC Bellamy after a violent struggle with a labourer, John Harding. The paper also reported an incident which involved PC Brown being kicked several times on the body and face, but this did not merit an attention-grabbing headline.
23 *MWN*, 15 March 1867. Robinson appeared at the York Assize charged with stabbing with intent to kill Amos Garbutt and with inflicting grievous bodily harm while resisting arrest, for which he received 5 years' penal servitude.
24 *MWN*, 8 Jan. 1859.
25 *SGMT*, 7 Feb. 1868, 1 May 1868. *MWN*, 6 May 1864 and 23 Aug. 1867.
26 In 1861 there had been 31, by 1868 the number had risen to 127, of whom 51 had been summoned and 48 convicted. Annual Report of Superintendent of police year ending 29 Sept. 1868. Middlesbrough Watch Committee, 1859–72, CB/M/C, 2/10 1, p. 229.
27 Ibid., 6 Jan. 1879.
28 Annual Report of Superintendent Saggerson, Middlesbrough Watch Committee, 29 Sept. 1861
29 *MWN*, 31 Dec. 1869 and 6 Sept. 1867.
30 *MWN*, 2 July 1869.
31 *MWN*, 4 Feb. 1860, 20 Sept. 1867, and 8 Nov. 1867. Similar incidents took place at other theatres, see e.g. 12 Nov. 1869 for a typical incident at the Royal Albert theatre.
32 *MWN*, 24 Sept. 1859 (the three men involved were each fined £5 for this attack), 29 Dec.1860 and 2 Sept. 1864..
33 *MWN*, 18 Feb., 31 March and 30 June 1860.
34 *MWN*, 5 July 1867 and 12 Nov. 1869. See also the report of a gang attack on the police in July 1872, *ME*, 4 July 1872.
35 Unfortunately the Watch Committee minutes do not detail the time lost from work as a result of such assaults. One can but speculate on both the short- and long-term effects.
36 Attacks upon individual policemen are open to differing interpretations. Inspector Thorpe, as he became, may have been assaulted 9 times because he was an assiduous and long-serving officer, but he might also have received more than his fair share of assaults because he was unpopular. It is impossible to say which is the more convincing interpretation, but anecdotal

evidence relating to early twentieth-century Middlesbrough indicates quite clearly that unpopular policemen were singled out for attack. See Middlesbrough Watch Committee, 25 June 1861, for a warning from Superintendent Saggerson that over-reaction by inexperienced officers led to serious consequences for the police.

37 *MWN*, 14 Oct. 1860. See also 24 Sept. 1859 for a similar incident.
38 C. Emsley, '"The Thump of Wood on a Swede Turnip": police violence in nineteenth century England', *Criminal Justice History*, 6, 1985, p. 143.
39 Ibid., p. 143.
40 *MWN*, 13 Aug. 1859.
41 For example, Samuel Bowes and Thomas James Ray. Midlesbrough Watch Committee, 1859–72. CB/M/C, 2/100, pp. 166 and 189.
42 Middlesbrough Watch Committee, 17 Feb. 1859, p. 146.
43 *MWN*, 23 Nov. 1866.
44 *MWN*, 25 Aug. 1865.
45 *Idem.*
46 Middlesbrough Watch. Committee, 14 Aug. 1865.
47 *MWN*, 1 Sept. 1865.
48 *MWN*, 8, 15 and 22 Feb. 1867.
49 *MWN*, 12 April 1867.
50 *SGMT*, 21 Nov. 1862.
51 *MWN*, 6 May 1864.
52 *MWN*, 8 July 1864.
53 *MWN*, 28 July 1860.
54 *MWN*, 12 April and 17 June 1867.
55 *MWN*, 17 March 1860.
56 *MWN*, 23 Nov. 1866.
57 *MWN*, 25 Aug. 1865.
58 H. R. P. Gamon, *The London Police Court Today and Tomorrow*, London, 1907, p. 25; see also S. Reynolds and B. and T. Woolley, *Seem So! A working-class view of politics*, London, 1911 and R. Roberts, *The Classic Slum*, London, 1971, for similar views.
59 *MWN*, 19 June 1868.
60 *MWN*, 17 July 1868.
61 See for example Middlesbrough Improvement Commission, Minute Book, 1841–53, CB/M/C, 1/1, 2 Sept. 1842. Middlesbrough Watch Committee, 14 Oct. 1856, May 1862 and 9 Sept. 1869.
62 For specific responses to particular middle-class fears regarding protection of property and Sunday drinking see Middlesbrough Watch Committee, 19 Oct. 1854 and 12 Sept. 1859.
63 *MWN*,4 Aug. 1860. See also 18 Feb. 1860.
64 *MWN*, 7 Dec. 1861.

Chapter 6: Urban and Industrial Growth

1 Much of this material is drawn from D. Taylor, 'The infant Hercules and the Augean Stables: a century of economic and social development in Middlesbrough, c.1840–1939', in A. J. Pollard, ed., *Middlesbrough: town and*

community, 1830–1950, Stroud, 1996. See also L. Polley, 'Housing the community, 1830–1914', also in Pollard, ed., *Middlesbrough*.
2 For further details of the consolidation and rationalisation of steel production in Middlesbrough, see Taylor 'Infant Hercules', p. 63.
3 P. Mathias, *The Retailing Revolution*, London, 1969; Fraser, *The Coming of the Mass Market*; and J. Benson, *The Rise of Consumer Society*.
4 D. Taylor, 'The Jamaican banana: or how to be a successful businessman in nineteenth-century Middlesbrough', *Bulletin of the Cleveland and Teesside Local History Society*, 1982.
5 Lady Bell, *At the Works: a study of a manufacturing town*, London, 1907.
6 A. A. Hall, 'Wages, earnings and real earnings in Teesside: a reassessment of the ameliorist interpretation of living standards in Britain, 1870–1914', *International Review of Social History*, 1981.
7 Cited in J. J. Turner, 'The frontier revisited: thrift and fellowship in the new industrial town, c.1830–1914', in Pollard, ed., *Middlesbrough*.

Chapter 7: Expansion and professionalisation

1 Steedman's major study finishes in 1880. See also W. J. Lowe, 'The Lancashire Constabulary, 1845–1870: the social and occupational function of a Victorian police force', *Criminal Justice History*, 4, 1983, and Swift, 'Urban policing'.
2 Emsley, *English Police*. Reiner, *The Politics of the Police*, provides a detailed analysis of the rise of police legitimacy after 1856.
3 H. Shpayer-Makov, 'The making of a police labour force', *Journal of Social History*, 26, 1990; 'A portrait of a novice constable in the London Metropolitan Police, c. 1900', *Criminal Justice History*, 12, 1991, and 'Career prospects in the London Metropolitan Police in the early twentieth century', *Journal of Historical Sociology*, 4, 1991; but see Welsh, 'The reform of urban policing'.
4 As in the earlier years, several local firms employed their own police officers. This practice peaked in the mid-1870s when the number of privately paid constables was equivalent to some 50 per cent of the authorized establishment. Thereafter numbers fell, but even in the early twentieth century privately paid policemen were equivalent in number to one-tenth of the official force.
5 Printed Council Minutes [hereafter PCM], CB/M/C, 1/63, 26 Feb. 1903.
6 Taylor, *The New Police*, pp. 77–82. T. Jefferson and R. Grimshaw, *Controlling the Constable: Police accountability in England and Wales*, London, 1984.
7 The interventions of the Watch Committee often involved relatively minor matters. For example, Chief Constable Ashe was ordered to issue a notice regarding the throwing of orange peel on the flags, the use of bad language in the streets, and to take action to stop children obstructing the footpaths. Middlesbrough Watch Committee, 29 March 1884, 30 May 1893 and 30 June 1898.
8 It is almost certain that those men for whom full career information is not available left within weeks or months of enlisting. Adjusting the figures on this assumption, almost 60 per cent of recruits in the 1850s and 1860s

served less than one year compared with 10 per cent of recruits in the 1880s and 1890s.

9 Figures for selected years in the 1870s show 21 per cent and 35 per cent of recruits serving for 5 years or more in Buckinghamshire and 24 per cent in Staffordshire (cf. Middlesbrough 31 per cent for 1870s), and for 1880 show 23 per cent and 44 per cent respectively (cf. Middlesbrough 48 per cent for 1880s): Steedman, *Policing the Victorian Community*, pp. 93–4. Some 30 per cent of recruits in Wolverhampton in 1859 served for 5 years or more. Philips, *Crime and Authority*, p. 68.

10 The absence of information, especially for the early years, is particularly frustrating. It is likely that the social origins of the local police force were similar to the social origins of the unskilled and semi-skilled men of the town, and would therefore have included men drawn for more distant parts of the country. It is difficult to see a pattern to the distribution of birth-places. Some men came from predominantly agricultural counties (Norfolk, Suffolk and Lincolnshire but also Devon), others came from industrial areas (Blackburn, Leicester, Liverpool, Leeds and Oldham) and yet others came, though not in great numbers, from London, Bombay and Philadelphia. Only a minority had served in the armed forces. For a general discussion of recruitment patterns among nineteenth-century English policemen see C. Emsley and M. Clapson, 'Recruiting the English Policeman, c. 1840–1940', *Policing and Society*, 3, 1994.

11 14 Nov. 1908, CB/M/C, 1/69.

12 Annual Report, 1913, CB/M/C, 1/74.

13 Riches was instrumental in June 1905 in making permanent the appointment of PC Morton, who was described as being 'an excellent photographer and one who is competent to take finger prints'. CB/M/C, 1/65, 29 June 1905.

14 *North Eastern Daily Gazette*, 16 Feb. 1900.

15 There was little clear-cut seasonal variation in the figures. Resignations were spread more or less evenly across the year with peaks in June and December.

16 Constables' Conduct Registers, CB/M/P, 32.

17 For example, L. Gott, F. Metcalf and J. Wood.

18 For example, A. F. Black, W. Gibbon, E. Hall, F. Smales and J. Turner.

19 For example, K. Garner and F. Pattison.

20 William Hannan, who had done so much to transform policing in Middlesbrough in the 1850s, also took a sideways shift, becoming chief constable of Huddersfield in 1862.

21 Cooper was superannuated after the annual inspection in 1881 'in conse-quence of his age and long service'. He was 55 years old and 'incapable from infirmity of body and mind'(Middlesbrough Watch Committee, 26 July 1881). Edward Saggerson was also broken in body when he retired. Although the worst cases of infirmity were to be found under men who served in the early days of the force, there were a number of sad cases found among later policemen. Chronic rheumatism and defective vision ended the career of Sergeant Peacock in 1907, while PC Oakley was incapacitated by sciatica in 1910. PC Bate was more fortunate and was able to continue despite his 'Tuberculus Inflammation' of the right testicle. PCM, CB/M/C, 1/67, 28 March 1907 and CB/M/C, 1/71, 21 Nov. 1910.

22 All the examples in the following paragraph are taken from the Constables' Conduct Registers.

23 For example, PC Hogg was dismissed (1883) for being drunk in the Victoria public house. See also PCs Hewitt and Wilson – the latter combined drunkenness with sick leave. In the late nineteenth century dismissals were often for the second offence – see PC Anderson and PC Gant dismissed in 1876 and 1874 respectively. PC Spark was treated with surprising leniency. He was dismissed for drunkenness and neglect of duty after a 17-year career punctuated by drink-related disciplinary offences and periods of sick leave. It would appear that (unsurprisingly) there was a drink culture among the town's policemen.

24 PC McKenzie fell asleep in the town railway station, PC Marsey in a cabin and probationer PC Barker in the Linthorpe Police Station during his half-hour supper break. PC Reveley was dismissed with disgrace (1893), having been found drunk on duty in a public house and later asleep in a cabin at the Newport Ironworks.

25 PC Brown assaulted a woman member of the public. PC Magee was found guilty of wife beating and PC Bickley smashed the window of his inspector's office.

26 See for example PC Laraman, who was dismissed in 1894. His gambling was compounded by drunkenness while on duty at the Theatre Royal.

27 PCM, CB/M/C, 2/105 21 Dec. 1910.

28 For a more detailed account see D. Taylor, 'The standard of living of career policemen in Victorian England: the evidence of a provincial borough force', *Criminal Justice History*, 12, 1991.

29 The successful men were: 1870s – William Nunn, William Peacock and Frederick Knowlson; 1880s – Richard Blakeborough, Robert Grey, Robert Hall, William Milestone and John Stones; 1890s – Robert Hird, Matthew Hodgson and William Seymour.

30 J. P. Martin and G. Wilson, *The Police: a study in manpower*, London, 1969, pp. 29–32. Obviously the average could obscure considerable variations. In both the Buckinghamshire and Staffordshire forces in the third quarter of the nineteenth century promotion to sergeant could take as long as 20 years. Steedman, *Policing the Victorian Community*, pp. 106–7.

31 Most sergeants were men of good character but there were exceptions. Robert Sparks' career was undermined by a drink problem that led to demotion and, eventually, dismissal. James Waller was promoted to sergeant at the age of 38 after 10 years' service. It appears that frustration at the absence of further promotion led to drink-related disciplinary problems. An assault on a fellow officer finally ended his career.

32 See also the career of James Hanson, though in his case death rather than dismissal terminated a career punctuated with drink-related offences.

33 There is evidence from other parts of the country, notably London, that disciplinary standards were eased in the latter part of the nineteenth century.

34 The position continued largely unchanged in the early twentieth century. Just under 40 per cent of the recruits who joined between 1900 and 1904 served 10 years or more before the disruption brought about by the Great War. Of these men, approximately 30 per cent were promoted once or more, i.e. an almost identical figure to that for the 1890s. This compares with

figures for London which show that, excluding short-stay men, roughly 25 per cent of recruits were promoted to sergeant, of whom two-thirds stayed at that rank. Shpayer-Makov, 'Career prospects . . .' pp. 393 and 398.
35 Taylor, *The New Police*, pp. 68–9.
36 A. A. Hall, 'Working class living standards in Middlesbrough and Teesside, 1870–1914', unpublished CNAA Ph.D. dissertation, Teesside Polytechnic, 1979.
37 It is difficult to do justice to the complexities of wage rates in the iron and steel industry in a short space. Hall, 'Working class living standards', charts the changes in detail.
38 Ibid., chap. 3.
39 Middlesbrough Watch Committee, 25 April 1893.
40 See Chapter 9 for further details.
41 See for example Middlesbrough Watch Committee, 26 Feb. 1903, 26 April 1906, 31 May 1906, 28 May 1908 and 16 Sept. 1909.
42 Silverside had been commended earlier in the same year for stopping a runaway horses.
43 Middlesbrough Watch Committee, 29 July 1884.
44 General Order Book, CB/M/P 25, p. 352
45 The new police station at the west end of Cannon Street was opened in the early 1870s. By the late 1870s there was another station in Linthorpe.

Chapter 8: The Police and Crime in Middlesbrough after 1870

1 The act extended the range of larceny trials that could be tried summarily. All juveniles under the age of 12, unless charged with murder or manslaughter, could be so tried, as could juveniles under the age of 16, if consenting, for larceny, embezzlement or receiving stolen goods; and it extended to all adults pleading guilty or consenting to be tried summarily for similar offences to the value of £2. See 42 & 43 Vict. C.49, 'An Act to Amend the Law Relating to the Summary Jurisdiction of Magistrates'. See Introduction, pp. 10–11 for a discussion of H. Taylor.
2 Gatrell, 'The decline of theft and violence'; Thompson, *Rise of Respectable Society*.
3 Petrow, *Policing Morals*.
4 Williams, 'Counting crimes', approaches the Home Office returns in a 'pessimistic' sense, seeing them as a potential indicator of public concern and 'determined more than anything else, by changes in police policy: between forces and over time'; p. 81.
5 Gatrell and Hadden, 'Criminal statistics'.
6 Although not commented upon at the time, murder was less common than suicide. In late nineteenth-century Middlesbrough the incidence of suicide was twice that of homicide.
7 Middlesbrough Watch Committee, 3 July 1873 and 9 July 1874.
8 Annual Report, 1878, *Middlesbrough Weekly Exchange*, 12 Oct. 1878 and Annual Report, 1879, PCM, CB/M/C, 1/39, 7 Oct. 1879, p. 356.
9 PCM, CB/M/C, 1/42, 25 July 1882, p. 132.

10 PCM, CB/M/C, 1/51, 7 Oct. 1891, CB/M/C, 1/70, 26 May 1910 and CB/M/C, 1/72 8 June 1912. See also CB/M/C 1/58, 24 Feb. 1898.

11 For attempted wife murder see the cases of Albert Olsen and Robert Robertson. PCM, CB/M/C, 1/62, 27 March 1902 and CB/M/C, 1/68, 30 April 1908.

12 PCM, CB/M/C, 1/71, 24 Nov. 1910.

13 Davis had carried on an affair with Esther Richards while her husband was away working. On his return Esther Richards and Walter David moved away from Middlesbrough, but she returned to Middlesbrough later the same year. Davis followed her and battered her to death with a hammer.

14 PCM, CB/M/C, 1/40 24 May 1881 and CB/M/C, 1/58 24 Feb. 1898.

15 For example, in 1912 Shamoza Furozesha, ship's cook, and Valles Mahomed, ship's fireman, were sentenced at York to 3 years' penal servitude and 12 months' hard labour for assaults on fellow crew members Tothee Gool and Sardar Khan. Charles Williams was tried at quarter session for an aggravated assault on Mary O'Brien and for living on her immoral earnings. PCM, CB/M/C, 1/68 24 Sept. 1908

16 Lady Bell, *At the Works*, London 1907, reprinted 1967, p. 18. Florence Bell's attempt 'to put a piece of prosperity under the microscope', as she described her study of Middlesbrough, has been widely seen as a major piece of early twentieth-century social enquiry. Her interest in social conditions in the town date from shortly after her marriage to Hugh Bell, a major industrialist, in 1876 and extended over the next quarter of a century during which time she visited over 1,000 working-class homes interviewing both women and men. There are problems with the book as a source largely because of her failure to detail her methodology, despite being an admirer of Charles Booth. The precise number of people interviewed is unknown, as is the nature of the interviews and the extent to which she was assisted in conducting them. Equally, she does not indicate the date at which her evidence was collected. The last shortcoming is particularly important when trying to assess the extent of change over time in, for example, drinking or gambling.

17 PCM, CB/M/C, 1/67, 22 Nov. 1907.

18 PCM, CB/M/C, 1/66 28 June 1906.

19 PCM, CB/M/C, 1/41, 24 May 1881 and CB/M/C, 1/43, 26 June 1883.

20 Annual Report, *Daily Exchange*, 9 Oct. 1884. There was no other case to compare with this, but in 1912 Herbert Morley was sentenced to 15 month's hard labour for feloniously wounding with intent to kill two girls.

21 PCM, CB/M/C, 1/69, 2 Oct. 1908. Mrs Suddick was sentenced to 3 years' penal servitude but her husband was discharged. See also CB/M/C, 1/63 18 June 1903 and CB/M/C, 1/70, 27 June 1910.

22 PCM, CB/M/C, 1/51, 25 Nov. 1890, CB/M/C, 1/58, 30 June 1898, CB/M/C, 1/65 30 March1905, CB/M/C, 1/66 28 June 1906, CB/M/C, 1/68 27 June 1908, CB/M/C, 1/69, 18 Feb. 1908, 29, CB/M/C, 1/70 4 June 1911, CB/M/C, 1/71 23 March 1911. See CB/M/C 1/71 7 Feb. 1911 for a case that involved abuse by a brother.

23 PCM, CB/M/C, 1/71 20 Sept. 1911.

24 There was also growing concern with 'abnormal' male sexual behaviour after 1885 which led to a number of cases for 'outrages to decency'. For typical examples, see PCM, CB/M/C, 1/67, John Bennett was sent to the

assize for gross indecency in Albert Park, and CB/M/C, 1/73 24 April 1913 when several men were committed to Leeds Assize for gross indecency in a public urinal. A number of such offences also involved sailors.

25 PCM, CB/M/C, 1/63 30 Nov. 1902. CB/M/C 1/60 25 June 1900 Susan Burns was tried for unlawfully wounding Daisy Lougheran and CB/M/C, 1/63 29 Jan. 1903 Mary Rowell and Catherine Scarl were committed for robbery with violence from Michael Smith.

26 In typical cases tried at York, Martin McKie was robbed of £6 by three men and Thomas Robinson of £1 10s. (£1.50). James Weatherall and Edward Carr, in comparison stole only 3s. 4d. (16p).

27 The pattern of crime at Northallerton was replicated at the Middlesbrough Quarter Sessions from 1910 onwards.

28 Annual Report, 1908, p. 6.

29 PCM, BB/M/C, 1/69, Probation Officer's report 21 Jan. 1909.

30 PCM, CB/M/C, 1/71, 20 Sept. 1911. See also 27 April 1911 for a case of a young woman who had been driven by poverty to steal clothes for her wedding.

31 The petty crime rate fell from 6,385 per 100,000 around 1871 to 3,796 around 1881.

32 The figure for 1891 was 3,289 (approximately 15 per cent below the figure for 1881) and for 1901 was 2,320.

33 Bell, *At the Works*, p. 246.

34 See his report for 1882 in which he noted a 10 per cent fall in the number of drunkenness cases but commented that this 'cannot be considered as satisfactory'. *ME*, 5 Oct. 1882.

35 Annual Report 1880, *ME*, 7 Oct. 1880.

36 Annual Report 1875, *MWN*, 15 Oct. 1875. See also 1880 Annual Report, *ME*, 7 Oct. 1880 and especially his comments in the 1874 Annual Report, *MWN*, 16 Oct. 1874, in which he commended 'deservedly severe sentences' passed on those found guilty of aggravated assaults upon women.

37 See also the Chapter 8 appendix for statistics relating to other police activities.

38 See for example the complaint received in June 1905 about boys and men 'continually gambling' in Thorn Street. Middlesbrough Watch Committee, 29 June 1905 and 28 Feb. 1908. Other complaints were received about adolescent behaviour and the limitations of the town's by-laws, for example, in not prohibiting roller-skating in the streets.

39 The most notable example of this was in Liverpool where anti-vice campaigners wanted an all out attack on brothels. The chief constable advised that this would lead to a scattering of brothels over the city but was overruled. He acted on instructions and the outcome he predicted occurred. When members of the watch committee complained about the presence of brothels in respectable areas, the chief constable simply said he had been implementing a policy decided by a superior body. Jefferson and Grimshaw, *Controlling the Constable*, pp. 39–45.

40 The subject is well covered in D. Dixon, *From Prohibition to Regulation: bookmaking, anti-gambling and the law*, Oxford, 1991and M. Clapson, *A Bit of a Flutter: Popular Gambling and English Society, c.1823–1961*, Manchester, 1992.

Petrow, *Policing Moral*, part V, deals specifically with the enforcement of anti-gambling legislation in London.

41 *MWN*, 7 May 1875. See also *Cleveland News*, 1 May 1880s, cited in M. Huggins, *A History of Flat-Racing*, London, 1999, p. 95. Indeed, an attempt by some council members to strengthen the by-laws regarding betting was defeated.

42 Middlesbrough Watch Committee, 29 June 1905 notes 'Boys and Men [are] continually Gambling in Thorn Street'. See also 28 Feb. 1907 and 21 Dec. 1910.

43 *North Eastern Daily Gazette*, 5 Aug. 1898.

44 Reports of Chief Superintendent to Watch Committee, CB/M/P 23, 10 June 1896.

45 The by-laws had been strengthened in 1896, but renewed concern led to new by-laws introduced in June 1906. Middlesbrough Watch Committee, 16 Dec. 1895 and 25 June 1906. See also the general orders relating to the playing of pitch-and-toss (July 1905) and Sunday betting (Dec. 1906), CB/M/P, 25, p. 174 and p. 230.

46 Annual Report 1909, p. 16.

47 Annual Report 1912, p. 14.

48 Bell, *At the Works*, p.255.

49 Ibid.

50 Ibid.

51 Middlesbrough Watch Committee, 8 Aug. 1893.

52 Middlesbrough Watch Committee, 21 Dec. 1910.

53 K. Nicholas, *The Social Impact of Unemployment on Teesside, 1919–39*, Manchester, 1986.

54 Gatrell, 'Decline'; Thompson, *Respectable Society*.

55 Annual Report 1871, *ME*, 12 Oct. 1871

56 Middlesbrough Watch Committee, 9 Jan. 1873.

57 1877 Annual Report, *ME*, 16 Oct. 1877.

58 *ME*, 5 Oct. 1882.

59 Annual Report 1884, *ME*, 9 Oct. 1884.

60 Ibid.

61 Matthews was not unique. See also the records of John Davies and Isaac Mather, who appeared before Northallerton magistrates in Jan. 1888 and April 1889 respectively.

62 T. Holmes, *Pictures and Problems from the London Police Courts*, London, 1900. Holmes actually took a sympathetic view of these women, but his compassion was not widely shared. See also L. Zedner, *Women, Crime and Custody in Victorian England*, Oxford, 1991, pp. 44–6.

63 See also Catherine O'Brien (June 1885), Sarah Carney (April 1887), Annie Ryan (Jan. 1888), Eliza Blakey (April 1888) and Jane Knight (1893). None were in the same class as the notorious Jane Cakebread who was prosecuted 280 times.

64 Generally speaking industrial schools have received a poor press from historians, but Linthorpe appears to have been an exception. According to the inspectors, the staff 'treated [the boys] with obvious kindness'. Physical punishment was not central to the running of the school and there were several leisure activities, ranging from gymnastics to choirs and a brass

band. Interestingly, the boys participated in a number of events within the town and, more importantly, had a good record of employment, albeit mainly in the armed services. Few boys absconded, and in the early twentieth century there were well-attended reunions of 'old boys'! Sue Maidens, 'The Linthorpe Industrial School: an agency of class control?', unpublished dissertation, Teesside Polytechnic, 1991.

65 G. Pearson, *Hooligan: a history of respectable fears*, Basingstoke, 1983. J. Springhall, *Youth, Popular Culture and Moral Panics: penny gaffs to gangsta-rap, 1830–1996*, Basingstoke, 1998. Gang membership was important for adolescent males seeking to prove their masculinity and was not confined to a rough residuum but included the sons of skilled men. A. Davies, 'Youth gangs, masculinity and violence in late-Victorian Manchester and Salford', *Journal of Social History*, 32, 1998.

66 Annual Report 1872, *ME*, 10 Oct. 1872.

67 Annual Report 1873, *MWN*, 17 Oct. 1873. See also Annual Report 1878, *ME*, 12 Oct. 1878.

68 Annual Reports 1874 and 1875, *MWN*, 16 Oct. 1874 and 15 Oct. 1875.

69 Annual Report 1880, *ME*, 7 Oct. 1880.

70 The striking feature of Ashe's surviving reports is the absence of any commentary on the state of crime in the town.

71 *North Eastern Daily Gazette*, 16 Feb. 1899.

72 Bell, *At the Works*, p. 139.

73 Ibid.

74 Ibid, p. 138.

75 *Middlesbrough Police Court Mission*, 2nd Annual Report, 1907, p. 3. See also 1911 annual report, p. 3, for similar sentiments.

76 Annual Report 1913, p. 7.

77 L. Radzinowicz and R. Hood, *The emergence of Penal Policy*, Oxford, 1990, pp. 629–33. See also V. Bailey, *Delinquency and Citizenship: reclaiming the young offender, 1914–1948*, Oxford , 1987.

78 *North Eastern Daily Gazette*, 4 June 1899, 6 Sept. 1900 and 10 Jan. 1904.

Chapter 9: The Police and the Public from the 1970s to 1914

1 *The Times*, 24 Dec. 1908.

2 This is very clearly seen in Reiner, *Politics of the Police*, which is primarily concerned with the crisis of police legitimacy in the late twentieth century and uses the creation of police legitimacy a century before as the basis for his explanation of the current problems in policing.

3 The cases that were tried at quarter session or assize usually involved another serious charge. For example, Arthur Chaplin was tried at Northallerton quarter session on a charge of inflicting grievous bodily harm on PC Venters and also assaulting James Copeland. PCM, CB/M/C, 1/66 27 Sept. 1906. Peter Hand was sent to Leeds assize on charges of warehouse breaking and inflicting grievous bodily harm on PC Yolland, who, incidentally, was awarded the badge of merit for his 'plucky action'. CB/M/C, 1/68 30 Jan. 1908, CB/M/P 30.

4 A crude measure of change can be gained by from the following index numbers.

	Population	Police force	Assaults against police
1871	100	100	100
1881	138	100	43
1911	263	217	150

5 Report of Chief Superintendent to the Watch Committee, CB/M/P, 23 6 Jan. 1870 and 3 July 1873.
6 *MWN*, 13 May 1870. PC Marsden was subjected to a kicking by two Irishmen the following month but the crowd did not take part in this incident. Ibid. 17 June 1870. See also ibid. 30 Sept. 1870 and 28 Nov. 1870.
7 *MWN*, 9 March 1872.
8 Report of Chief Superintendent to the Watch Committee, CB/M/P 23 3 July 1873.
9 Middlesbrough Watch Committee, 8 Dec. 1875.
10 Middlesbrough Watch Committee, 4 Oct. 1876. As noted in Chapter 8 faction fighting among the Irish remained a problem throughout the decade and into the early 1880s.
11 PCM, CB/M/C, 1/44 27 Dec. 1883.
12 PCM, CB/M/C, 1/47 27 March 1887.
13 Reports of Chief Superintendent to the Watch Committee, CB/M/P 24, 24 Sept. 1889 and 7 Oct. 1889. PCM, CB/M/C, 1/50 26 Nov. 1889.
14 PCM, CB/M/C, 1/63 27 Nov. 1902 and 1/65 20.
15 For routine incidents see for example PCM CB/M/C 1/61 24 April 1902, CB/M/C 1/64 25 Feb., 20 April and 26 May 1904, CB/M/C 1/66 26 April 1906, CB/M/C 1/68 10 Feb. 1908, CB/M/C 1/69 14 Nov. 1908, CB/M/C 1/70 20 May 1909, CB/M/C 1/70 23 Dec. 1909, CB/M/C 1/71 21 Nov. 1910, CB/M/C 1/72 21 Dec. 1911 and 29 Feb. 1912, CB/M/C 1/72 16 May and 8 June 1912 and CB/M/C 1/74 6 March 1913. See also *Middlesbrough Gazette*, 14 Nov. 1908, 19 Nov. 1909, 22 Feb. 1912, 27 March 1912, 8 June 1912, 31 Jan. 1913 and 4 July 1913 for examples of typical incidents involving assaults on the police.
16 PCM, CB/M/C, 1 Nov. 1905.
17 Report of Chief Superintendent to Watch Committee, CB/M/P24 28 Nov. 1893. See PCM, CB/M/C, 1/66 1 Nov. 1905 for a more typical but less humorous incident.
18 PCM, CB/M/C, 1/60 27 March 1902, CB/M/C, 1/64 20 April 1904 and 2 May 1904.
19 For example, PCM, CB/M/C, 1/67 26 Aug. 1907 and CB/M/C, 1/69 9 May 1909. The first incident led to PC Henderson being awarded the badge of merit for his bravery. In the second Naven attacked two constables. PCM, CB/M/C, 1/70, 23 Dec. 1909, CB/M/C, 1/71 24 Nov. 1910 and CB/M/C, 1/73, 6 March 1913.
20 Chaplin's career has already been noted, but in addition he attacked two constables, PCs Dobson and Goddard, for which he was found guilty of grievous bodily harm at Northallerton quarter sessions in 1905. PCM, CB/M/C, 1/65, 30 March 1905. For other cases sent to quarter session see CB/M/C, 1/66 19 Aug. 1906 and CB/M/C, 1/70 27 June 1910. Annie Lee

'viciously kicked' the unfortunate PC Bate when he arrested her for drunk and disorderly behaviour. CB/M/C, 1/70 27 June 1910.

21 PCM, CB/M/C, 1/72, 27 June 1912.

22 PCM, CB/M/C, 1/72 17 Sept. 1912. *Middlesbrough Gazette,* 17 Sept. 1912. The woman, Catherine Fearns, was the wife of a Durham policeman, but the men were ordinary members of the public.

23 Printed Council Minutes, CB/M/C, 1/74 23 March 1914. *Middlesbrough Gazette,* 9 March 1914.

24 There were some unusual incidents. For example, Inspector Thorpe was temporarily blinded by a stone thrown in the parliamentary election of 1880. More typical was the broken rib suffered by PC Bennett. *Middlesbrough Gazette,* 1 March 1880. PCM, CB/M/C, 1/40 23 March 1880 and Middlesbrough Watch Committee, 8 December 1875. See also *MWN,* 3 and 10 March 1871, 6 June and 4 July 1872 for typical incidents in the 1870s and *MG,* 19 Nov. 1908, 19 Nov. and 13 Dec. 1909, 22 March and 12 May 1912, and 4 July 1913 for remarkably similar incidents from the early twentieth century.

25 PCM, CB/M/C, 1/67 27 June 1907, CB/M/C, 1/70 13 Dec. 1909 and CB/M/C, 1/71 27 June 1910. Bate, like Gatenby before him, had a mixed career. Dismissed for improper conduct in 1903, he rejoined the force and in August 1908 took the teetotal pledge. By June 1910 he had been promoted to the third rank, having rescued an old woman from a fire. Thereafter he suffered a series of misfortunes. He underwent two operations for tuberculosis of the testicles, was found hiding an empty spirits bottle in the station lavatory, and finally found guilty of improper conduct in a railway carriage while in uniform on the way to York assize. He was dismissed in July 1912.

26 Reports of Chief Superintendent to the Watch Committee, CB/M/P 24 25 July 1901 and Middlesbrough Watch Committee, 24 Nov. 1908. This is in addition to the dangers encountered in arresting people using knives on other members of the public. In two separate incidents, for example, Elias Blackburn and Robert Gatenby were promoted to the merit class for arresting men thus armed.

27 Middlesbrough Watch Committee, 19 July 1906

28 Chief Constable's Annual Reports. Riches gave figures for overall time lost for every year from 1904 to 1914. Unfortunately, this was broken down between sickness and injury in only 5 of the years.

29 There are few commendations to be found for the 1870s, but see Middlesbrough Watch Committee, 5 April 1876. For later examples see PCM, CB/M/C, 1/56 27 Aug. 1896, CB/M/C, 1/65 9 Feb. 1904, CB/M/C, 1/66 30 Nov. 1905, CB/M/C, 1/68 27 June 1907 and CB/M/C, 1/74 20 Feb. and 16 July 1914.

30 PCM, CB/M/C, 1/69 16 Sept. 1909. CB/M/C, 1/70 26 May 1910 and 22 June 1910.

31 PCM, CB/M/C, 1/71 27 April 1911.

32 PCs Bromyard and Davison were simply praised, PCs Silverside and Grimmett were each paid a guinea (£1.05) in addition to the commendation, while PC Rennison was praised, paid half a guinea and promoted. In the most publicised incident PC Freeman's 'gallant and very noble attempt'

to stop a runaway horse resulted in serious injury. Freeman's little finger was amputated and his career was brought to an end somewhile later. PCM, CB/M/C, 1/66 26 April 1906 and 1/68 28 May 1908, CB/M/C, 1/71 25 May 1911 and CB/M/C, 1/73 25 Sept. 1913. CB/M/C, 1/66 3 May 1906 and CB/M/C, 1/69 16 Sept. 1909.

33 Reiner, *Politics of the Police*, ch. 2.
34 Middlesbrough Watch Committee, 5 Sept. 1872 and 11 May 1874. Constables' Conduct Registers CB/M/P 30 and 31.
35 Constables' Conduct Registers, CB/M/P, 29,30 & 31 and PCM, CB/M/C, 1/64 25 Feb. 1904.
36 See individual entries in Constables' Conduct Registers, CB/M/P 29, 30 and 31. Both the Blakeborough brothers, William and Richard, were found guilty of assaulting members of the public in the 1890s, but this did not prevent them from being promoted to sergeant later. Richard went on to become an inspector. See also entries for PCs E. Caddy, Hart and Spenceley for similar incidents.
37 There were a small number of cases (three in total) in which a charge of assault against a police officer was rejected by the Watch Committee.
38 Middlesbrough Watch Committee, 2 March 1877 and 2 March 1877. In this case neither of the two men was censured for the lapse in behaviour.
39 Constables' Conduct Registers, CB/M/P, 29, 30 and 31
40 This did not apply to PC Magee, who was dismissed when found guilty of assaulting his wife.
41 Constables' Conduct Registers, CB/M/P 30. In fact Weaver did not stay long in the force. Fined 15s. (75p) for being drunk on duty in January 1900, he resigned two months later.
42 I am particularly indebted to Mr Tom Bainbridge for his recollections of his and his father's experiences of policing Middlesbrough in the late nineteenth and early twentieth century. See also S. Humphries, *Hooligans or Rebels? An oral history of working-class childhood and youth, 1888–1939*, Oxford, 1981, and Roberts, *Classic Slum*.
43 But see for example Middlesbrough Watch Committee, 6 Jan. 1870. See also 4 July 1872 for an example of a grateful shopkeeper giving a £2 reward to PC Spence for arresting a thief and 5 April 1876 for praise from the stipendiary magistrate for the bravery of PC Bennett who arrested a man who had violently assaulted him.
44 *ME*, 3 Oct. 1872.
45 Middlesbrough Watch Committee, 4 Oct. 1878.
46 *ME*, 28 March 1872.
47 PCM, 28 April 1891, 28 Feb. 1894, 23 and 26 Jan. 1897 and 17 and 23 July 1895, 3 Jan. 1903
48 PCM, CB/M/C, 1/52 24 May 1892. Similar complaints were made by other members of the public. See 28 Feb. 1907 and 24 Feb. 1910. In the latter case the complainant was particularly agitated by shouting outside the Foreign Meat shop in Cannon Street.
49 PCM, CB/M/C, 1/56 28 May 1895.
50 PCM, CB/M/C, 1/62 23 June 1902 and General Order Book Dec. 1906.
51 General Order Book, CB/M/P 25 p. 74. Much of this paragraph is based on this source.

52   See Middlesbrough Watch Committee, 26 Feb. 1895, 15 Oct. and 27 Nov.
     1902, 28 May, 24 Sept. and 30 Dec. 1903, 23 Feb. 1905, 26 Sept. 1907 and
     30 Jan. 1908. PCM,Cb/M/C, 1/67, 26 Aug. 1907 and CB/M/C, 1/69, 6 Oct.
     1909. The sums involved usually varied from 10s. (50p) to £1.
53   Middlesbrough Watch Committee, 30 May 1893.
54   *Middlesbrough Year Book*, 1901, p. 53.
55   *Middlesbrough Year Book*, 1905.
56   *North Eastern Daily Gazette*, 9 Feb. 1900.
57   The point is often made that the Welsh community in Middlesbrough was
     from the outset more integrated and more law-abiding, not least because
     whole families had moved into the town.

Bibliography

1 Major primary sources

1.1 Cleveland County Record Office, Middlesbrough

Middlesbrough Improvement Commission Minutes, 1841–53, CB/M/C, 1/1.
Middlesbrough Improvement Commission Minute Book, 1846–53, CB/M/C, 1/2.
Middlesbrough Improvement Commission Draft Minute Book, 1841–47, CB/M/C, 1/3.
Middlesbrough Improvement Commission Draft Minute Book, 1848–53, CB/M/C, 1/4.
Middlesbrough Commission, Light, Watching and Police Committee Minute Book, 1848–53, CB/M/C, 1/5.
Borough of Middlesbrough, Minutes of the Watch, Police, and Lighting Committee, 1853–59, CB/M/C, 2/100.
Borough of Middlesbrough, Minutes of the Watch, Police and Lighting Committee, 1859–72, CB/M/C, 2/101.
Borough of Middlesbrough, Minutes of the Watch Committee, 1872–1911, CB/M/C, 2/102.
Borough of Middlesbrough, Printed Council Minutes, 1977, CB/M/C, 1/129.
Borough of Middlesbrough, Printed Council Minutes, 1879–1914, CB/M/C, 1/39–1/74.
Borough of Middlesbrough, Bye-laws, CB/M/C, 7/1.
Miscellaneous Newspaper Cuttings, CB/M/C, 12/1.
Reports of Chief Superintendent to Watch Committee, 1867–73, 1889–1900, 1902–11, CB/M/P. 3–12, 23, 24.
General Order Book, 1885–1910, CB/M/P, 25.
Constables' Conduct Registers, 1855–1911, CB/M/P, 29–31.
Policeman's Notebooks, 1892–6 and n.d., CB/M/P, 33–35.
*Middlesbrough Improvement Act, 4 & 5 Victoria, Cap.*lxviii, CB/M/P, 58.
Middlesbrough Police Beats, 1885, CB/M/P, 67.
Borough of Middlesbrough, Quarter Sessions Calendar of Prisoners, 1910–14.

1.2 Middlesbrough Public Library, Local History Section

M. M. Taylor, *Notes of Old Middlesbrough*, 1876.
Middlesbrough Police Court Mission Annual Reports, 1907–1914 .
Middlesbrough Year Book, 1900, 1901,1905, 1907–12.

Newspapers

Middlesbrough Daily Exchange
Middlesbrough Weekly Exchange
Middlesbrough Exchange and North Ormesby News
Middlesbrough Times
Middlesbrough Weekly News & Cleveland Advertiser

Middlesbrough & Stockton Gazette
North Eastern Daily Gazette
Stockton Guardian & Middlesbrough Times
The Dominie

Directories

Kelly's, 1879, 1885/6, 1887, 1893, 1897, 1901, 1905, 1909, 1913.
Ward's, 1861, 1896/7, 1898/9, 1900/01, 1910/11, 1912/13.
Middlesbrouh Directory and Guide, 1862/3.
White's Directory of the North Riding, 1867 .
Handbook and Directory of Middlesbrough, 1873.
Directory of Middlesbrough, 1874.
Slater's Directory, Cleveland District, 1876/7.
Directory of Stockton, Middlesbrough and Hartlepool, 1880.
Middlesbrough Directory and Guide, 1884/5.

W. Ranger, *Report to the General Board of Health on a preliminary enquiry into the sewerage, drainage, and supply of water, and the sanitary conditions of the inhabitants of the Borough of Middlesbrough in the North Riding of the County of York,* 1854.

1.3 North Yorkshire County Record Office, Northallerton

Cleveland Association for the Protection of Persons and Property and for the prevention of Poaching and Vagrancy, 1839–42.
North Riding of Yorkshire, Northallerton Quarter Sessions Judicial Records/Minute Books, 1834–59 and 1859–81.
North Riding of Yorkshire, Northallerton Quarter Sessions Special Order Book, 1833–45.
Calendar of Prisoners, North Riding of Yorkshire, Northallerton Quarter Sessions, 1830–99.
York Assize Calendars, 1832–45, 1855–82 and 1882–1914.

1.4 Parliamentary Papers

Annual Reports of Her Majesty's Inspectors of Constabulary, Parliamentary Papers, 1857–1914.
Report from the Select Committee on Police Superannuation Funds, 1875 (352), vol.xv.

1.5 Public Record Office

Annual Police Returns, 1858–69, HO 63/4,6,8,10,12,14,16,18,20,22,24.

2 Unpublished theses

A. A. Hall, 'Working class living standards in Middlesbrough and Teesside, 1870–1914', CNAA Ph.D., Teesside Polytechnic, 1979.
D. W. Hadfield, 'Political and social attitudes in Middlesbrough, 1853–1889, with special reference to the role of the Middlesbrough Ironmasters', CNAA, Ph.D., Teesside Polytechnic, 1981.

J. Leonard, 'Urban and demographic change in Middlesbrough, 1841–1871', D.Phil., University of York, 1974.

K. Mourby, 'The social effects of unemployment on Teesside, 1919–1939', CNAA, Ph.D., Teesside Polytechnic, 1982.

J. J. Turner, 'Friendly societies in South Durham and North Yorkshire, c.1790–1914', CNAA, Ph.D., Teesside Polytechnic, 1992.

D. R. Welsh, 'The reform of urban policing in Victorian England: a study of Kingston upon Hull, 1836 to 1856', Ph.D., University of Hull, 1997.

3 Books and articles

M. Anderson, *Family Structure in Nineteenth Century Lancashire*, Cambridge, 1971.

O. Anderson, *Suicide in Victorian and Edwardian England*, Oxford, 1987.

Anon, *1856–1956: the first hundred years of the North Riding Constabulary*, Guisborough, n.d.

Anon., *The Police and Constabulary List, 1844*, reprinted 1990.

J. E. Archer, 'Men behaving badly? Masculinity and the use of violence, 1850–1900', in D'Cruze, ed., *Everyday Violence*.

D. Ascoli, *The Queen's Peace*, London, 1979.

P. Bailey, ed., *Policing and Punishment in the Nineteenth Century*, London, 1981.

V. Bailey, *Delinquency and Citizenship: reclaiming the young offender, 1914–1948*, Oxford, 1987.

V. Bailey, *This Rash Act Suicide across the Life Cycle in the Victorian City*, Stanford, 1998.

C. Bauer and L. Ritt, '"A Husband is a Beating Animal": Frances Power Cobbe confronts the wife-abuse problem in Victorian England', *International Journal of Women's Studies*, 6, 1983.

C. Bauer and L. Ritt, 'Wife-abuse, late-Victorian English feminists and the legacy of Frances Powere Cobbe', *International Journal of Women's Studies*, 6, 1983.

D. H. Bayley, ed., *Police and Society*, London, 1977.

Lady Bell, *At the Works: a study of a manufacturing town*, London, 1907 (reprinted 1967).

J. Benson, *The Rise of Consumer Society in Britain, 1880–1980*, London, 1994.

W. Booth, *In Darkest England and the Way Out*, London, 1890.

E. J. Bristow, *Vice and Vigilance: Purity Movements in Britain since 1700*, Dublin, 1977.

A. Briggs, *Victorian Cities*, London, 1963.

M. Brogden, *The Police: autonomy and consent*, London, 1982.

A. Brundage, 'Ministers, magistrates and reform: the genesis of the rural constabulary act of 1839', *Parliamentary History*, 5, 1986.

B. D. Butcher, *A Movable Rambling Force: an official history of policing in Norfolk*, Norwich, 1989.

D. Cannadine, *Class in Britain*, London, 2000.

P. J. Cain and A. G. Hopkins, *British Imperialism: Innovation and Expansion, 1688–1914*, London, 1993.

M. Carpenter, *Juvenile Delinquents: their condition and treatment*, London, 1853.

M. Carpenter, *Our Criminals*, London, 1864.

M. Chase, 'Chartism 1838–1858: Responses in Two Teesside Towns', *Northern History*, 24, 1988.

M. Chase, 'Dangerous People? The Teesside Irish in the 19th century', *North East Labour History Bulletin*, 28, 1994.

K Chesney, *The Victorian Underworld*, London, 1974.

M. Clapson, *A Bit of a flutter Popular Gambling and English Society, c.1823–1961*, Manchester, 1992.

J. Clay, 'On the Relation between Crime, Popular Instruction, Attendance on Religious Worship and Beerhouses', *Journal of the Statistical Society*, 20, 1857.

A. Clark, 'Domesticity and the problem of wifebeating in nineteenth-century Britain: working-class culture, law and politics', in D'Cruze, ed., *Everyday Violence*.

A. A. Clarke, *The Policemen of Hull*, Beverley, 1992.

A. A. Clarke, *Country Coppers: the story of the East Riding Police*, Bridlington, 1993.

C. T. Clarkson and J. H. Richardson, *Police!*, London, 1888.

F. P. Cobbe, 'Wife Torture in England', *Contemporary Review*, 1878.

W. R. Cockcroft, 'The Liverpool Police', in S. P. Bell, ed., *Victorian Lancashire*, Newton Abbott, 1974.

S. Cohen and A. Scull, eds, *Social Control and the State*, Oxford, 1983.

C. Conley, *The Unwritten Law: criminal justice in Victorian Kent*, Oxford, 1991.

N. F. R. Crafts, *British Economic Growth during the Industrial Revolution*, Oxford, 1985.

T. A. Critchley, *A History of Police in England and Wales*, London, 1967.

A. Croll, 'Street disorder, surveillance and shame: regulating behaviour in the public space of the late-Victorian British town', *Social History*, 24, 1988.

S. D'Cruze, ed., *Crimes of Outrage*, London ,1998.

S. D'Cruze, ed., *Everyday Violence in Britain, 1850–1950*, London, 2000.

B. J. Davey, *Lawless and Immoral: policing a county town, 1838–1857*, Leicester, 1983.

A. Davies, 'The Police and the people: gambling in Salford, 1900–1939', *Historical Journal*, 34, 1991.

A. Davies, 'Youth Gangs, Masculinity and Violence in Late-Victorian Manchester and Salford', *Journal of Social History*, 32, 1998.

A. Davies, 'Youth gangs, gender and violence, 1870–1900' on D'Cruze, ed. *Everyday Violence*.

G. Davis, *The Irish in Britain, 1815–1914*, Dublin, 1991.

J. Davis, 'From "Rookeries" to "Communities": Race, Poverty and Policing in London, 1850–1985', *History Workshop Journal*, 1991.

D. Dixon, '"Class Law": the Street Betting Act of 1906', *International Journal of the Sociology of Law*, vol.8, 1980 .

D. Dixon, *From Prohibition to Regulation: Book-making, Anti-gambling and the Law*, Oxford, 1991.

Bob Dobson, *Policing in Lancashire, 1839–1989*, Staining, 1989.

M. E. Doggett, *Marriage, Wife-beating and the Law in Victorian England*, London, 1992.

A. P. Donajgrodski, ed., *Social Control in Nineteenth Century Britain*, London, 1977.

D. Eastwood, *Government and Community in the English Provinces, 1700–1870*, Basingstoke, 1997.

D. J. Elliot, *Policing Shropshire, 1836–1967*, Studley, 1984.

C. Emsley, *Policing and its Context*, Basingstoke, 1983.

C. Emsley, 'The thump of wood on a swede turnip: police violence in nine-teenth-century England', *Criminal Justice History*, 6, 1985.

C. Emsley, 'Detection and Prevention: the old English police and the new', *Historical social Research*, 37, 1986.

C. Emsley, *Crime and Society in England*, London, 1987.

C. Emsley, *The English Police: a social and political history*, Hemel Hempstead, 2nd edition, 1996.

C. Emsley and M. Clapson, 'Recruiting the English Policeman, c.1840–1940', *Policing and Society*, 3, 1994.

J. Field, 'Police, Power and Community in a provincial English town', in Bailey, ed., *Policing and Punishment*.

F. Finnegan, *Poverty and Prejudice: a study of Irish immigrants in York, 1840–1875*, Cork, 1982.

R. Floud and D. N. McCloskey, *The Economic History of Britain since 1700*, Cambridge, 1994.

D. Foster, *The Rural Constabulary Act, 1839*, London, 1982.

D. Foster, 'The East Riding Constabulary in the nineteenth century', *Northern History*, 21, 1985.

W. H. Fraser, *The Coming of the Mass Market*, Basingstoke, 1981 .

H. R. P. Gamon, *The London Police Court Today and Tomorrow*, London, 1907 .

V. A. C. Gatrell and T. B. Hadden, 'Criminal statistics and their interpretation', in E. A. Wrigley, ed., *Nineteenth-Century Society: essays in the use of quantitative methods for the study of social data*, Cambridge, 1972 .

V. A. C. Gatrell, B. Lenman and G. Parker, eds, Crime *and the Law: a social history of crime in Western Europe since 1500*, London, 1980.

V. A. C. Gatrell, 'The decline of theft and violence in Victorian and Edwardian England', in Gatrell, Lenman and Parker, *Crime and the Law*.

V. A. C. Gatrell, 'Crime, authority and the policeman-state', in F. M. L. Thompson, ed., *The Cambridge Social History of Britain*, vol. 3, Cambridge, 1990.

V. A. C. Gatrell, *The Hanging Tree: Execution and the English People, 1770–1868*, Oxford, 1994.

J. R. Gillis, 'The Evolution of Juvenile Delinquency in England, 1890–1914', *Past & Present*, 67, 1975.

B. Godfrey, 'Law, Factory Discipline and "Theft": the Impact of the Factory on Workplace Appropriation in mid to late Nineteenth-Century Yorkshire' *British Journal of Criminology*, 39, 1999 .

B. Godfrey, 'Judicial impartiality and the use of criminal law against labour: the sentencing of workplace appropriators in Northern England, 1840–1880', *Crime, History and Societies*, 3, 1999.

A. A. Hall, 'Wages, Earnings and Real Earnings in Teesside: a reassessment of the ameliorist interpretation of living standards in Britain, 1870–1914', *International Review of Social History*, 26, 1981.

A. J. Hammerton, *Cruelty and Companionship: conflict in nineteenth-century married life*, London, 1992.

M. Hann, *Policing Victorian Dorset*, Wincanton, 1987.

D. Harding, 'Sir Hugh Gilzean Reid and the Daily Gazette', *Cleveland History*, 1994.

B. Harrison, *Drink and the Victorians: the temperance question in Victorian England, 1815–1872I, London*, London, 1971.

J. Hart, 'Reform of the borough police, 1835–56', *English Historical Review*, 70, 1955.

D. Hay and F. Snyder, eds, *Policing and Prosecution in Britain, 1750–1850*, Oxford, 1989.

C. Hempstead, ed., *Cleveland Iron and Steel*, BSC, Teesside, 1979.

S. Holdaway, ed., *The British Police*, London, 1979.

T. Holmes, *Pictures and Problems from London Police Courts*, London, 1900.

T. Holmes, *Known to the Police*, London, 1908.

B. Howell, *The Police in Late-Victorian Bristol*, Bristol Historical Association Pamphlet, 1986.

P. Hudson, *The Industrial Revolution*, London, 1992.

M. Huggins, *A History of Flat Racing*, London, 1999.

S. Humphries, *Hooligans or Rebels? An Oral History of Working-class Childhood and Youth, 1888–1939*, Oxford, 1981.

L. C. Jacobs, *Constables of Suffolk*, Ipswich, 1992.

O. Jay, *Life in Darkest London*, London, 1891.

O. Jay, 'The East End and Crime', *New Review*, 1894.

T. Jefferson and R. Grimshaw, *Controlling the Constable: Police accountability in England and Wales*, London, 1982.

R. Jervis, *Chronicles of a Victorian Detective*, 1907, reprinted Runcorn, 1995.

D. J. V. Jones, 'Thomas Campbell Foster and the rural labourer: incendiarism in East Anglia in the 1840s', *Social History*, 12, 1976.

D. J. V. Jones, *Crime, Protest, Community and Police in Nineteenth-Century Britain*, London, 1982.

D. J. V. Jones, 'The New Police, Crime and People in England and Wales, 1829–1888', *Transactions of the Royal Historical Society*, 33, 1983.

D. J. V. Jones, *Crime in Nineteenth Century Wales*, Cardiff, 1992.

J. Jones, '"She resisted with all her might": sexual violence against women in late-nineteenth century Manchester and the local press', in D'Cruze, ed., *Everyday Violence*.

J. E. King, '"We could eat the police": popular violence in the north Lancashire cotton strike of 1875', *Victorian Studies*, 28, 1985.

P. King, 'Prosecution associations and their impact in eighteenth-century Essex', in Hay and Snyder, eds, *Policing and Prosecution*.

W. L. M. Lee, *A History of Police in England*, London, 1901.

W. Lillie, *The History of Middlesbrough*, Middlesbrough, 1953.

W. J. Lowe, 'The Lancashire Constabulary, 1845–70: the social and occupational function of a Victorian police force', *Criminal Justice History*, 4, 1983.

T. J. Madigan, *The Men Who Wore Straw Hats: policing Luton, 1870–1974*, Dunstable, 1993.

A. H. Manchester, *A Modern Legal History of England and Wales, 1750–1950*, London, 1980.

A. H. Manchester, *Sources of English Legal History: law, history and society in England and Wales, 1750–1950*, London, 1984.

J. P. Martin and G. Wilson, *The Police: a study in manpower. The evolution of the service in England and Wales, 1829–1965*, London, 1969.

P. Mathias, *The Retailing Revolution*, London, 1967.

R. McKibbin, 'Working-class gambling in Britain, 1880–1939', *Past & Present*, vol.82, 1979.

W. McWilliams, 'The Mission to the English Police Courts', 1876–1936', *The Howard Journal*, 22, 1983.

A. Mearns, *The Bitter Cry of Outcast London*, 1883.

E. Midwinter, *Law and Order in early-Victorian Lancashire*, York, 1968.

W. R. Miller, *Cops and Bobbies: Police Authority in New York and London, 1830–1870*, Chicago, 1977.

W. R. Miller, 'Never on Sunday: Moralistic Reformers and the Police in London and New York', in Bayley, ed., *Police and Society*.

R. J. Morris and R. Rodger, *The Victorian City: a reader in British urban history*, Harlow, 1993.

K Nicholas, *The Social Impact of Unemployment on Teesside, 1919–39*, Manchester, 1986.

M. Ogborn, 'Ordering the city: surveillance, public space and the reform of urban policing in England, 1835–56', *Political Geography*, 12, 1993.

R. Paley, '"An Imperfect, Inadequate and Wretched System"?: Policing London before Peel', *Criminal Justice History*, 10, 1989 .

S. H. Palmer, *Police and Protest in England and Ireland, 1780–1850*, Cambridge, 1988.

G. Pearson, *Hooligan: a history of respectable fears*, London, 1985.

S. Petrow, *Policing Morals: the Metropolitan Police and the Home Office, 1870–1914*, Oxford, 1994.

D. Philips, 'The Black Country Magistracy, 1835–60: a changing elite and the exercise of its power', *Midland History*, 3, 1976.

D. Philips, 'Riots and Public Order in the Black Country, 1835–60', in Stevenson and Quinault, *Popular Protest*.

D. Philips, *Crime and Authority in Victorian England*, London, 1977.

D. Philips, 'A new engine of power and authority: the institutionalization of law enforcement in England, 1780–1830', in Gatrell, Lenman and Parker, eds, *Crime and the Law*.

D. Philips, 'Crime and Punishment', in Cohen and Scull, eds, *Social Control*.

D. Philips, 'Good Men to Associate and Bad Men to Conspire: Associations for the Prosecution of Felons in England, 1760–1860', in Hay and Snyder, *Policing and Prosecution*.

D. Philips and R. D. Storch, 'Whigs and Coppers: the Grey Ministry's national police scheme, 1832', *Historical Research*, 67, 1994.

D. Philips and R. D. Storch, *Policing provincial England, 1829–1856 the politics of reform*, Leicester, 1999.

A. J. Pollard, ed., *Middlesbrough: town and community, 1830–1950*, Stroud, 1996.

L. Polley, *The Other Middlesbrough: a study of three nineteenth-century suburbs*, University of Teesside, 1993.

L. Polley, 'Housing the Community, 1830–1914', in Pollard, ed., *Middlesbrough*.

C. Postgate, *Middlesbrough, Its History, Environs and Trade*, Middlesbrough, 1898.

N. Pringle and J. Treversh, *150 Years Policing in Watford District and Hertfordshire County*, Luton, 1991.

L. Radzinowicz, *A History of Criminal Law*, 4 volumes, London, 1948, 1956 and 1968.

L. Radzinowicz and R. Hood, *The Emergence of Penal Policy in Victorian and Edwardian England*, Oxford, 1990.

H. G. Reid, ed., *Middlesbrough and Its Jubilee,* Middlesbrough, 1881.

R. Reiner, *The Politics of the Police*, Hemel Hempstead, 3rd edition 2000.

C. Reith, *The Police Idea*, Oxford, 1938.

C. Reith, *The British Police and the Democratic Ideal*, Oxford, 1943.

C. Reith, *A Short History of the Police*, Oxford, 1948.

C. Reith, *A New Study of Police History*, London, 1956.

E. A. Reynolds, *Before the Bobbies: the night watch and police reform in Metropolitan London, 1720–1830*, Basingstoke, 1998.

S. Reynolds and B. and T. Woolley, *Seems So! A working-class view of politics*, London, 1911.

A. F. Richter, *Bedfordshire Police, 1840–1990*, Kempston, 1990.

D. Richter, *Riotous Victorians*, Ohio, 1981.

M. J. D. Roberts, 'Public and private in early nineteenth-century London: the vagrant act of 1822 and its enforcement', *Social History*, 13, 1988.

R. Roberts, *The Classic Slum*, London, 1971.

L. Rose, *'Rogues and Vagabonds': the vagrant underworld in Britain, 1815–1985*, London, 1988.

E. Ross, '"Fierce Questions and Taunts": married life in working-class London, 1840–1914' *Feminist Studies*, 8, 1983.

E. Ross, *Love and Toil*, Oxford, 1993.

G. Rude, *Protest and Punishment*, Oxford, 1978.

G. Rude, *Criminal and Victim: crime and society in early nineteenth-century England*, Oxford, 1985.

M. Scolan, *Sworn to Serve: Essex Police*, Chichester, 1993.

R. B. Shoemaker, *Gender in English Society 1650–1850*, London, 1999.

H. Shpayer-Makov, 'The making of a police labour force', *Criminal Justice History*, 24, 1990.

H. Shpayer-Makov, 'A portrait of a novice constable in the London metropolitan Police, c.1900', *Criminal Justice History*, 12, 1991.

H. Shpayer-Makov, 'Career prospects in the London Metropolitan Police in the early twentieth century', *Journal of Historical Sociology*, 4, 1991.

R. Sindall, *Street Violence in the Nineteenth Century: Media Panic or Real Danger?*, Leicester, 1990.

J. Springhall, *Youth, Popular Culture and Moral Panics: penny gaffs to gansta rap, 1830–1996*, Basingstoke, 1998.

P. T. Smith, *Policing Victorian London*, Connecticut, 1985.

M. Stallion and D. S. Wall, *The British Police: Police Forces and Chief Officers, 1829–2000*, Gateshead, 1999.

P. J. Stead, 'The New Police', in Bayley, ed., *Police and Society*.

P. J. Stead, *The Police of Britain*, London, 1985.

C. Steedman, *Policing the Victorian Community: the formation of the English provincial police from 1856 to 1880*, London, 1984.

J. Stevenson and R. Quinault, eds, *Popular Protest and Public Order*, London, 1974.

J. Stevenson, *Popular Disturbances in England*, London, 1992.

S. Stevenson, 'The "habitual criminal" in nineteenth-century England: some observations on the figures', *Urban History Yearbook*, 14, 1986.

R. D. Storch, 'The Plague of Blue Locusts: police reform and popular resistance in northern England, 1840–57' *International Review of Social History*, 20, 1975.

R. D. Storch, 'The policeman as domestic missionary', *Journal of Social History*, 9, 1976.

R. D. Storch, 'Police Control of Street Prostitution in Victorian London', in Bayley ed., *Police and Society*.

R. D. Storch, ed., *Popular Culture and Custom in Nineteenth-Century England*, London, 1980.

R. D. Storch, 'Policing rural southern England before the police: opinions and practice, 1830–1856', in Hay and Snyder, eds, *Policing and Prosecution*.

R. Swift, 'Another Stafford Street Row' *Immigrants and Minorities*, 3, 1984.

R. Swift, *Police Reform in Early-Victorian York*, York, 73, 1987.

R. Swift, 'Urban Policing in Early-Victorian England, 1835–1856: a reappraisal', *History*, 73, 1988.

R. Swift, 'The English Urban magistracy and the Administration of Justice during the early-nineteenth century: Wolverhampton 1815–60', *Midland History*, 17, 1992.

R. Swift, 'Heroes or Villains? The Irish, Crime and Disorder in Victorian England', *Albion*, 29, 1997.

R. Swift and S. Gilley, eds, *The Irish in Britain, 1815–1939*, London, 1989.

J. Styles, 'The Emergence of the Police – Explaining Police Reform in eighteenth and nineteenth century England', *British Journal of Criminology*, 27, 1987.

D. Taylor, *999 And All That*, Oldham, 1968.

D. Taylor, 'The Jamaican banana: or how to be a successful businessman in nineteenth-century Middlesbrough', *Bulletin of the Cleveland and Teesside Local History Society*, 1982.

D. Taylor, 'The Antipodean Arrest: or how to be a successful policeman in nineteenth-century Middlesbrough' *Bulletin of the Cleveland and Teesside Local History Society*, 58, 1990.

D. Taylor, 'Crime and Policing in early-Victorian Middlesbrough, 1835–55', *Journal of Regional and Local Studies*, 11, 1991.

D. Taylor, 'The standard of living of career policemen in Victorian England: the evidence of a provincial borough force', *Criminal Justice History*, 12, 1991.

D. Taylor, *'A Well-chosen, effective body of men': the Middlesbrough police force c.1841–1914*, University of Teesside, 1995.

D. Taylor, *The New Police in the Nineteenth Century: crime, conflict and control*, Manchester, 1997.

D. Taylor, 'The Infant Hercules and the Augean Stables: a century of economic and social development in Middlesbrough, c.1840–1939', in Pollard, ed., *Middlesbrough*.

D. Taylor, 'Policing and the Community: late-twentieth century myths and late-nineteenth century realities', in K Laybourn, ed., *Social Conditions, Status and Community*, Stroud, 1997.

D. Taylor, *Crime, Policing and Punishment in England, 1750–1914*, Basingstoke, 1998.

H. Taylor, 'Rationing crime: the political economy of criminal statistics since the 1850s', *Economic History Review*, 51, 1998.

F. M. L. Thompson, *The Rise of Respectable Society*, London, 1988.

F. M. L. Thompson, ed., *The Cambridge Social History of Britain*, 3 vols, Cambridge, 1990.

J. J. Tobias, *Crime and Industrial Society in the Nineteenth Century*, London, 1972.

N. Tomes, '"A Torrent of Abuse": crimes of violence between working-class men and women in London', *Journal of Social History*, 11, 1978.

J. Tosh, *A Man's Place: masculinity and the middle-class home in Victorian England*, London, 1999.

J. J. Turner, 'The Frontier Revisited: Thrift and Fellowship in the New Industrial Town, c.1830–1914, in Pollard, ed., *Middlesbrough*.

R. Vogler, *Reading the Riot Act*, Milton Keynes, 1991.

J. Walkowitz, *Prostitution and Victorian Society: women, class and the state*, Cambridge, 1980.

M. Weaver, 'The new science of policing: crime and the Birmingham Police Force, 1839–1842', *Albion*, 26, 1994.

B. Weinberger, 'The police and the public in mid-nineteenth century Warwickshire', in Bailey, *Policing and Punishment*.

B. Weinberger, *The Best Police in the World: an oral history of English policing*, Cambridge, 1995.

M. J. Wiener, 'Judges v. Jurors: Courtroom Tensions in Murder Trials and the Law of Criminal Responsibility in Nineteenth-Century England', *Law and History Review*, 17, 1999.

M. J. Weiner, 'The sad story of George Hall: adultery, murder and the politics of mercy in mid-Victorian England' *Social History*, 14, 1999.

C. A. Williams, Counting crimes or counting people: some implications of mid-nineteenth century British police returns' *Crime, History & Societies*, 4, 2000.

J. Woodgate, *The Essex Police*, Lavenham, 1983.

E. A. Wrigley, *Continuity and Change: the character of the Industrial Revolution in Britain*, Cambridge, 1988.

L. Zedner, *Women, Crime and Custody in Victorian England*, Oxford, 1994.

Index

accidents, street, 170, 176–7
Acklam, 84
age profile of community, 22, 165
agricultural sector, 2
Albert Club, 160
Albert Park, 28, 105, 148, 158, 177, 204
Albert Road, 19, 20, 23
Alder, Robert, 60
Allick, Robert, 59
Alney, William, 44
Amber Street, 106
Amos, James, 30
Amos Hinton & Sons, 104
Anderson, M., 186
Anderson, O., 193
Anderson, PC, 201
Angle Street, 106
animals, dangers from, 132, 177
Appleby, Thomas, 60
Arthur, Prince, 105
Ashe, William
    attacks on, 86, 87
    career, 46, 47, 116, 181
    Close case, 48–9
    cricket matches, 134
    crime statistics, 155
    experience, 114
    petty crime, 159, 160, 180
    relationship with Watch
        Committee, 113, 199
    reports, 9, 166
Atkins, Mary, 192
Atkinson, F., 90, 91
Atkinson, Harriet, 58
Atkinson, PC, 178
Atkinson, William, 47, 116
attempted murder, 57, 64, 84, 144,
    145, 146–7
attempted suicide, 64–5, 144
Ayresome, 109
Ayresome Green Lane, 180
Ayresome Street, 106
Ayrton Ironworks, 102

Bailey, Alfred, 44
Bailey, V., 193, 206
Bainbridge, PC, 147, 178
Bainbridge, Tom, 209
Baker, William, 59
bakery trade, 104
Baldwin, Elizabeth, 147
Bames, Richard, 60
Bamford, Thomas, 43
Barber, Joseph, 150
Barker, PC, 174, 201
Barnes, PC, 132, 176
Barrow, PC, 119
Basham, PC, 119
Bate, PC, 175, 176, 200, 208
Bauer, C., 194
Baxtor, Councillor, 93
Beamire, PC, 178
beats, 131–2, 133, 137
Bedfordshire, 189
beerhouses, 18, 64, 85, 154
begging, 154, 157, 168
Belk, J. T., 47
Bell, Alfred, 122
Bell, Florence, Lady, 105, 147, 154,
    160, 161, 166–7, 199, 203, 204,
    205
Bell, Hugh, 105, 203
Bell, John, 61, 147
Bell, Lothian, 62
Bellamy, Inspector, 118, 173, 197
Bell Brothers, 16, 102
Bennett, John, 203–4
Bennett, PC, 208, 209
Benson, J., 186, 199
bias, police, 89–97
Bickley, PC, 201
Black, A. F., 200
Black, Thomas, 49
Blackburn, Arthur, 146
Blackburn, Elias, 122, 208
Black Country, 55, 56, 57, 61, 113
Blackpool, 186

Blakeborough, Richard, 119, 201, 209
Blakeborough, William, 178, 209
Blakey, Eliza, 205
'Bloody Code', 5
boiler-makers, 127, 128
boiler works, 18
Bolckow, Henry, 15, 24, 37, 105
Bolckow & Vaughan, 15–16, 17, 18,
    61, 102
watchmen, 30, 31, 36, 43, 45, 46
'Bold Venture' quarry, 16
Bolton, 2, 38
Bone, Jessy, 194
Booth, Charles, 203
Booth, Sergeant, 175
Booth, William, 187
Borough Road, 105, 134
borstals, 165
bottle washing, 101
Botton, John, 59
Boundary Road, 20
Bowes, Charles, 35, 45, 70
Bowes, Samuel, 44, 80, 86, 89, 198
Boynton, John, 43
boys' brigade, 165, 167
boys' clubs, 167
Bradford, 38, 56, 135, 136
Brett, George, 133
Bridge public house, 123
Bridnorth, 29, 190
Brierly, Joseph, 73
Briggs, Asa, 2, 53, 185, 186, 188, 189
Briggs, Mr (dock contractor), 63
Britannia Iron Co., 17
Britannia Ironworks, 102
British and Colonial Meat Company,
    104
Brockett, Thomas, 62
Bromyard, PC, 208
Brooks, Vincent, 132
brothels, *see* prostitution
Brothers of London, 59
Brown, Christopher, 32
Brown, John, 59
Brown, PC, 178, 197, 201
Brown, Robert, 89–91, 92, 94
Brown, Timothy, 90–1
Brownless, Mary Ann, 73
Buckinghamshire, 113, 200, 201

Buckle, Richard, 44, 64
Buckton, William, 190
building industry, 110, 130
Bull, James, 173
bull-running, 5
Burdon, William, 60
Burgess, Peter, 174
Burgess, William, 174
Burke, John, 62
Burke, Michael, 61
Burney, PC, 174
Burnley, 2
Burns, Agnes, 65
Burns, Father, 197
Burns, James, 31
Burns, Susan, 149, 204
Burton, Montagu, 105
Burton, PC, 86–7
Burton, Robert, 148–9
Burtt, Charles, 150
butchers, 104
Butler, Rebecca, 71
Byers, James, 59
by-laws, 28, 65, 66, 79, 106, 154, 156
Byworth, PC, 86

cabinetmakers, 18
Caddy, E., 119, 209
Cain, P. J., 186
Cairn, Robert, 174
Cakeworth, Jane, 164, 205
Callaghan, Michael, 70
Campbell, James, 89
Campbell, Mary, 164–5
Cane, Margaret, 71
Cannadine, D., 186
Cannon Street, 20, 105, 107, 134,
    174, 182, 202, 209
Cannon ward, 107, 109
Caraher, PC, 177
Cargo Fleet, 132, 141
Carney, Sarah, 205
Carpenter, Mary, 187
Carr, Edward, 204
Carroll, John, 193
Carter, Francis, 178
Carter, John, 75
Cassidy, John, 72
Castle, PC, 120

Castle Howard reformatory, 193
catchpits, 107
Chaplin, Arthur, 174, 206, 207
Chapman, George, 195
Chapman, S., 193
Chapman, William, 31
Chapman's Yard, 20
Charles Ephgrave, 104
Charlton, Mary, 71
chemical industry, 18
children
  criminals, 165–9
  labour, 167
  neglect, 148, 166
  safety concerns, 177
Children Act (1908), 145, 168
cholera, 7, 23, 24
Church of England, 6
cinemas, 105
circus, 72
Clapson, M., 196, 200, 204
Clarendon Road, 134
Clark, Henry, 76
Clark, William, 86
Clarke, A. A., 185
Clarke, Mary, 62
class factors, 4–5
  community, 24, 105–6
  criminals, 56
  see also middle classes; working
    classes
Clay, Reverend John, 187
Cleveland Association, 27
Cleveland General Association, 26
Cleveland Ironmasters' Association,
  16
Cleveland Street, 138
Cleveland Works, 102
Close, John, 62
Close, Thomas Cameron, 47–9
clothing trade, 104–5
coal industry, 14–15, 19, 97
  larceny, 61, 75
Coates, Francis, 64
Cochrane family, 16
Cockburn, George, 61
Codey, John, 86
Cole, Frederick, 117
Cole, James, 59

Collinson, PC, 179
Colne, 78, 80
Commercial Street, 145, 174
Conafrey, Matthew, 149
conduct problems, *see* policemen,
  conduct problems
Congleton, 29
Conley, C., 64, 193, 194
consumerism, 111, 152
Cook, Thomas, 44
Co-op, 104
Cooper, John, 46, 119, 131
Cooper, Mary, 148
Copeland, James, 206
corner shops, 104
Corporation Road, 20, 103
corruption, police, 119–20, 159–60,
  182
costermongers, 186
Coughlin, Margaret, 59
Coulon, Edward, 44, 89
County and Borough Police Act
  (1856), 7, 37, 41–2, 50, 53, 98
Cowan, Robert, 149
Cowley, Robert, 193
Cox, PC, 174
Coyle, John, 60
Coyle, Margaret, 59
Crafts, N. F. R., 186
crime, 52–77, 142–70
  attempted suicide, 64–5, 144
  child neglect, 148, 166
  drunkenness, 53, 66–9, 72, 77, 84–6,
    93, 95, 97, 153–5, 174, 187
  press coverage, 53, 64, 68–9, 71, 76
  against property, 56–7, 74, 144,
    149, 151–2
  records and statistics, 9–11, 52–3,
    80, 89, 143
  street offences, 157–8
  trends, 54–5, 143, 150–1
  see also larceny; moral crime;
    violent crime
Crimean war, 16
Criminal Justice Act (1855), 9
Criminal Law Amendment Act
  (1885), 145
Criminal Law Amendment Act
  (1912), 145

criminals, 163–5
    career, 62, 164
    ethnicity, 56
    female, 71, 147–8, 149, 164–5
    gender factors, 55–6, 59, 61, 63, 66,
        69, 71, 72, 163
    hanging, 147
    Irish immigrants, 56, 69, 145–6,
        163–4
    juvenile, 165–9
    social circumstances
        class factors, 56
        education, 56, 163
        overcrowding, 71
        poverty, 63, 71, 166–7, 168
        unemployment, 56, 163
Critchley, T. A., 79, 196
Croll, A., 186
Crompton, Samuel, 70
Crookes, J., 65
Crosby, William, 192
Cross, George, 148
Cross Street, 68
Cubitt, Thomas, 15
Cudworth, William, 18
cutlasses, 35, 80, 84

Daily Exchange, 163
Daley, Michael, 61
Darley, PC, 177
Darlington, 104
Davey, B. J., 185, 190, 196
David, Walter, 203
Davies, A., 206
Davies, John, 205
Davis, G., 196
Davis, J., 196
Davis, Walter, 147, 203
Davison, Margaret, 72
Davison, PC, 208
Dawson, Elizabeth, 60
Dawson, George, 44
Dawson, John, 60
D'Cruze, S., 194
De Brus, 18
demographic development, 8, 14,
    19–24, 27, 37, 105–12, 154, 165
demotions, 89, 123–4, 179
Dempsey, Isabella, 146

Dennis, PC, 133
detective work, 116–17
Dewsbury, 112, 135
Diamond Street, 134
diarrhoea, 23, 108
Dickens, Charles, 1, 52
Dickinson, John, 177
disease issues, 7, 22, 23–4, 108–9
    mortality rate, 23, 108–9
dismissals, 43–4, 89, 117–20, 123–4,
    177, 178
Ditchburn, John, 149
Dixon, D., 204
Dixon, George, 123–4
Dobson, Mason, 122
Dobson, PC, 207
dock, 15, 18, 35, 143, 153
    1840 riot, 7, 24, 29, 53, 54, 63
Doherty, James, 62
domestic violence, 70, 84–5, 146–7
Dominie, 69
Donajgrodzki, A. P., 196
Doncaster, 51, 135
Dorking, Michael, 60
Dorman Long, 102
Dowlais Iron Company (Merthyr
    Tydfil), 193
drainage system, 107
drunkenness, 53, 66–9, 72, 77, 84–6,
    93, 95, 97, 153–5, 174, 187
    police, 43–4, 47, 93, 119, 123–4,
        179–80
Duffield, Eleanor, 75
Duffy, Catherine, 71
Durham, 41, 104, 113, 126, 189
Durham City, 126
Durham Street, 22, 71, 86, 104, 138
dysentery, 108

Eales, Mr, 179
Eastman's, 104
East Street, 104
economic and industrial develop-
    ment, 2–3, 7–8, 14–19, 97–8,
    100–5, 142, 171
education, 56, 157, 163, 166
Education Acts, 154
Eland, PC, 90
Emerald Street, 106

Emmerson, Isabella, 58
Employment of Children Act, 168
Emsley, C., 1, 79, 185, 196, 198, 199, 200
engineering industry, 17–18, 101, 103
  wages, 110, 127, 128, 130
enteric fever, 108
Eston, 185
Eston Hills, 16
Eston Junction, 83, 102
Evans, Ernest, 178
Evans, Patrick, 83
Evesham, 29, 190
Exeter, 38, 78
Explosives Act, 170
Extension and Improvement Act (1866), 73
Extension Hotel, 75

Fall, Peter, 70
Farndale, Sergeant, 118
Farrell, Fanny, 178
Fearns, Catherine, 208
Fenianism, 81, 83–4, 197
Ferguson, Ann, 76
Feuring, Erestina, 75
Feversham Street Boys' Club, 167
Finnegan, F., 196
fires, 132–3, 176
fishmongers and fried fish dealers, 104
Flavell, Sergeant, 37
Flinn, Peter, 70
Floud, R., 186
Folkstone, 29
food retailing, 104
football, 5, 158
Forbes and Sparks, 104
Fortitude, The, 18
Fothergill, Nathan, 84
foul language, 66
founding fathers, 7, 8, 15, 19, 65, 67, 97, 183
Fox, Head & Co., 17, 101
Francis, James, 91
Franco-Prussian War, 17, 102
Fraser, W. H., 186, 199
Freeman, Edward, 70
Freeman, PC, 208–9

Freeman, Percy, 132
Freeman, Hardy and Willis, 105
Frost, PC, 84, 118
Fruish, James, 147
Fuller, PC, 174
Furozesha, Shamoza, 203

Galbraith, William, 147
Galloway, John, 34–5
gambling, 74, 93, 149, 154, 158, 159–62, 168, 180, 182
  by police, 120, 161
Gamon, Hugh R. P., 94, 198
gang violence, 64, 145–6, 148, 150
Gant, PC, 201
Garbutt, Amos, 84, 197
Garbutt, John, 62
Garland, Patrick, 70
Garner, K., 200
Garnett, Thomas, 75–6
Garon, Hugh, 194
Gatenby, Robert, 50, 87, 173, 175, 208
Gatrell, V. A. C., 1, 9, 185, 187, 192, 202, 205
Gauntlett Street, 132, 176
gender profile of community, 22, 101, 162
General Order Book, 158, 178, 180
Gibbon, W., 200
Gilkes, Edgar, 17
Gilkes & Wilson, 16
Gilkes, Wilson, Pease & Co., 17
Gilley, S., 196
Gladstone, William, 14, 23, 24
Gladstone Street, 173
Globe Inn, 70
Goddard, PC, 207
Godfrey, B., 193
Gofton, Ralph, 44
Gool, Tothee, 203
Gott, L., 200
Gould, John Henry, 147, 172
Gould, Walter, 117
Graham, Eleanor, 71
Graham, George, 71
Graham, John, 32
Graham's Yard, 20
Grainger, John, 44

Grange Road, 20
gratuities, 45, 46, 50, 96, 130–1
greengrocery trade, 104
Green Lane, Acklam, 84
Grey, Robert, 120, 201
Gribbin, John, 59
Griffiths, John, 146
Grimmett, PC, 208
Grimshaw, R., 199, 204
grocery trade, 103–4
Grove Hill, 21, 77, 95, 109, 111
Guisborough, 27
Gurney Street, 103

Hackney, Patrick, 84–5
Hadden, T. B., 9, 185, 192, 202
Halifax, 2, 78, 135, 136
Hall, A. A., 129, 199, 202
Hall, E., 200
Hall, Robert, 201
Hammerton, A. J., 194
Hammond, John, 43
Hand, Peter, 206
Hannan, William, 35, 37, 41, 98, 169
  career, 200
  enlarged police force, 38, 53, 54
  petty crime, 66, 76
  relationship with Watch
    Committee, 34
  serious crime, 77
Hanson, James, 201
Harding, John, 197
Hardwick, John, 60
Hardy, Jewitt, 44, 83
Hargreaves, Albert, 118
Hargreaves, Cornelius, 174
Hart, PC, 173, 209
Hartlepool, 15
Hartlepool and Dock Railway
  Company, 15
Hatfield, PC, 175
Haw, William, 61
Hay, D., 189, 193
Hays, Alice, 75
Hazel, James, 59
health and disease, 7, 22, 23–4, 108–9
  mortality rate, 23, 108–9
  suicide, 23
Heaton, Superintendent, 196

Hedley, James, 91
Hempstead, C., 188
Henderson, PC, 147, 172, 174, 181,
  207
Henley, 29
Hennessey, Kate, 164
Hepworth's and Dunn, 105
Her Majesty's Inspectors, 133
Hessel, Robert, 147
Hester, James, 195
Hewitt, PC, 201
Heyburn, PC, 86
Hildreth, Richard, 65
Hill, Ernest, 179
Hinton, Amos, 104
Hippodrome, 132–3, 176
Hird, Michael, 146
Hird, Robert, 121, 132, 176, 201
Hirst, Edwin, 44
Hobson, Frederick, 122
Hobson, Hannah, 71
Hobson, Harriet, 62
Hobson, John, 44, 89, 93
Hodgson, Ernest, 132
Hodgson, Matthew, 117, 121, 201
Hogg, PC, 201
Holmes, Thomas, 164, 205
Holting, John, 149
Home, Inspector, 44
Home and Colonial, 104
Home Rule, 197
Hood, R., 206
Hopkins, A. G., 186
Hopkins & Co., 17
Hopkins, Gilkes & Co., 17–18
Hopper, Charles, 49, 91
Hopper, PC, 179
Hopper's Yard, 23
Horncastle, 32–3, 78
Horner, Mrs, 86
Horsfield, PC, 85, 90
housing, 98, 109, 143
  development, 7, 19–21, 23–4, 105–7
  employment, 18
  overcrowding, 22–3, 106–7
  police, 125, 134
  sanitary issues, 107–8
Huddersfield, 2, 78, 135, 136, 196
Hudson, Francis, 124, 178

Hudson, P., 186
Huggins, M., 205
Hughes, Barnard, 61
Hughes, Catherine, 60
Hughes, Henry, 64
Hughes, PC, 196
Hull, 34
Humphries, S., 209
Hunter, Sarah, 59
Hurley, Susan, 164
Hutchinson, PC, 120

ice-cream vendors, 186
illness, 7, 22, 23–4, 108–9
    mortality rate, 23, 108–9
immigrant workers, 14, 21–2, 98, 164
    see also Irish immigrants
Imperial Ironworks, 102
Improvement Act (1841) 7, 24, 27–8,
    33, 79, 98
    appointments, 29
    petty crime, 65
    police/population ratio, 38
    Robinson, John, 190
    watchmen, 36
Improvement Commission, 9, 11, 29,
    30, 32, 33
Incender, Ignatez, 62
Incest Act (1908), 145
indecency, 187
India, SS, 120
industrial and economic develop-
    ment, 2–3, 7–8, 14–19, 97–8,
    100–5, 142, 171
infant mortality rates, 108, 109
inns and public houses, 18, 64, 85,
    154
insanitation, 107–8, 109
inspectors of weights and measures,
    157
Irish immigrants, 14, 21–2
    attitudes of police towards, 95
    attitudes to police, 78, 79, 81–4, 95,
        98, 173
    crimes committed by, 56, 69,
        145–6, 163–4
    dock strike (1840), 63
    health issues, 23
    police conduct issues, 178

    as policemen, 82
    police seen as discipliners of, 12
iron and steel industry, 8, 15–18, 98,
    100–3, 143, 159
    wages, 109–10, 127, 128–30
Ironmasters' District, 17, 18, 108
itinerant salesmen, 5, 157
itinerant shows, 72

Jackson, Gill & Company, 102
Jay, Reverend Osborn, 187
Jefferson, T., 199, 204
Jewison, Thomas, 60
Jobson, Thomas, 49
Johnson, Jane Ann, 71
Johnson, John, 59
Johnson, William, 43, 86
Jones, David J. V., 2, 9, 52, 185, 188,
    191, 192
Jones, William, 117
Jones Brothers & Co., 102
Jordison, PC, 179
Joseph, Andrew, 193
juvenile courts, 165, 168–9
juvenile offenders, 165–9
Juvenile Offenders Act (1847), 9
Juvenile Offenders Act (1850), 9

Kay, James, 150
Kelly, Patrick, 195
Kelly, Thomas, 190
Kent, 189, 194
Keogan brothers, 85, 196–7
Khan, Sardar, 203
Kidd, John, 44
Kidson, Robert, 150
Kilburn, William, 61
Kilvington, Alice, 174
Kilvington, William 'Tin-Ribs', 30, 33,
    34
King, P., 189
Kingston upon Hull, 34
Kirby Moorside, 26
Kirk, Richard, 36
Kneeshaw, Thomas, 192
Knight, Jane, 205
Knowlson, Frederick, 116, 117, 121,
    201
Knox, John, 35

Lacey, Father, 197
Lacy, Councillor, 40
Lamb, Alice, 60
Lancashire, 55
Lancaster, Joseph, 122
Land League, 197
Langbaurgh, 27
Langley, Rebecca, 147
Laramon, PC, 201
larceny, 56–63, 66, 74–6, 143, 149–54,
  156, 202
  of clothing and footwear, 58, 74,
    75, 151–2, 153
  of food and drink, 62, 75, 152, 168
  from household, 59–60, 150
  industrial, 60–1, 75, 152
  by juveniles, 168
  of money and jewellery, 59–60, 62,
    74, 152, 153
  from shops, 58–9, 62
Laurel Street, 134
Lavender, Jackson, 74–5
Lawrence, PC, 175
Leach, Dolly Reed, 58–9
Leach, James, 193
Lee, Annie, 174, 207–8
Lee, James, 149
Lee, W. L. Melville, 196
Leeds
  assizes, 49, 149, 204, 206
  attitudes to police, 78, 80
  criticisms of police, 51
  police/population ratio, 38, 136
  sanitary issues, 108
  size of force, 135
leisure, 18, 72, 103, 105, 143
  police, 34, 134–5, 177
length of service, 32–3, 41–2, 45–7,
  49, 113–23
Lenman, B., 185
Lennard, Robert, 59
Leonard, J. W., 21, 188, 192
Leyburn, Hannah, 60
library, police, 34, 134–5
licensed clubs, 154
lighting, street, 35, 82, 175
Light, Watching and Police
  Committee (later Watch
  Committee), 29, 33

Linthorpe
  Blackburn's caution, 122
  industrial school, 165, 205–6
  Police Station, 201, 202
  suburbanisation, 105, 111
Linthorpe Road, 20, 85, 195
Little, Peter, 72
Liverpool, 3, 14, 113, 148, 204
Local Government Act (1858), 106
local press
  crime coverage, 53, 64, 68–9, 71, 76
Lockeran, Michael, 145
lodger population, 21, 22, 106
London
  attitudes to police, 78
  costermongers, 186
  gambling, 205
  hooliganism, 165
  immigrant population, 14
  Jennings Building, 81
  police discipline, 201
  police force, 6
  police promotions, 202
  urban growth, 3
  see also Metropolitan Police
London Boot Co., 105
Long, James, 177
Long, Robert, 70
long-service class, 122, 123, 124, 125
Lougheran, Michael, 83
Loughran, Daisy, 149, 204
Lowe, W. J., 199
Lower Commercial Street, 35
Lyme Regis, 190
Lynch, Thomas, 174

MacArdle, Charles, 174
MacArdle, Patrick, 174
Maccane, William, 62
McCann, Ann, 72
Maccarron, Neil, 43
McCarthy, Bridget, 85
McCarthy, John, 85
McCarthy, Mrs, 146
McCarthy, Patrick, 146
McCloskey, D. N., 186
McCormick, William, 194
McCoy, James, 73
McCoy, Sophia, 73

McCulley, David, 145
McEvoy, PC, 119
MacEwan, Patrick, 173
McGrall, Catherine, 62
McIntyre, Patrick, 70
McKenzie, PC, 201
McKie, Martin, 204
McNally, Jemima, 75
Magee, PC, 201, 209
Mahomed, Valles, 203
Maidens, Sue, 206
Manchester, 3, 14, 38
Mann, George, 46, 114, 133
manslaughter, 57, 145, 146–7
Mardon, Henry, 44
Mardon, PC, 179
Market Place, 18, 65, 132, 139
Markey, Edward, 44
Markle, John, 148
Marron, Patrick, 62
Marron, Philip, 62
Marsden, PC, 207
Marsey, PC, 201
Marshes, 132, 140
Marsh Road, 107, 180
Marsh ward, 107, 108
Martin, J. P., 201
Marton Lane, 93
Mary Street, 82
masculinity, construction of, 5
Mason Street, 20
Mather, Isaac, 205
Mathias, P., 199
Matthews, Patrick, 164, 205
Mawer, Matthew, 46–7, 114, 116
Maypole Dairies, 104
Mearns, Reverend Andrew, 187
measles, 23
Meggison, Mary, 71
Melber, PC, 120
men's clothing trade, 104–5
merit class, 39, 47, 50, 122–3, 126,
    127, 191
Merthyr Tydfil, 14, 20, 52, 191, 193
Messiter, Robert, 194
Metcalf, F., 119, 200
Metcalf, James, 49–50
Metropolitan Police, 6, 30, 94, 112,
    114, 117

Metropolitan Police Act (1829), 25
middle classes
    attitudes to police, 78, 92–3, 96, 97,
        99, 181
    complaints about police, 12, 96, 99
    consumption, 152
    housing, 105, 106
    living standards, 110
    as targets for thieves, 21
Middlesbrough
    by-laws, 28, 65, 66, 79, 106, 154,
        156
    community
        age profile, 22, 165
        class issues, 24, 105–6
        gender profile, 22, 101, 162
        immigrants, 14, 21–2, 98, 164
        see also Irish immigrants
    development
        demographic, 8, 14, 19–24, 27,
            37, 105–12, 154, 165
        economic and industrial, 7–8,
            14–19, 97–8, 100–5, 142, 171
        dock, 15, 18, 35, 143, 153
        founding fathers, 7, 8, 15, 19, 65,
            67, 97, 183
        health and disease, 7, 22, 23–4,
            108–9
        mortality rate, 23, 108–9
        suicide, 23
    housing, 98, 109, 143
        development, 7, 19–21, 23–4,
            105–7
        employment, 18
        overcrowding, 22–3, 106–7
        sanitary issues, 107–8
    incorporation, 33
    police station, 19, 30
    reputation, 8, 24, 41, 53, 63, 67, 69,
        143
    sanitary conditions, 107–8, 109
    stocks, 65
    town hall, 19, 30
    water supply, 108
Middlesbrough and Cleveland Boys'
    Brigade, 167
Middlesbrough Exchange, 179, 180
Middlesbrough Extension and
    Improvement Act (1856), 106

Middlesbrough Ironworks, 17
Middlesbrough Pneumonia, 109
Middlesbrough Pottery, 18
Middlesbrough Weekly News, 24
  attitudes to police, 92, 93, 94, 97
  bias by police, 90, 91
  violence against police, 82
  violence by police, 89
Middleton, 78
migration patterns, 4
  see also immigrant workers; Irish
    immigrants
Milestone, William, 201
Mitford, Thomas, 88
Moniken, John, 63
Moody, Stephen, 60
Moore, Inspector, 118
Moore, Thomas, 150
moral crime, 27–8, 68–9, 76, 174, 180
  begging, 154, 157, 168
  foul language, 66
  gambling, 74, 93, 149, 154, 158,
    159–62, 168, 180, 182
  indecency, 187
  prostitution, 73–4, 76, 147, 154,
    157, 158, 174, 181, 204
  soliciting, 195
  vagrancy, 27, 66, 72, 153–4, 157,
    158, 160
moral issues, 5–6, 79, 93, 97, 142
  police conduct problems, , 44, 119,
    120, 123, 161
Morgan, PC, 120
Morley, Herbert, 203
Morris, James, 193
Morris, PC, 118
Morris, R. J., 186
Morrison, Daniel, 84
Morrow, Robert, 59
mortality rate, 23, 108–9
Morton, Detective Constable, 175
Morton, PC, 200
Morton, William, 89
Mouncer, Thomas, 147
M'Quillan, Daniel, 70
Mulvey, Michael, 195
Municipal Corporation Act (1835), 25
Municipal Corporations Act (1853),
    24, 33

murder, 57, 64, 144, 145, 147–8, 202
  attempted, 57, 64, 84, 144, 145,
    146–7
Murray, Ellen, 72, 73
music-halls, 105
Myrtle Street, 134

Nash, PC, 120
National Anti-Gambling League, 159
Naven, Richard, 174, 207
Neesam, PC, 173
neglect of duty, 44, 119
Neill, Hugh, 122
Nelson, Barnard, 62
Nelson's, 104
Newcastle-upon-Tyne, 104, 127
Newcombe, Sarah, 85
Newport Ironworks, 17, 201
Newport Road, 20
Newport Rolling Mill, 101
Newport ward, 107, 108, 109
Newsome's Circus, 72
Nicholas, K., 205
Nicholson, Thomas, 150
night patrol, 35
Nile Street, 93, 108
Nixon, PC, 87
Nolan, John, 149
Northallerton quarter sessions, 27,
    53–8, 63, 80–1, 91, 147, 150–1,
    164, 177, 206
North-Eastern Co., 102
North Eastern Daily Gazette, 111, 166,
    181
Northern, Ann, 58–9
North Ormesby Hospital, 133
North Ormesby Road, 75, 146
North Riding of Yorkshire
  consolidation of forces, 37
  inefficiency of force, 27
  police recruits, 113
  police wages, 41, 126
  private policing initiatives, 26
  serious crime, 54, 56
North Street, 19
Nunn, William, 201

Oakley, PC, 200
O'Brien, Catherine, 205

O'Brien, Mary, 203
Ogborn, M., 186
Ogle, PC, 80
Oliver, Elizabeth, 59
Oliver, James, 26
Oliver Street, 107
Olsen, Albert, 203
Onions, Frank, 132
Ord, Richard, 29, 30, 31, 33, 63
Ormesby, 16
Otley, Richard, 18, 19, 98
overcrowding, 4, 22–3, 106–7
    and criminal behaviour, 71
Owners of the Middlesbrough Estate,
    see founding fathers
Oxford Music Hall, 86

Packet Wharf, 137
Parker, G., 185
Parkin, Henry, 122
Parliament Road, 106
Pattison, F., 200
Pattison, James, 44
Patton, Ellen, 193
pawnbrokers, 157
Peacock, William, 116, 190, 200, 201
Pearl Street, 106
Pearson, G., 206
Pease, Joseph, 15, 19
Pease, Joseph, Jnr, 59
Peel, Sir Robert, 6
pensions, 45, 46–7, 130–1
perks, 125
Petroleum Act, 170
Petrow, S., 195, 202, 205
Philips, David, 1–2, 6, 9, 52, 56, 67,
    185, 187, 188, 189, 192, 193, 200
Piercy, Mr, 179
Place, Joseph, 124
Police and Constabulary List (1844), 29
Police Bill (1832), 25
Police Committee, 32, 33
Police Guardian, 133
Police House, 30
policemen
    career paths, 44–50, 113–25
    demotions, 89, 123–4, 179
    dismissals, 43–4, 89, 117–20,
        123–4, 177, 178

length of service, 32–3, 41–2,
    45–7, 49, 113–23
long-service class, 122, 123, 124,
    125
merit class, 39, 47, 50, 122–3,
    126, 127, 191
promotions, 45–7, 49–50, 118,
    120–9, 135, 201–2
recruitment, 12, 29–32, 35–7,
    114, 125
resignations, 43, 45, 117–19, 123,
    178
retirement, 45, 118, 133
service class, 125
turnover, 12, 35, 39–43, 50, 89,
    114
conduct problems, 30, 32, 43–4, 50,
    89–94, 119–20, 123, 178–82
bias, 89–97
complaints, 12, 179–81
corruption, 119–20, 159–60, 182
drunkenness, 43–4, 47, 93, 119,
    123–4, 179–80
fines, 130, 178
gambling, 120, 161
insubordination, 44, 119
moral issues, 44, 119, 123
neglect of duty, 44, 119
prosecutions, 177
theft, 120
violence, 44, 72, 88–9, 119,
    177–9
cutlasses, 35, 80, 84
emergence and development of
    policing, 6–8, 13, 26–9
functions, 39, 170
detective work, 116–17
inspectors of weights and
    measures, 157
night patrol, 35
river police, 153
surveillance, 170
welfare, 12, 176–7
home life
housing, 125, 134
wives, 125
image, 177
local press's attitudes, 11, 176,
    179–80

policemen (*continued*)
  public attitudes, 12, 78–99, 171–82
  leisure, 134–5
  library, 34, 134–5
  police band, 34, 134, 177
  sports, 134
  praise, 31, 51, 92, 96, 176, 179, 181
    for Ashe, 48, 181
    for Knowlson, 117
  merit class, 39, 47, 50, 122–3,
    126, 127, 191
  promotions, 45, 46, 47, 49, 50,
    118, 120–9, 135, 201–2
  private, 36, 39, 40, 114, 199
  remuneration
    gratuities, 45, 46, 50, 96, 130–1
    merit badge scheme, 122
    pensions, 45, 46–7, 130–1
    perks, 125
    rewards, 123, 181
    salaries and wages, 29–35, 39–46,
      125–30
    sickness fund, 39
    superannuation scheme, 34, 39,
      130
  staves, 84
  structure of force, 37, 42, 116
    numbers, 37, 38–9, 42, 112, 135
    police/population ratio, 37–9,
      112–13, 136
  working conditions, 34, 125, 131–4
    beats, 131–2, 133, 137
    breaks, 132, 176–7
    dangers, 131–3
    esprit de corps, 125, 133–4
    holiday leave, 132
    journals, 133
    shifts, 131, 132
    sick leave, 175–6
    violence by public, 20, 27, 47,
      66–7, 70, 79–88, 132, 147,
      155, 172–5, 182, 207
Police Office, 89
police/population ratio, 37–9,
  112–13, 136
Police Review and Parade Gossip, 133
Police Service Advertiser, 133
Pollard, A. J., 188, 189, 198, 199
Polley, L., 188, 199

Pontefract, 29
population growth, *see* demographic
  development
Port Clarence, 16
Port Darlington, 18
Postgate, C., 18, 188, 194
Potter, John, 59
poverty, criminals, 63, 71, 166–7, 168
Preston, 56, 186
Prevention of Crime Act (1879), 9
Princess Street, 107
private police, 36, 39, 40, 114, 199
private prosecution associations, 26–7
prize fights, 70
Probation Act (1907), 168
probation orders, 169
promotions, 45–7, 49–50, 118, 120–9,
  135, 201–2
property, crimes against, 56–7, 74,
  144, 149, 151–2
prostitution, 73–4, 76, 147, 154, 157,
  158, 174, 181, 204
protests, 5
Proudlock, PC, 179
public attitudes to police, 12, 78–99,
  171–82
Public Benefit Boot Co., 105
Public Health Act (1848), 23
Public Health Act (1855), 106
Public Health Act (1875), 23
public houses and inns, 18, 64, 85, 154
Puck, 69, 93–4, 96
Pulleine, James, 31
Purvis, Henry, 131
Pybus Brothers, 104

Quakers, 15
Quinn, Catherine, 71

Radzinowicz, L., 196, 206
railways, 14–16, 17, 19
Raisbeck, Thomas, 122, 173, 174, 181
Rake Kimber & Co., 18
Ranger Report (1854), 23, 189
rape and sexual assaults, 144, 145,
  148–9
Ray, Thomas James, 44, 198
Raylton Dixon & Co., 18, 103
recruitment, 12, 29–32, 35–7, 114, 125

Redding, PC, 173
Reece, Elizabeth, 147–8
Reed, John, 45, 114, 133
Reiner, R., 196, 199, 206, 209
Reith, Charles, 79, 187, 196
religious issues, 6, 22, 81–2
  organisations for children, 167
Rennison, PC, 208
resignations, 43, 45, 117–19, 123, 178
respiratory diseases, 109
retailing, 8, 18, 103–5, 143
retirement, 45, 118, 133
Reveley, PC, 201
rewards, 123, 181
Reynolds, E. A., 185, 187
Reynolds, S., 198
Richards, Esther, 203
Richardson, Alderman, 40
Richardson, David, 70
Richardson, PC, 87
Richardson, Thomas, 60
Riches, Henry, 11, 187
  career, 181
  children's safety, 177
  on crime, 152
  crime statistics, 155
  detective work, 200
  petty crime, 159, 160, 162
  police/population ratio, 113
  relationship with Watch
    Committee, 113
  sick leave, 133, 208
  street offences, 157
  turnover of police, 114
Riches, Norman, 167
Richmond, 29
riots, 5, 80
  1840 dock riot, 7, 24, 29, 53, 54, 63
Ripon, 29
Rising Sun public house, 32
Ritt, L., 194
river police, 153
Roberts, M. J. D., 187
Roberts, R., 198, 209
Robertson, Robert, 203
Robinson, John, 86–7, 190
Robinson, Johnson, 84, 197
Robinson, PC, 119, 175
Robinson, Peter, 60

Robinson, Thomas, 204
Robson, Hannah, 86
Robson, PC, 86
Rodger, James, 132
Rodger, PC, 176
Rodger, Richard, 186
Rogers, Bernard, 75
Rogers, Michael, 73
Rooney, Thomas, 173
Rortch, Peter, 63
Ross, E., 194
Rowell, Mary, 149, 204
Rowland, Reverend, 148
Royal Albert theatre, 197
Ruby Street, 106, 134
Rudé, George, 9, 52, 185, 192
Rural Constabulary Act (1839), 6–7,
  25, 26, 189
Ryan, Annie, 205
Ryan, James, 85
Ryder, Anne, 147s

Saggerson, Edward, 99, 169, 192
  attack on, 85–6
  bias by police, 91, 96
  Close's arrest, 48–9
  crime statistics, 155
  criminals, 162
  drunkenness, reports on, 85, 155
  experience, 114
  independence, 34
  Irish community, 84, 173
  juvenile offenders, 165, 166, 167
  merit class, 39
  optimism, 163
  petty crime, 76, 159
  police/population ratio, 38–9
  pragmatism, 95
  public attitudes to, 92
  reassurance of Watch Committee, 50
  relationship with Watch
    Committee, 113
  reports, 9
  retirement, 133, 200
  serious crime, 57, 64, 77
  unsolved murder, 148
  violence, reports on, 156
  violence against police, 82, 145–6,
    198

sailors, 72, 147, 149, 204
Sailors' Trod, 93
St Helens, 188
St Hilda's church, 180
St Hilda's ward, 108, 109
St John's School, 174
St Peter's, 148
salaries and wages, 29–35, 39–46,
    125–30
salesmen, itinerant, 5, 157
Salford, 38
Salvation Army, 180
Sample, Andrew, 86, 114, 179
Samuel, David, 75
Samuelson, Sir Bernard, 16, 17
Sanderson, Thomas, 62
Sanitary Committee, 45
sanitary issues, 107–8, 109
Saxton, Abraham, 31
Sample, Andrew, 46
Scales, Thomas, 147
Scarl, Catherine, 149, 204
School Board, 46–7, 116, 166
Scott, James, 123
scouting movement, 165, 167
Scully, John, 173
Sedgwick, Joseph, 190
self-control, 5
service class, 125
services sector, 2–3
sewage flooding, 107
sexual assaults and rape, 144, 145,
    148–9
Seymour, William, 201
Shannon, Thomas, 149
Shean, Philip, 72
Sheffield, 108, 135, 136
shifts, 131, 132
shipbuilding industry, 17, 18, 101,
    102, 103, 128
Shipley, Ann, 73
Shoemaker, R. B., 187
Short, Mary, 193
shows, travelling, 72
Shpayer-Makov, H., 112, 199, 202
Shrovetide football, 5
sickness fund, 39
Sigsworth, James, 31
Silversides, Arthur, 117, 132, 202

Silverside, PC, 208
Sindall, R., 187
Skillen, Frederick, 178
Sledge, PC, 173
Smales, F., 200
smallpox, 7, 23
Smith, Christopher, 190
Smith, Elizabeth, 147
Smith, Jacob, 149
Smith, Michael, 149, 204
Smith, William, 62, 149
Smith's Dock, 103
Snowden & Hopkins Ironworks, 16,
    17, 36
Snowden Road, 160
Snyder, F., 189
Society for the Conviction of Felons, 26
soliciting, 195
South Bank, 16, 103
Southfield Villas, 21, 77
South Shields, 126
South Street, 103
Spark, PC, 201
Spark, Robert, 123, 124, 201
Sparks, PC, 178
Spawforth, Sarah, 83
Spence, PC, 209
Spenceley, Mary, 193
Spenceley, Matthew, 44
Spenceley, PC, 209
Springhall, J., 206
Staffordshire, 61, 113, 200, 201
Stainsby, Joseph, 83, 86, 88, 90, 190,
    197
Stainthorpe, PC, 173
Stallion, M., 190
Stamford, 5, 29, 190
staves, 84
Steedman, C., 1, 185, 187, 191, 196,
    199, 200, 201
steel, *see* iron and steel industry
Stephenson, William, 58
Stewart, Charles, 44
Stewart, James, 60
Stewart's the 'King Tailors', 105
stocks, 65
Stockton, 83, 104, 108–9
Stockton & Darlington Railway
    Company

dock riot (1840), 63
economic developments, 14, 15, 16
police officers, 190
thefts from, 61, 75
Stockton Gazette and Middlesbrough Times, 92
Stockton Street, 68, 140, 194, 161, 180
Stokes, David, 148
Stokes, Elizabeth, 148
Stokesley, 27
Stones, John, 117, 121, 201
Storch, R. D., 6, 79, 185, 187, 188, 189, 196
Storey, Thomas, 43
Street Betting Act (1906), 159, 160
street lighting, 35, 82, 175
street offences, 157–8
street traders, 5
Suddick, John, 148, 203
Suddick, Mary Ann, 148, 203
suicide, 23, 64–5, 202
   attempted, 64–5, 144
Summary Jurisdiction Act (1879), 151
summary justice, extensions to, 9, 53, 55, 74, 142, 143, 151, 153
Sunderland, 104, 127
superannuation scheme, 34, 39, 130
surveillance, 170
Sussex Street, 132, 139
Sutherland, PC, 173
Sutton Brothers, 104
Swift, R., 1, 56, 81, 185, 188, 192, 196
Swinburne, Richard, 26–7

Talbot Inn, 16
tank works, 18
T. Appleton & Co., 103
Tate, John Gladstone, 124
Tavistock, 29, 190
Taylor, Christopher, 118
Taylor, D., 38, 185, 187, 188, 189, 193, 198, 199, 201, 202
Taylor, Howard, 9–10, 53, 142, 187, 192, 202
Taylor, Thomas, 44

Taylor, William, 122
Tees, River, 15, 108, 153
Tees Engine Works, 16
Tees Ironworks, 16
Teesside Bridge & Engineering Works, 18
Teesside Iron and Engine Works, 18
Teesside Ironworks, 17, 102
temperance movement, 79
Temple, Thomas, 44, 46, 130
Theatre Royal, 201
theatres, 72, 105
theft, *see* larceny
Thetford, 29
Thomas, Elizabeth, 176
Thomas, George, 195
Thomas, John, 29–30, 31, 32, 97
Thompson, F. M. L., 147, 185, 205
Thompson, George, 58, 149
Thompson, John, 44
Thompson, Mary Ann, 71
Thorn Street, 204, 205
Thorpe, Robert
   attacks on, 86, 87, 88, 197, 208
   bias, 91
   career, 46, 116
   death, 133
   experience, 114
   Fenians, 84
Tobias, J. J., 185, 187
Todd, John, 62
Tomes, Nancy, 70, 194
Tomlin, Joseph, 49, 85, 130
Tosh, J., 187
Tow Law, 185
Town Hall, 19, 30
Toynbee Trust, 94
Trainor, R. H., 146, 193
travelling salesmen, 5, 157
travelling shows, 72
Trodden, Francis, 149
Turner, J. J., 199, 200
turnover of police, 12, 35, 39–43, 50, 89, 114
typhoid, 108
typhus, 23

unemployment, criminals, 56, 163
Union Street, 105

vagrancy, 27, 66, 72, 153–4, 157, 158, 160
Vagrancy Act (1898), 145, 159
Vaughan, John, 15, 24, 33, 37
Vaughan, Thomas, 83
Venters, PC, 206
Victoria Dock (Hartlepool), 15
Victoria public house, 201
Victoria Road, 134
violent crime, 53, 57, 63–4, 67–72, 77, 144–50, 153–6
  attempted murder, 57, 64, 84, 144, 145, 146–7
  attitudes to, 5, 6
  domestic, 70, 84–5, 146–7
  gangs, 64, 145–6, 148, 150
  manslaughter, 57, 145, 146–7
  murder, 57, 64, 144, 145, 147–8, 202
  against police, 20, 27, 47, 66–7, 70, 79–88, 132, 147, 155, 172–5, 182, 207
  by police, 44, 72, 88–9, 119, 177–9
  prize fights, 70
  rape and sexual assaults, 144, 145, 148–9
  by women, 71, 147–8, 149
Vulcan Street, 15, 16
Vulcan ward, 107

wages and salaries, 29–35, 39–46, 125–30
Wake, William, 35
Wakefield, 135, 136
Walker, Ann, 58
Walker, Robert, 60
Wall, D. S., 190, 191
Waller, James, 123, 201
Walsall, 190
Walton, Eutychus, 60
Warters, Joseph, 44, 89
Watch Committee, 33–7
  bias by police, 90, 91
  commendations and praise, 39, 176, 179
  complaints, 180
  conditions of work, 132
  criminals, 162, 166
  discipline issues, 119–20, 124, 177, 178, 179, 181

Fenians, 84
gang fights, 146
historical record, 9
juvenile offenders, 166
long-service class, 123
petty crime, 68, 76, 158, 160, 161
police pay, 39, 40, 43, 46, 125, 130
police/population ratio, 38
public attitudes to police, 92
recognition of individual policemen, 96
relationship with police, 113, 159
serious crime, 57, 77
violence against police, 87, 145, 197, 198
violence by police, 89, 209
Wilson's leadership, 98
wishes mediated by police, 12
watchmakers, 18
watchmen, 36
Waterloo Road, 134
water supply, 108
Watson, George, 104
Wayland, John, 60
Weatherall, James, 204
Weaver, PC, 179, 209
Wedgewood, Josiah, 5
Weinberger, Barbara, 196
welfare functions of police, 12, 176–7
Wellington Street, 104
Welsh, D. R., 191, 199
West Bromwich, 188
West Ham, 188
West Riding of Yorkshire, 41, 61, 126
West Street, 68
Westwood, Thomas, 64
Wheatley, Mary Ann, 71
Whitby Abbey Inn, 70
White, John, 44
Whitehouse, John, 58
White's Directory, 18
Wiener, M. J., 187
Wigan, 38
Wilds, Charlotte, 148
Wilds, Rebecca, 148
Wilkinson, James, 44, 83, 85
Wilkinson, William, 122, 133
Williams, C. A., 9, 187, 202
Williams, Caroline, 75

Williams, Charles, 203
Williams, PC, 119
William Wolfenden & Son, 104
Wilson, Eliza, 62
Wilson, G., 201
Wilson, Isaac, 33–4, 98, 169
  discipline issues, 177
  ironworks, 17
  police wages, 40, 43, 125, 130, 191
  Watch Committee's reputation, 192
Wilson, James, 192
Wilson, Jane, 58
Wilson, PC, 119, 120, 201
Wilson, Richard, 60
Wilson Street, 20, 104
wire industry, 18
Wolverhampton, 14, 38, 51, 188, 200
Wood, Anthony, 148
Wood, J., 200
Wood, William, 62
Woolley, B., 198
Woolley, T., 198
Woodford, Lieutenant-Colonel, 37
Woodgate, J., 185
Workhouse Hospital, 146
working classes
  alcohol consumption, 72
  attitudes of police towards, 94–5, 96, 162–3
  attitudes to police, 78, 79, 86, 95, 171, 176
  gambling, 159, 160
  general behaviour, 183

housing, 106, 109
leisure, 105, 174, 182
living standards, 105, 109, 111, 142–3, 152, 182
moral issues, 6, 142
petty crime, 67, 77
police brutality and insensitivity, 12, 93
police conduct issues, 178–9
as policemen, 45–6
police seen as discipliners of, 12
serious crime, 77
threat posed by, 4–5
Worsted Acts, 61
Wright, Robert, 45
Wright, William, 44, 60
Wrigley, E. A., 185, 186

Yelland, PC, 147
Yolland, PC, 206
York
  assizes, 53, 62, 64, 120, 146–50, 197, 203, 204
  attitudes to police, 78
  police/population ratio, 38, 136
  size of force, 135
York & Darlington Railway Co., 17
Younger, Ernest, 147
Young Man's Temperance Brigade, 167

Zedner, L., 205
Zetland Inn, 88